4. Recalls details from a short story or picture

5. Identifies cause and effect relationship in stories, events, or pictures

6. Predicts outcomes in stories, events, or pictures

7. Draws inferences from stories, events, or pictures

8. Distinguishes reality from fantasy

9. Creates stories based on a described or pictured situation

II. Pre-Writing

A. **Distinguishes top from bottom**

B. **Follows top-to-bottom progression**

C. **Distinguishes left from right**

D. **Follows left-to-right progression**

E. **Recognizes basic shapes in an object or picture**

F. **Names basic writing strokes: top-to-bottom line, left-to-right line, slant left line, slant right line, backward circle, forward circle.**

G. **Recognizes basic writing strokes in an object or picture**

H. **Traces and writes basic strokes**

I. **Traces upper and lower-case letters and numerals 0–10**

J. **Writes letters of name beginning with initial upper-case letter followed by lower-case letters**

III. Pre-Arithmetic

A. **Matching**

1. Matches sets containing the same number of objects (1–10)

2. Matches like coins: penny, nickel, dime, quarter

B. **Identification**

1. Identifies larger of two groups containing unequal numbers of objects (1–10)

2. Associates numeral with corresponding group of objects (1–10)

3. Associates numeral 0 with an empty set

4. Names coins: penny, nickel, dime, quarter

C. **Sequencing**

1. Counts from 1 to 10

2. Arranges numerals 1 to 10 in correct sequence

3. Identifies objects in sequence using: first, last, next, middle

4. Identifies objects in a sequence using ordinal numbers first to fifth

5. Follows directions to complete a task consisting of numbered steps

Basic Skills in Kindergarten

Basic Skills in Kindergarten:
Foundations for Formal Learning

edited by
Walter B. Barbe
Michael N. Milone, Jr.
Virginia H. Lucas
Jack W. Humphrey

Zaner-Bloser, Inc.
Columbus, Ohio

Designed by Thomas M. Wasylyk.

ISBN No. 0-88309-104-6
Reorder No. 250050-8

Contents

SECTION TWO

The importance of the kinde is agreed upon by educators, parents, and others concerned with y nildren. Despite this agreement, there is little consensus on how best to educate the child during this vitally important year. Should the child enjoy the unfettered life to which he or she had become accustomed and progress through naturally occurring stages of development, or should the structure of the later school years be introduced so as to take advantage of the learning potential of the child?

Quite obviously, neither of these extremes is the answer for all children. To elicit a child's full potential during the kindergarten year, some degree of structure must be imposed; but there must be sufficient freedom to allow naturally occurring development to take place. It is to these propositions that this book is dedicated.

In compiling the readings that constitute this text, we leaned heavily on those authors who favored a formal approach to kindergarten education. Our reason for so doing is that pre-academic skill instruction is the less well-developed of the prevalent kindergarten methods. Traditional, informal kindergarten procedures date from the early 19th century, at which time Froebel coined the term and inititated such practices. As a consequence of this long history, informal approaches are comparatively well-established. The formal approach, on the other hand, had its start in the middle of the 20th century and is therefore still in its nascent stage.

Although our selections overwhelmingly reflect pre-academic skill instruction, we repeatedly make the point that such instruction must be complemented by an equal emphasis on informal activities. The child who acquires prerequisite perceptual, motor, and cognitive skills without developing parallel language, affective, and social abilities is at a great disadvantage. Educating the whole child is our goal, and we believe that the best way to attain it is through a kindergarten program that reflects the synthesis of the traditional and formal schools of thought.

Overview

INTRODUCTION

Kindergarten is one of the most important school years. It is the time when a child's motivation to learn is at its highest, and when environmental factors that impede later educational progress have not yet taken their toll. The combination of enthusiasm and ability that is characteristic of the kindergarten child is rarely equalled in subsequent years.

The foundation of future academic success is laid during the kindergarten year. Basic readiness skills become part of the child's repertoire, attitudes toward school and learning are formed, and interpersonal and linguistic abilities are put to the test within the context of a cultural institution. A child who experiences a productive and enjoyable kindergarten year is well on the way to a successful learning experience.

Two Perspectives on Kindergarten

There are two schools of thought concerning kindergarten education. One of these, the traditional, informal approach, is based on the premise that an unstructured environment rich in linguistic expression will promote the acquisition of common knowledge as a consequence of observing or participating in natural events (Moore, 1977). The second approach is more formal, and comprises focused academic activities. Learning to learn and skill mastery are the broad goals of this latter method (Moore, 1977).

These two schools of thought are not necessarily antithetical. They can, in fact, complement each other, and if kindergarten is to be a strong foundation for future academic success, then both formal and informal educational experiences must be offered to each child.

Although we advocate a middle of the road position reflecting the synthesis of formal and informal methods of kindergarten education, this book focuses on pre-academic skill instruction. Our reasons for this emphasis are as follows:

1. Incidental learning of affective and linguistic skills, the goals of traditional instruction, can be brought about by many experiences. Pre-academic skills, on the other hand, are rarely learned incidentally, and require direct instruction. The selections that constitute this book can provide kindergarten teachers with a framework within which pre-academic skill instruction may be undertaken.

2. The literature is replete with references that treat the traditional approach to kindergarten instruction. Quite the opposite is true of skill instruction. The teacher, administrator, or teacher in training who wishes to become familiar with skill instruction must do a good deal of library research before a substantial number of pertinent references are amassed.

3. Delineating the goals of traditional kindergarten instruction is difficult. General statements can be made as to which overarching purposes are consistent with the informal approach, but identifying specific objectives is problematic. With skill instruction, however, establishing objectives is straightforward. It is a relatively simple task, therefore, to develop a curriculum which relies upon pre-academic skill instruction.

4. Direct pre-academic skill instruction appears to bring about better cognitive growth than does traditional instruction. As King (1978) has pointed out:

> . . . the majority of studies reported the direct approach to be more effective, especially with children who might be classed as low achievers (p. 505).

It is necessary here to reiterate that by adopting as our topic pre-academic skill instruction, we are not belittling the importance of the affective or linguistic skills that are consistent with traditional instruction. We agree that:

> Increasing amounts of psychological research reveal the affective and cognitive components of growth to be so inextricably bound together that we can no longer think of working with the child as a disengaged intellect (Weber, 1973, p. 269).

Pre-academic skill instruction is not the be-all and end-all of kindergarten. It is, however, an essential element that must be included in the curriculum if we are to prevent kindergarten from becoming a ". . . laissez-faire situation . . . with little direct adult intervention" (Foerster, 1975, p. 81).

Kindergarten and the Concept of Readiness

Readiness entered into professional vocabularies and the curriculum in the 1920s, when it was believed that readiness was solely the product of maturation (Durkin, 1970). Psychologists and educators of the time were caught up in the mental measurement movement spawned by Terman's revision of Binet and Simon's scales. The search for the behavioral correlates of readiness was instigated by the belief that once these correlates were isolated, education would experience a quantum leap of progress.

Today's concept of readiness is far removed from that of the 1920s. It can be defined as "... various combinations of abilities which result from or are the product of nature and nurture interacting with each other" (Durkin, 1970, p. 530). Ausubel (1959) offers a functionally related definition: readiness is "... the adequacy of existing capacity in relation to the demands of a given learning task" (p. 147).

Kindergarten is a readiness year, but it must be realized that readiness and kindergarten are not synonymous. At each level of education, there are certain skills that fall under the heading "readiness." In other words, "... whatever comes before 'readies' the individual for what comes after" (Foerster, 1975, p. 81). Consistent with this definition, kindergarten is best regarded as the proving ground in which skills necessary for the primary grades are developed and practiced.

Beller (1970) has interpreted readiness in a way that is helpful in maintaining a realistic perspective on kindergarten:

> ... activities and operations which define readiness relate in some logical way to new activities and operations which are to be learned or to the educational method by means of which the new operations are to be taught (p. 729).

Kindergarten, then, as a readiness year, should consist of activities that prepare the child for the information or methods that are to come later. Formal instruction in reading, writing, and arithmetic have a decidedly minor place in the kindergarten curriculum, whereas pre-reading, pre-writing, pre-arithmetic, linguistic, affective, and other related skills should predominate.

Cognitive Abilities of Kindergarten Children

It has only been in the past few years that the potential of kindergarten children has been appreciated. In times past, the child who had not yet entered school was considered cognitively inept and egocentric. Evidence has begun to pile up against this view (Gelman, 1979), and today it is generally acknowledged that the abilities of pre-first grade children are more than adequate for the pre-academic skills proposed in this book.

Just as it is inappropriate to assume that all kindergarten children are cognitively inept, it is also incorrect to take for granted that they all have attained the same level of developmental maturity. As Lesiak (1978) has suggested, "... children will continue to enter kindergarten with varied abilities, experiential backgrounds, and interests. Therefore, educators must implement kindergarten based on a real consideration of differences" (p. 137).

3

Conceptual and perceptual abilities relate to kindergarten performance in two ways. First and foremost, these abilities govern whether or not the child can accomplish the task. Of this consideration we are well aware. But, there is also a second, more subtle factor in operation. The child's level of cognitive maturity also determines whether or not the task is understood.

Hardy, Stennett, and Smythe (1974) examined in detail the development of auditory and visual language concepts as they related to instructional strategies. The results of their work were both impressive and useful. For example, they found that over 90 percent of the participants in their study entered kindergarten with the ability to follow the direction "draw a circle around." This in itself is hardly a major discovery, but it takes on added meaning when it is contrasted with another finding that only 51 percent of their participants could follow the direction "underline." The implication is that children's errors on tasks in which the necessary response was underlining may reflect the inability to follow directions rather than a weakness in the skill of interest.

A by-product of the study conducted by Hardy and her colleagues is that they obtained some indication of the concepts that develop incidentally over the course of the kindergarten year. One instance is the temporal use of the term *middle*. At entry into kindergarten, 25 percent of the children could correctly follow directions involving the term *middle*. By the end of kindergarten, 40 percent could do so correctly, even though direct instruction was provided to only 10 percent of the participants.

This research on the language of instruction points out that cognitive development is more than a vague construct whose applicability is marginal. As Hardy and her associates (1974) have shown, the concepts and terminology which children can understand relate directly to their functioning in the classroom.

The variability in cognitive skills of young children bears importantly on the kindergarten curriculum in that the same procedures may be introductory instruction for some and refinement for others. Simply put, there is enough difference among the characteristics of kindergarten children to warrant differential programming. Both Beller (1970) and Weinberg (1979) support this position by asserting that sensitivity to individual differences in cognitive styles, learning patterns, and motivational variables is necessary for successful kindergarten instruction.

Given that the purpose of kindergarten is to prepare the child for the primary grades, formal academic instruction in reading, writing, and arithmetic should be held to a minimum at this critical time. The learning activities that do take place must be developmentally appropriate and articulated with later content and methodology. It is equally important that individual differences in style as well as rate of learning be recognized at this time (Weber, 1973), and that

4

instruction be implemented in a way that is consistent with each child's abilities and needs. By keeping these considerations in mind, we can avoid making "... unwarranted statements about the nature of preschool curricula" (Gelman, 1979, p. 905).

As is true of many academically related variables, socioeconomic status has been found to relate significantly and positively with the skill level of entering kindergarten children (Hall, Moretz, and Statom, 1976; Miller, 1969). Children who learned to write prior to formal instruction in kindergarten or grade one most often came from homes in which at least one parent was a college graduate (Hall, Moretz, and Statom, 1976). Letter and word recognition, picture interpretation, sequencing, discrimination, and rhyming abilities of middle-class children were somewhat better than those of upper lower-class children, and considerably better than those of children from lower lower-class families (Miller, 1969).

Parents in the middle class and above have the resources, opportunities, and motivation to provide their children with experiences that promote skill development. Among these experiences are family trips followed by discussions, the use of manipulative materials, and reading to children. Lower-class children encounter these experiences much less frequently, so the skills fostered by the experiences are not so likely to emerge.

Before proceeding to a discussion of the skills upon which kindergarten should be based, it is important to note that although we are advocating that direct pre-academic skill instruction be made available to all kindergarten children, such instruction is even more essential for lower socioeconomic children. Only then can they begin making up the deficit they have experienced as a consequence of a comparatively impoverished environment.

Kindergarten Skills

There are fundamentally four classes of skills that relate to kindergarten age children: cognitive, affective, psychomotor, and linguistic (Foerster, 1975). Cognitive and psychomotor skills are dominant in direct, formal instructional programs, while affective and linguistic abilities are favored by traditional, informal instruction.

Another way to view kindergarten competencies is to relate them to hemispheric specialization theory. Analytic and linear sequential tasks, which are left-hemisphere functions, are best learned through the structured activities of a formal kindergarten. The synthetic, parallel skills most often associated with right-hemisphere functioning seem to develop incidentally as a consequence of early childhood experiences or traditional, unstructured kindergarten programs.

Emery (1975) has divided the skills that preface reading into two categories: primary and secondary. Primary indicators are oral vocabulary, reading curiosity, auditory discrimination, and visual discrimination. Secondary indicators include attention, compliance, memory, copying ability, and page turning. From Emery's hierarchy and comments, one can infer that primary indicators may require direct instruction, while secondary indicators can be strengthened through natural informal experiences.

Piagetian theory also provides a taxonomy useful in organizing skills appropriate for kindergarten children. Kirkland (1978) groups relevant skills under three headings: organic development, social development, and symbolic development. She also asserts that cognitive maturity, as reflected by directionality, distinguishing letter features, classification, attention, and association, is the key to learning to read. One can presume, therefore, that activities that engender cognitive maturity are suitable topics for kindergarten instruction.

Hoffman and Fillmer (1979) advocate a curriculum based on learning experiences. The skills that they deem essential fall into the following categories: problem solving, understanding concepts, and functional language. The essence of Hoffman and Fillmer's position is that kindergarten should be a time when children are learning rather than teachers teaching.

Yet another scheme for classifying kindergarten goals has been offered by Yawkey and Silvern (1976). They divided kindergarten goals into content and process categories. An example of a content goal is associating a letter with its most frequent sound. A process goal, of which problem solving or classification are instances, lacks a specific referent.

These classification systems are just a few of the many that have been proposed in recent years. The proliferation of methods of organizing kindergarten skills suggests that there is no best way of accomplishing this task, and that a skill list is as much a reflection of an author's orientation as it is a description of the reality of childhood. Any list of skills and the structure by which they are systematized are serviceable if they contribute to the education and development of young children.

The Zaner-Bloser Kindergarten Check Lists: Foundation and Companion Skills

The skills that we are proposing reflect several sources: other lists of skills, the objectives promulgated by state departments of education, the results of past research, and the contributions of practitioners. They are organized into *foundation skills* and *companion skills*. Foundation skills are primarily cognitive and psychomotor, and are best promoted through direct instruction. Companion skills are no less important, but are of a type that are often acquired incidentally. They require direct instruction only when the opportunity to assimilate them has not been provided by the environment or classroom activities.

FOUNDATION SKILLS

I. Pre-Reading

A. Matching

1. Matches familiar objects
2. Matches basic colors: red, yellow, blue, green, orange, purple, black, brown
3. Matches basic shapes: square, circle, triangle, rectangle
4. Matches objects by other features: taste, size, smell, texture, etc.

B. Labeling

1. Names familiar objects
2. Names basic colors
3. Names basic shapes

C. Classification

1. Classifies objects by color
2. Classifies objects by shape
3. Classifies objects by other characteristics

D. Sequencing

1. Sequences objects by size
2. Sequences four pictures to make a story

E. Symbolic ability

1. Recognizes own name in print
2. Names upper-case letters
3. Names lower-case letters
4. Matches upper-case letters with their lower-case correspondents
5. Associates printed words with objects
6. Groups spoken words by final sounds
7. Groups spoken words by initial sounds
8. Recognizes final sounds in spoken words
9. Recognizes initial sounds in spoken words
10. Associates letters with their most frequent sounds

F. Closure

1. Completes a picture in which a part is missing
2. Completes a spoken sentence in which one familiar word is missing

G. Comprehension

1. Follows directions involving spatial relationship words: under, over, in, out, near, far, up, down, left, right, front, back, top, bottom, above, below, inside, outside, beginning, end, on, off, before, after
2. Understands opposites: under-over, in-out, near-far, up-down, left-right, front-back, top-bottom, above-below, inside-outside, beginning-end, on-off, before-after
3. Recalls main idea and main characters from a short story or a picture
4. Recalls details from a short story or picture
5. Identifies cause and effect relationship in stories, events, or pictures
6. Predicts outcomes in stories, events, or pictures

7

7. Draws inferences from stories, events, or pictures

8. Distinguishes reality from fantasy

9. Creates stories based on a described or pictured situation

II. Pre-Writing

A. Distinguishes top from bottom

B. Follows top-to-bottom progression

C. Distinguishes left from right

D. Follows left-to-right progression

E. Recognizes basic shapes in an object or picture

F. Names basic writing strokes: top-to-bottom line, left-to-right line, slant left line, slant right line, backward circle, forward circle.

G. Recognizes basic writing strokes in an object or picture

H. Traces and writes basic strokes

I. Traces upper- and lower-case letters and numerals 0–10

J. Writes letters of name beginning with initial upper-case letter followed by lower-case letters

III. Pre-Arithmetic

A. Matching

1. Matches sets containing the same number of objects (1–10)

2. Matches like coins: penny, nickel, dime, quarter

B. Identification

1. Identifies larger of two groups containing unequal numbers of objects (1–10)

2. Associates numeral with corresponding group of objects (1–10)

3. Associates numeral 0 with an empty set

4. Names coins: penny, nickel, dime, quarter

C. Sequencing

1. Counts from 1 to 10

2. Arranges numerals 1 to 10 in correct sequence

3. Identifies objects in sequence using: first, last, next, middle

4. Identifies objects in a sequence using ordinal numbers first to fifth

5. Follows directions to complete a task consisting of numbered steps

COMPANION SKILLS

I. Task Orientation

A. Attention span is adequate for age appropriate assigned tasks

B. Follows directions

C. Makes decisions

D. Marks responses

E. Works independently

F. Works cooperatively

G. Interacts appropriately with peers and adults

H. Asks help of an adult when appropriate

II. Affect

A. Expression

1. Interprets feelings given pictures or facial expressions

2. Expresses emotions appropriately

3. Expresses self spontaneously

4. Shares personal experiences

B. Attitudes

1. Respects others

8

2. Has a positive attitude toward self

3. Has a positive attitude toward school and learning

III. General Readiness

A. Perceptual and motor skills

1. Gross and fine motor skills are adequate for age appropriate tasks

2. Recognizes familiar textures, tastes, smells, sounds, and sights

3. Localizes the source of an auditory stimulus

4. Follows moving auditory and visual stimuli

5. Recognizes that objects and events have characteristics in more than one modality

B. Self Awareness

1. Identifies body parts: head, arms, hands, legs, feet, eyes, ears, nose, mouth, fingers, toes

2. Matches body parts with their function

C. Memory

1. Long and short term memory are adequate for age appropriate assigned tasks

2. Gives name and address upon request

D. Cognition

1. Identifies the disparity in a set in which only one element is different: B B A B

2. Progresses from concrete to abstract

3. Understands part to whole relationship

4. Seeks new information

5. Grasps fundamentals of conservation of mass and number

E. Time concepts

1. Understands morning, afternoon, day, night

2. Understands the seasons and their weather

3. Associates time with events: in the morning, you go to school

F. Language

1. Auditory

a. Is interested in spoken language

b. Enjoys being read to

c. Reproduces pronounced familiar words

d. Communicates using sentences

e. Recognizes minimal differences in spoken words: hit—sit; cap—cup; cat—cab

f. Differentiates between spoken words on the basis of length

g. Reproduces a spoken sentence consisting of five familiar words

h. Retells a story in own words

2. Visual

a. Is interested in written language

b. Knows that the purpose of written language is to communicate

c. Recognizes boundaries of printed words

d. Paces dictation to the writing speed of the person recording

e. Has book awareness skills

   1. Distinguishes top of book from bottom

   2. Distinguishes front of book from back

   3. Holds book with right side up and cover facing front

   4. Distinguishes among pictures, letters, numerals, and words

The skills in the Zaner-Bloser Check List are intended to assist in the management of kindergarten instruction. We are not recommending that each skill be taught in isolation. Rote learning of linear sequential skills has not been shown to be generalizable to the academic skills that follow in the later years (Wingert, 1969). Instead, we propose that traditional, informal activities be used to help the child apply these skills in such a way that a transition occurs from preoperational to concrete operational thinking.

Several strategies can be used to accomplish this transition. Sigel (1979) asserts that the process of guided inquiry is a critical element in fostering representational thinking. As the child examines events and experiences inquisitively, distance is established from the ongoing present. The child can then begin to ". . . transcend the immediate, evoke the past, as well as anticipate the future" (Sigel, 1979, p. 70). Representational thinking is intimately related to the ability to read.

Kirkland (1978) advances the proposition that teaching strategies should cultivate the logical abilities necessary for reading. Nevius (1977) agrees, stating that abstract thinking contributes to good reading, so pre-reading programs should include teaching for logical thought. The methods Nevius suggests are grouping by common characteristics, patterning, comparing, classifying, predicting, and learning to transfer problem solving skills from one situation to another.

Reading aloud to children, one of the mainstays of traditional early childhood education, can be invaluable in teaching children both pre-academic skills and problem solving strategies. Crowell and Au (1979) have developed a scale of questions that can transform the reading aloud of stories into a program for the systematic development of comprehension skills. The questions increase in difficulty, beginning with general inquiries concerning the theme of the story and progressing to queries about the relationship of the story to other tales. The authors recommend that the questions teachers ask be at or beyond the level of the child to assure that the child will become an active processor of information. Further suggestions as to how storytelling can be used as a structured teaching tool are made by Schickedanz (1978), who notes that elementary but critical abilities such as memorization of story lines, locating print in books, and matching letters and sounds can be outcomes of this enjoyable activity.

The taxonomy of skills we have assembled and the selections that have been incorporated in this text can serve as the basis of a curriculum that occasions the development of the cognitive, psychomotor, linguistic, and affective abilities necessary for academic success in the primary grades. By borrowing from both formal and traditional approaches to kindergarten education, the teacher can promote in an enjoyable way the specific skills, problem solving strategies, and abstract thinking abilities that underlie academic success in the later grades.

Modality Strengths of Kindergarten Children

Of all of the characteristics of young children, their perceptual or modality strengths are perhaps the least understood. A modality is a sensory channel through which information is received and processed; the most efficient channel corresponds to a child's modality strength. Vision, audition, and kinesthesia are the educationally relevant modalities. A child may have a strength in any one of these modalities, or may evidence a mixed modality strength which comprises two or more channels (Barbe, Swassing, and Milone, 1979).

In the neonate, kinesthesia seems to be in a more advanced stage of development than audition or vision (Schiebel and Schiebel, 1964). Subsequent years, however, see a shift to the auditory modality, and in the pre-first grade child, audition is dominant (Barbe et al., 1979; Niemark, 1975). Vision eventually becomes the most important perceptual channel.

At the same time that the modality shift described above is occurring, another change is taking place. Whereas in the young child the modalities are comparatively distinct and independent, in adolescents and adults the modalities tend to become integrated with one another. As a result of maturation, strategies are developed to transfer information from one modality to another (Chalfant and Scheffelin, 1969).

The contention that audition is the favored modality of kindergarten children seems to conflict with the statement of Paradis and Peterson (1975) that children of this age have better visual than auditory discrimination abilities. These authors base their statement on the finding that children could discriminate among pictures, designs, letters and printed words, but were less able to differentiate between spoken words on the basis of initial and final sounds.

By examining the steps involved in visual and auditory discrimination, one can see that these two seemingly equivalent tasks are quite disparate in terms of difficulty for the child. Visual discrimination requires only that a point by point comparison be made between two continually present stimuli. It is not necessary that memoric images be matched. In contrast, differentiating between two spoken words means that first one, then the other, must be stored in short term memory, and then a feature by feature comparison must be attempted. In other words, the auditory task of comparing two minimally different words of three letters each is the cognitive equivalent of identifying differences between two remembered visual images of three aspects each in which only one aspect is distinctive. It seems, therefore, that Paradis and Peterson

(1975) based their argument on non-equivalent tasks, and that the superiority of the auditory modality of kindergarten children still holds.

How can knowledge of kindergarten children's modality characteristics be of practical use in the classroom? First, reliance upon the auditory modality will bring about better responses than will visual clues. Kindergarten children are accustomed to interacting with their peers and the adults in their life through the oral/aural mode. When it is important that a message get across to the child, audition is the mode of preference.

Second, use multisensory materials with caution. There is no doubt that integration of the modalities can be fostered in the kindergarten child. It is important, however, that such integration not be initiated at the expense of other, more age appropriate skills. There is ample time in the later school years to promote modality integration.

Third, if multisensory materials are being used, give the child the option of using them in only one modality at a time. This will give those children with mixed modality strengths the chance to capitalize upon their higher level of cognitive maturity, while at the same time allowing other children the opportunity to learn through their single modality strength.

Pre-Reading Instruction

Reading is undoubtedly the most important academic skill. All other subjects are dependent upon the ability to extract meaning from written symbols. The child who has reading difficulties invariably manifests correlative problems in other disciplines.

By extension, pre-reading skills are of similar importance. The frequency with which articles dealing with pre-reading skills appear in the literature attests to this. More journal space is devoted to pre-reading than to pre-writing and pre-arithmetic combined.

A survey of teachers conducted by La Conte (1968) supports the argument that kindergarten children are not yet ready to read. Respondents reported overwhelmingly, however, that they taught preliminary skills such as naming letters of the alphabet and associating sounds with printed letters.

The chief reason that pre-reading skills must be taught in kindergarten is because many children are ". . . not able to acquire proficiency in the reading readiness skills in the time that could be allotted in the first grade" (Stanchfield, 1971, p. 701). There is so much material to be presented in the first grade that either antecedent skills are presumed learned and not taught, or the reading skills that should be learned in the first grade are ignored. Kindergarten, then, gives some children the chance to learn elements of reading they might otherwise miss (MacGinitie, 1976).

The kindergarten reading curriculum should comprise developmentally appropriate language learning activities and perceptual training (Caldwell, 1973). Further, it should instill in the child an enjoyment of the spoken and written word. Only through this combination of skill instruction and enhancement of positive attitudes will the child become an able and enthusiastic reader in subsequent school years.

In planning pre-reading instruction, the teacher should maintain an awareness of what takes place in the first grade, for at no point do pre-reading skills end and reading skills commence (Durkin, 1969). Education is a continuum, and the more closely kindergarten pre-reading is aligned with first grade reading, the more likely it is that a child will become a good reader.

Although it seems that skill in reading is dependent in a general way upon prior development in the areas of perceptual and conceptual ability and language use (Sawyer, 1975), there appears to be little direct and identifiable transfer between perceptual skills as such and reading ability. In other words, the ability to match figures, sequence objects, identify basic shapes, and so on has been found to relate only in an ill-defined way to later reading achievement. What, then, are some of the effective measures we may undertake to build reading ability upon a pre-reading base?

One is teaching problem solving. As was mentioned previously, the logical thinking component of problem solving is closely intertwined with reading ability (Sigel, 1979). Direct instruction, natural experiences, or contrived circumstances in which logical thought is developed are likely to enhance later reading ability.

A second is promoting word perception (Sawyer, 1975). The child who learns to recognize individual words as the basic unit of communication is better prepared to begin reading than is the child who cannot identify the boundaries of a spoken or written word.

Enhancing pattern recognition abilities is a third measure. Montgomery (1977) describes an assessment tool and instructional procedures based on patterns which consist of the strokes of the printed alphabet. Children who were trained with the pattern recognition materials were reported to have improved significantly in reading performance.

Another measure, teaching to children's learning strengths, is not so well documented as those cited above, but shows promise as an effective instructional technique. The concept is not difficult to understand: "teachers should make efforts to design and use instructional materials, as well as employ teaching methodologies, that accommodate the child's perceptual learning abilities level'' (Gilberg and Gilberg, 1979, p. 43). Certain children favor one or the other sensory channels, and it makes sense to capitalize upon this preference or strength to teach pre-reading skills. Barbe, Swassing, and Milone (1979) describe teaching to children's modality strengths, Dunn and Dunn (1978) discuss how instruction can be made to coincide with children's individual learning styles, while Wheatley (1979) and Restak (1979) advocate a curriculum that reflects hemispheric specialization.

In discussing measures that further later reading performance, the obvious must not be overlooked. For example, discriminating among letters, numerals, words, and pictures is necessary if the child is eventually to read. So, too, is the knowledge that written language is meant to communicate, and that it parallels spoken language. Finally, the child must know how to use printed material, such as, which is the front of a book as opposed to the back, and the top versus the bottom, where a line of print starts and ends, how one page leads to another. As elementary as these skills sound, they are of such importance that they cannot be taken for granted. They are usually incidental outcomes of home or school learning activities, but if they are not present, they should be the objects of direct instruction.

The pre-reading curriculum should be compatible with kindergarten children's abilities, engender a love of reading, and begin to lead children from the preoperational stage to concrete operational thinking. But, it should not be overly regimented, nor should it consist entirely of pencil and paper activities. Such practices are likely to cause information overload (Tutolo, 1979), and will most assuredly dampen the child's enthusiasm.

Pre-Writing Instruction

The back to basics movement in contemporary education has prompted a new interest in handwriting. Handwriting is again being viewed as a fundamental competency and, increasingly, pre-handwriting skills are being introduced in kindergarten.

Hall, Moretz, and Statom (1976) have identified factors that are characteristic of children who begin writing prior to direct instruction. These children observed others writing, had access to reading matter and materials necessary to write, evidenced the desire to communicate, and had been introduced to letter names. Not surprisingly, these factors can be readily converted to an informal curriculum suitable for handwriting instruction.

Pre-handwriting skills might emerge in an unstructured but conducive situation; a planned, sequential curriculum is much to be preferred. In the latter curriculum, it is more likely that poor handwriting habits will be avoided and prerequisite skills learned. These prerequisite skills were identified by Lamme (1979):

- small muscle development
- eye hand coordination
- holding a writing tool
- basic strokes
- letter perception
- orientation to printed language

Lamme cautions that it is important to introduce these skills but not to rush the child into them.

The steps that make up pre-handwriting instruction are clear. The child first learns directions (top and bottom, left and right), and then to recognize basic strokes (vertical line, horizontal line, slanted lines, and circles). Basic stroke production follows, which serves as a direct preface to the production of the manuscript alphabet and numerals. We feel that writing letters and numerals is optional in kindergarten. Research neither supports nor rejects the notion of teaching letter and numeral production in kindergarten, so it is best left to the discretion of the teacher.

In reviewing the literature and polling teachers, it is apparent that most teachers feel children either enter kindergarten with the ability to recognize their own first name, or acquire the skill soon after entry. They also agree al-most universally that kindergarten children can learn to write the letters of their name, either using a model or from memory. It seems realistic, therefore, to treat name recognition and writing as separate from pre-handwriting and pre-reading instruction, and to pursue these skills independently.

One other aspect of pre-handwriting instruction is worth noting. Motivation is the key to pre-handwriting (and handwriting) success. Children who want to learn to write, and whose enthusiasm to write is maintained, become good writers, from both penmanship and composition perspectives. There is no bet-ter time to establish a good motivation to write than in kindergarten. Pre-hand-writing instruction is gamelike, and results in a permanent product of which the child can be proud. If there is one area in which every child in the class can excel, it is in pre-handwriting instruction.

Pre-Arithmetic Instruction

As was mentioned previously, we have traditionally underestimated the com-petence of young children. Nowhere is this more apparent than in the realm of pre-arithmetic skills. Piaget's contentions have contributed to this situation, as have the unsystematic observations of educators.

Child development researchers, however, have suspected for some time that the numeric concepts of pre-schoolers are fairly well developed. Ginsberg (1969) found that five-year-olds attended to number and not color dimensions, while Watson (1977) reported that the pre-schoolers in her sample described events using number rather than shape or color descriptions. Thus, experimental evidence suggests that number is more meaningful to kindergarten children than is color, the cue most often used to teach number concepts.

Conservation is an ability that most experts agree is beyond the ken of pre-school children. Yet, Gelman (1979) has shown that ". . . given appropriate training, one can elicit conservation behavior in children who initially fail to conserve on classical conservation tests" (p. 184). We are not recommending that conservation be taught to all kindergarten children; no practical purpose would be served by so doing. Gelman's (1979) quote is mentioned in the heuristic sense that it expands the acknowledged pre-arithmetic potential of the kindergarten child.

As is true with most cognitive abilities, mathematic concepts are not grasped with a flash of insight, but proceed instead through several stages. D'Mello and Williamson (1969) have described the sequence by which one concept, cardinal correspondence, is acquired:

1. Numerals are recited in sequence.
2. Visual arrays of equal quantity are matched.
3. Spoken numerals are matched with quantities.
4. Printed numerals are matched with quantities.

Schwartz (1969) argues that ". . . children come to kindergarten with considerable knowledge upon which the school can build an interesting, challenging, and sequential curriculum" (p. 67). To identify what body of knowledge they possess, he has devised an inventory to assess the mathematical achievement of pre-school children. The results of the validation research for his assessment inventory substantiate his claim of children's arithmetic competence. Likewise, Williams (1965) found that kindergarten children manifested a substantial number of mathematical concepts, skills, and abilities. These skills were related to some circumstances and conditions in the pre-school environment such as familial socioeconomic status. Williams concluded that kindergarten children can benefit from appropriate mathematics instruction.

One of the problems faced by early childhood educators is deciding which elements should form the kindergarten pre-arithmetic curriculum. Kurtz (1978) surveyed kindergarten teachers, and attempted to class pre-arithmetic skills into those that were clearly kindergarten competencies, those that were questionable, and those that were clearly not kindergarten competencies. The results of his survey can serve as a useful guide in developing a kindergarten pre-arithmetic curriculum. The work of Holmes (1963) serves a similar function, and can assist in deciding the order in which kindergarten pre-arithmetic competencies should be introduced.

Conclusion

When the young child enters kindergarten, he or she is embarking on a journey that will require a significant amount of time and effort for more than a decade. The direction the child receives during this critical year will determine to a great extent the outcome of the journey.

It should be obvious to anyone who cares about young children that a regimen consisting entirely of either pointless play or endless hours of pencil and paper activities is not the best way for the journey to begin. Weber (1973) cautions that such a singleness of purpose ". . . tends to crowd out recognition of the complexity of human growth" (p. 268). The child needs a synthesis of the skill instruction that has been proven to contribute to cognitive and psychomotor growth, and the unstructured interaction whose end product is affective and linguistic competence. A curriculum that embodies the best features of both formal and traditional kindergarten approaches will most likely set the stage for a successful school experience.

Several fundamental principles underlie the curriculum recommendations we support:
1. Children possess a level of cognitive ability that allows them to benefit from direct instruction.
2. This level of ability is not the same for all children. An important first step in curricular planning is assessing entry level competencies.
3. There are certain skills that the child must learn to become ready for the formal academic activities of the later primary grades. These skills should serve as the basis of both direct instruction and the unstructured activities intended to promote incidental learning.
4. Formal instruction in reading, writing, and arithmetic is not the proper emphasis of kindergarten. Some children may acquire formal academic skills incidentally in kindergarten, but it is not until the first grade that direct instruction of these skills should occur.
5. Phenomenal growth in several domains takes place during the kindergarten year. If ambiguous goals are in effect, this growth will be "undirected and haphazard" (Yawkey and Silvern, 1976, p. 25).

Throughout this overview, and in selecting contributions for this text, we have avoided dictating teaching methods. Instead, we have attempted to establish a set of principles or guidelines within which the teacher can shape a program of instruction that best suits the needs of his or her students. By adhering to these principles, teachers can ensure that kindergarten will be a place where children are ". . . challenged, their needs met, and in which each child is considered . . ." (Foerster, 1975, p. 83).

REFERENCES

Ausubel, D.P. Viewpoints from related disciplines: human growth and development. *Teachers College Record,* 1959, *60,* 245–254.

Barbe, W.B., Swassing, R.H., and Milone, M.N. *Teaching through modality strengths: concepts and practices.* Columbus: Zaner-Bloser, 1979.

Beller, E.K. The concept readiness and several applications. *The Reading Teacher,* 1970, *23,* 727–737.

Caldwell, B.M. Just what is kindergarten for? *Instructor,* 1973, *83* (2), 134–135.

Chalfant, J.C. and Scheffelin, M.A. *Central processing dysfunctions in children: a review of research.* U.S. Department of Health, Education, and Welfare, National Institute of Neurological Diseases and Stroke, 1969.

Crowell, D.C. and Au, K.H. Using a scale of questions to improve listening comprehension. *Language Arts,* 1979, *56,* 38–43.

D'Mello, S. and Williamson, E. The development of the number concept: a scalogram analysis. *Child Development,* 1969, *40,* 681–688.

Dunn, R. and Dunn, K. *Teaching students through their individual learning styles: a practical approach.* Reston, VA: Reston, 1978.

Durkin, D. *Pre-reading skills.* Paper presented at the Convention of the International Reading Association, 1969.

Durkin, D. Reading readiness. *The Reading Teacher,* 1970, *23,* 528–534, 564.

Emery, D.G. *Teach your preschooler to read.* New York: Simon and Schuster, 1975.

Foerster, L.M. Kindergarten—what can it be? What should it be? *Elementary English,* 1975, *52,* 81–83.

Gelman, R. Preschool thought. *American Psychologist,* 1979, *34,* 900–905.

Gilberg, L.J. and Gilberg, S.F. Sight or sound? *Early Years,* 1979, *9* (1), 42–43, 59.

Ginsberg, R. Number and color response in the young child. *Journal of Experimental Child Psychology,* 1969, *7,* 265–273.

Hall, M.A., Moretz, S.A., and Statom, J. Writing before grade one—a study of early writers. *Language Arts,* 1976, *53,* 582–585.

Hardy, M., Stennet, R.G., and Smythe, P.C. Development of auditory and visual language concepts and relationship to instructional strategies in kindergarten. *Elementary English,* 1974, *51,* 525–532.

Hoffman, S. and Fillmer, H.T. Thought, language, and reading readiness. *The Reading Teacher*, 1979, *33*, 290–294.

Holmes, E.E. What do pre-first-grade children know about number? *Elementary School Journal*, 1963, *63*, 397–403.

King, E.M. Prereading programs: direct vs. incidental teaching. *The Reading Teacher*, 1978, *31*, 504–510.

Kirkland, E.R. A Piagetian interpretation of beginning reading instruction. *The Reading Teacher*, 1978, *31*, 497–503.

Kurtz, V.R. Kindergarten mathematics—a survey. *Arithmetic Teacher*, 1978, *25*, 51–53.

LaConte, C. Reading in kindergarten. *The Reading Teacher*, 1968, *23*, 116–120.

Lamme, L.L. Handwriting in an early childhood curriculum. *Young Children*, 1979, *34* (1), 20–27.

Lesiak, J. Reading in kindergarten: what the research doesn't tell us. *The Reading Teacher*, 1978, *32*, 135–138.

MacGinitie, W.H. When should we begin to teach reading? *Language Arts*, 1976, *53*, 878–882.

Miller, W.H. Home prereading experiences and first-grade reading achievement. *The Reading Teacher*, 1969, *22*, 641–645.

Montgomery, D. Teaching prereading skills through training in pattern recognition. *The Reading Teacher*, 1977, *30*, 616–623.

Moore, S.G. Old and new approaches to preschool education. *Young Children*, 1977, *33* (1), 69–72.

Nevius, J.R. Teaching for logical thinking is a prereading activity. *The Reading Teacher*, 1977, *30*, 641–643.

Niemark, E.D. Intellectual development during adolescence. In F.D. Horowitz (Ed.) *Review of child development research, Volume 4*, Chicago: University of Chicago Press, 1975, 541–594.

Paradis, E. and Peterson, J. Readiness training implications from research. *The Reading Teacher*, 1975, *28*, 445–448.

Restak, R.M. *The brain: the last frontier*. Garden City, NY: Doubleday, 1979.

Sawyer, D.J. Readiness factors for reading: a different view. *The Reading Teacher*, 1975, *28*, 620–624.

Schickedanz, J.A. "Please read that story again!" Exploring relationships between story reading and learning to read. *Young Children*, 1978, *33* (5), 48–55.

Schiebel, M.A. and Schiebel, A.B. Some neural substrates of postnatal development. In M.L. Hoffman and L.W. Hoffman (Eds.) *Review of child development research, Volume 1*. New York: Russell Sage Foundation, 1964, 481–579.

Schwartz, A.N. Assessment of mathematical concepts of five-year-old children. *The Journal of Experimental Education*, 1969, *37* (3), 67–74.

Sigel, I.E. On becoming a thinker: a psychoeducational model. *Educational Psychologist*, 1979, *14*, 70–78.

Stanchfield, J.M. Development of pre-reading skills in an experimental kindergarten program. *The Reading Teacher*, 1971, *24*, 699–707.

Tutolo, D. Attention: necessary aspect of listening. *Language Arts*, 1979, *56*, 34–37.

Watson, J.M. The influence of context on referential description in children. *British Journal of Educational Psychology*, 1977, *47*, 33–39.

Weber, E. The function of early childhood education. *Young Children*, 1973, *28*, 265–274.

Weinberg, R.A. Early childhood education and intervention—establishing an American tradition. *American Psychologist*, 1979, *34*, 912–916.

Wheatley, G.H. *The educational implications of hemispheric specialization theory.* Paper presented to the San Diego County teachers, Oct. 19, 1979.

Williams, A.H. Mathematical concepts, skills, and abilities of kindergarten entrants. *The Arithmetic Teacher*, 1965, *12*, 261–268.

Wingert, R.C. Evaluation of a readiness training program. *The Reading Teacher*, 1969, *22*, 325–328.

Yawkey, T.D. and Silvern, S.B. Kindergarten goals and contemporary education. *The Elementary School Journal*, 1976, *77*, 25–32.

Rationale

- The time has come for us to turn our attention to what young children can do as well as to what they cannot do. Without a good description of what young children do know, it's going to be exceedingly difficult, if not impossible, to chart their course as they travel the path of cognitive development. What's worse, we run the serious risk of making unwarranted statements about the nature of preschool curricula.

  Rochel Gelman

- Kindergarten goals . . . recognize the child's ability for early cognitive learning, yet they also recognize his need to learn through the playing-out of real situations.

  Thomas D. Yawkey
  Steven B. Silvern

- Even more important for the concept of readiness to be meaningful is the requirement that the activities and operations which define readiness relate in some logical way to new activities and operations which are to be learned or to the educational method by means of which the new operations are to be taught.

  E. Kuno Beller

- Because so much of the learning experience in the so-called formative years affects development in major domains of behavior—perceptual–cognitive, language, social, and affective—it is no surprise that early education practices have been shaped by the accumulated scientific knowledge base of developmental psychology.

  Richard A. Weinberg

INTRODUCTION

The selections that compose this chapter serve as a rationale supporting pre-academic skill instruction in kindergarten. Gelman's contribution is important because it indicates that kindergarten children possess the cognitive abilities necessary to profit from skill instruction. Weinberg notes that the practice of providing educational services to children before first grade has become an accepted part of the American culture.

The goals that are appropriate for kindergarten are discussed by Yawkey and Silvern, who comment that education has progressed beyond the stage where a single simply stated goal is ample structure upon which to build a program. Beller treats the concept of readiness in kindergarten as a preparation for the later primary grades, and Paradis and Peterson assert that considerable variability exists with respect to the readiness of kindergarten children.

The purpose of kindergarten is the focus of Foerster's article. She concludes, as does Genishi, that the most effective curriculum is one that promotes skill development within the context of appropriate language development and communication.

Preschool Thought

ROCHEL GELMAN

I find it noteworthy that this special issue has provided for a separate essay on preschool thought. Until very recently, almost all researchers of cognitive development have made a habit of contrasting the preschooler with the older child. Preschoolers have been characterized as lacking the classification abilities, communication skills, number concepts, order concepts, memorial skills, and a framework for reasoning about causal relationships between events that older children are granted. Indeed, had one written an essay on preschool thought five years ago, the conclusion might have been that preschoolers are remarkably ignorant. In this essay I review some of the evidence that has begun to pile up against the view that preschoolers are cognitively inept. I then consider why we failed to see what it is that preschoolers can do and possible misinterpretations of the recent findings.

It is commonplace to read about the egocentrism of preschool children. The idea is that the young child either is unable to take the perspective of another child or adult or, worse yet, believes his or her own perspective is the same as that of others. Such general statements derive support from a variety of studies. When asked to describe an abstract shape for another child, a preschooler will sometimes use private labels, for

From *American Psychologist*, Vol. 34, No. 10, pp. 900–905. Copyright 1979 by the American Psychological Association. Reprinted by permission.

example, "mommy's hat" (Glucksberg, Krauss, & Weisberg, 1966). The child's talk in the presence of others often goes on without any attempt to coordinate this talk with that of other speakers; the child seems not to care who else is speaking, what they say, or whether he or she is being listened to. "He feels no desire to influence his listener nor to tell him anything; not unlike a certain type of drawing room conversation where everyone talks about himself and no one listens" (Piaget, 1955, p. 32). When asked to choose a picture that represents the view of a mountain seen by someone opposite the child, the child selects the representation that matches what the child sees (Piaget & Inhelder, 1956)!

In 1973, Marilyn Shatz and I reported on our studies of the speech used by 4-year-olds when they talked to 2-year-olds, peers, or adults. We found that our subjects generally used short and simple utterances when they described the workings of a toy to their 2-year-old listeners. In contrast, these same 4-year-old children used longer and more complex utterances when describing the same toy to their peers or adults (Shatz & Gelman, 1973). Was it possible that these children, who were presumed to be egocentric speakers by the research community at large, were adjusting their speech in accordance with their perception or conception of their listeners' different abilities and needs? As it turns out, yes. We (Gelman & Shatz, 1977) found that 4-year-olds' speech to a 2-year-old serves different functions and contains somewhat different messages than does their speech to adults. Speech to 2-year-olds serves to show and tell, to focus, direct, and monitor attention; speech to adults includes talk about the child's own thoughts and seeks information, support, or clarification from adults. Adult-directed speech also contains hedges about statements of fact, indicating that the child recognizes that he or she may be wrong and that the adult could challenge his or her statements. The children in our experiments were clearly taking the

different needs and capacities of their listeners into account when talking to them. They hardly seem egocentric!

What about the claim that preschoolers think their visual perspective is the same as that of another person? Here again the presumed is contradicted. In an elegant series of experiments with 1–3-year-old children, Lempers, Flavell, and Flavell (1977) demonstrated over and over again that it is simply wrong to deny preschoolers an ability to distinguish their perspective from that of others. In the "show-toy task," 1½–3-year-old children showed toys to adults so that the front side was visible to the adult. This means they turned away from themselves the front of the toy and thereby deprived themselves of their original perspective. When asked to show pictures, almost all the 2- and 3-year-olds turned the front side to the adult and thereby ended up seeing the blank back of the picture. Still younger children showed the picture horizontally rather than egocentrically, that is, they did not simply hold the picture upright and thus show the back to their adult cohort in the task.

More recently, Flavell, Shipstead, and Croft (Note 1) dispelled the rumor that preschoolers believe that the closing of their own eyes deprives others of visual information about them. In fact, there is so much evidence now coming in about the perspective-taking abilities of preschoolers (for reviews, see Gelman, 1978; Shatz, 1978) that I find it hard to understand how I or anyone else ever held the belief that preschoolers are egocentric.

In retrospect one might argue that the perspective-taking abilities of preschoolers make sense. Young children do interact with others and they do talk. If they did not have any perspective-taking abilities, how could they ever communicate (cf. Fodor, 1972)? The argument might continue that we may have been wrong on the perspective-taking front, but surely we were correct in our characterization of other cognitive abilities. After all, number concepts seem much removed from the daily interactions of a preschooler. Besides, they constitute abstract ideas—the kind of ideas that everyone knows are very late in cognitive development. All of this may well be true; nevertheless, preschoolers know a great deal about the nature of number. I and my collaborators have shown that children as young as 2½ years honor the principles of counting and are able to use a counting algorithm to reason numerically, for example, to determine that an unexpected change in the numerical value of a set occurred because of surreptitiously performed addition or subtraction. (See Gelman & Gallistel, 1978, for a review of the arithmetic reasoning abilities of preschoolers.)

Successful counting involves the coordinated application of five principles (Gelman & Gallistel, 1978). These are as follows: (1) The one-one principle—each item in an array must be tagged with one and only one unique tag. (2) The stable-order principle—the tags assigned must be drawn from a stably ordered list. (3) The cardinal principle—the last tag used for a particular count serves to designate the cardinal number represented by the array. (4) The abstraction principle—any set of items may be collected together for a count. It does not matter whether they are identical, three-dimensional, imagined, or real, for in principle, any discrete set of materials can be represented as the contents of a set. (5) The order-irrelevance principle—the order in which a given object is tagged as one, two, three, and so on, is irrelevant as long as it is tagged but once and as long as the stable-order and cardinal principles are honored. Number words are arbitrary tags. The evidence clearly supports the conclusion that preschoolers honor these principles. They may not apply them perfectly, the set sizes to which they are applied may be limited, and their count lists may differ from the conventional list, but nevertheless the principles are used. Thus, a 2½-year-old may say "two, six" when

counting a two-item array and "two, six, ten" when counting a three-item array (the one—one principle). The same child will use his or her own list over and over again (the stable-order principle) and, when asked how many items are present, will repeat the last tag in the list. In the present example, the child said "ten" when asked about the number represented by a three-item array (the cardinal principle).

The fact that young children invent their own lists suggests that the counting principles are guiding the search for appropriate tags. Such "errors" in counting are like the errors made by young language learners (e.g., "I runned"). In the latter case, such errors are taken to mean that the child's use of language is rule governed and that these rules come from the child; we are not likely to hear speakers of English using such words as *runned, footses, mouses, unthirsty,* and *two-six-ten.* We use similar logic to account for the presence of idiosyncratic count lists.

Further facts about the nature of counting in young children support the idea that some basic principles guide their acquisition of skill at counting. Children spontaneously self-correct their count errors, and perhaps more important, they are inclined to count without any request to do so. If we accept the idea that the counting principles are available to the child, the fact that young children count spontaneously without external motivation fits well. What's more, the self-generated practice trials make it possible for a child to develop skill at counting.

Still other cognitive domains exist for which it has been possible to reveal considerable capacity on the part of the young child. There are conditions under which preschoolers classify according to taxonomic categories (Rosch, Mervis, Gray, Johnson, & Boyes-Braem, 1976), classify animate and inanimate objects separately (Keil, 1977; Carey, Note 2), and use hierarchical classifications (Keil, 1977; Mansfield, 1977; Markman & Siebert, 1976). They can be taught to use a rule of transitive inference (Trabasso, 1975). They can be shown to be sensitive to temporal order (Brown, 1976). They believe, as do adults, that causes precede their effects (Bullock & Gelman, 1979; Kun, 1978). They use rules to solve problems (Siegler, 1978), and so on. In short, they have considerable cognitive abilities. Why, then, has it taken us so long to see them? I think there are two related reasons.

First, we simply did not look. Indeed, we seemed to choose to ignore facts that were staring us in the face. Consider the case of counting prowess in the young child. It is now clear that preschoolers can and do count. But many of us, myself included, who researched number concepts in children started out with the view that preschoolers were restricted to the use of a perceptual mechanism for number abstraction. The idea was that their representation of number was governed by the same pattern-recognition abilities that are used to distinguish one object from another. Just as they distinguish "cowness" and "treeness," they presumably distinguished "twoness" and "threeness." I don't remember how many times I saw preschoolers counting in my various experiments before I finally recognized they were indeed able to count, no matter what our theories led us to believe. I do remember one 3-year-old telling me that he much preferred one task over another, that being the one in which it was possible to count! And it took us a while to recognize the ubiquitous tendency for 4-year-olds to talk down to 2-year-olds.

The failure to recognize facts that contradict existing theories is not unique to those who study cognitive development. Time and time again we read in the history of science of similar cases. It seems as if we have a general tendency to resist new facts if their recognition means giving up a theory without being able to come up with another that will account for the new as well as the old facts. I believe that we now know enough about the nature of the development of number concepts to be able to deal with the apparent contradictions between the new and old research findings. The young child seems unable to reason about number without reference to representations of specific numerosities, representations obtained by counting. With development, the child's reasoning moves from a dependence on specific representations to an algebraic stage in which specific representations of numerosity are no longer required. In the conservation task, the child has to make inferences about equivalence and nonequivalence on the basis of one-to-one correspondence. It matters not what the particular numbers of items in the two displays are. If they can be placed in one-to-one correspondence, then they are equal by definition. If we are correct, then the abilities we have uncovered can be seen as the beginning understanding of number. In this light their existence need not be seen as contradictory findings. Indeed, once one begins to talk about precursors of later cognitive abilities it is no longer unreasonable to start the search for those concepts and capacities the preschooler must have if he or she is to acquire complex cognitive abilities. We should expect to find domains in which they are quite competent—if only we look.

Recent work on the learning and memorial abilities of young children endorses my belief that there are many cases in which it will suffice to decide to look for competence in order for us to take note of it. As Carey (1978) pointed out, young children perform an incredible task by learning the lexicon of their native language. She estimated that 6-year-old children have mastered to some degree about 14,000 words. To do this, the children need to learn about nine new words a day from the time they start speaking until the time they reach their sixth birthday. This is truly a remarkable accomplishment. So what if the preschooler fails on a task that requires him or her to sort consistently by taxonomic category? The same child has to have some classification abilities in order to learn the lexicon so rapidly. To be sure, the child probably does not learn the full meaning of every new word the first time that word is heard. But as Carey showed, "One or a very few experiences with a new word can suffice for the child to enter it into his or her mental lexicon and to represent some of its syntactic and semantic features." Given this and the continued exposure to that word, it is then possible for a child to learn more about it and to reorganize his or her lexicon and the conceptual framework involved therein.

Nelson (1978) made it clear that young children readily learn the scripts that describe the class of events they encounter. Others (e.g., Mandler, in press) have shown young children to have excellent memories for stories—a fact that really should not surprise us, given the young child's interest in hearing stories.

Although some abilities are so pervasive that simply deciding to attend to them will make them evident, this is not true for a wide variety of cognitive skills, for example, reading and metacognitive skills. This brings me to the second reason for our failure, until recently, to acknowledge the cognitive capacities of preschoolers.

Many of the young child's cognitive abilities are well concealed and require the modification of old tasks or the development of new tasks for their revelation. I return to the question of early number concepts. Young children systematically fail Piaget's number conservation task. With this task, they behave as if they believe that the number of objects in a row changes when items are pushed together or spread apart. They thus begin by agreeing that two rows placed in one-to-one correspondence represent equal amounts; when they see one row lengthened, however, they deny the continued equivalence.

In an effort to control for a variety of variables that might have interfered with the child's possible belief in the invariance of the numerical value of a set de-

spite the application of a lengthening transformation, my colleagues and I developed what we call "the magic task" (Gelman, 1972). The task involves two phases. The first establishes an expectancy for the continued presence of two sets of two given values, say, 3 and 2, despite the repeated covering and uncovering of those sets. To avoid reference to number or the use of ambiguous terms such as *more* or *less,* one of these displays is designated "the winner," and the other "the loser." These are covered and children have to find the winner and tell us why they have or have not done so once they uncover a display. As luck would have it, preschoolers decide on their own that numerical value is the determinant for winning and losing status. They thus establish an expectancy for two particular numerical values. Then, unbeknownst to the child, the second phase of the experiment begins when the experimenter surreptitiously alters one of the expected displays. Across different conditions and experiments, the changes involve addition, subtraction, displacement, change in color of the original objects, and even a change in identity of the original objects. Children who encounter a change in number produced by subtraction or addition say that the expected number has been violated, typically identify the number of elements present and the number that should be present, and make explicit reference to the transformation that must have been performed—even if they did not see it. In contrast, children who encounter the effects of irrelevant transformations say the number of elements is as expected despite the change in length of a display, or in the color, or in the identity of an element in that display.

According to the results of the magic task, preschoolers know full well that lengthening or shortening an array does not alter the numerical value of a display. Still, these same children fail the conservation task. But note how different these tasks are. In the conservation task the child has to judge equivalence on the basis of one-to-one correspondence, correctly interpret questions that are ambiguous, watch the transformation being performed, and then ignore the effect of that transformation. In the magic task the child need not make judgments of equivalence based on one-to-one correspondence, he or she need not (indeed cannot) see the transformation being performed, and there are no ambiguous terms to misinterpret. In other words, the magic task is a very stripped down version of the conservation task. Likewise, many other tasks that show preschoolers in a positive light have downgraded the complexity of the tasks that they fail, altered the instructions, changed the stimuli used, embedded the question of interest in games preschoolers play, provided extensive pretraining before testing on the target task—In short, in many cases it has been necessary to develop tasks and experimental settings to suit the preschool child (Gelman, 1978). This is easier said than done. Consider the magic game which *was* designed to meet our best guesses as to how to elicit the number-invariance rules honored by the young child.

Bullock and Gelman (1977) modified the magic task in order to determine whether preschoolers could compare two number pairs. In particular, the question was whether they would recognize that the number pair 1 and 2 was like 3 and 4 insofar as 1 and 3 were both "less" and 2 and 4 were both "more." Children between the ages of 2½ and 4 were first shown one-item and two-item displays, and they established expectancies for a set of one and a set of two items. Half the children were told that the one-item array was the winner; half were told that the two-item array was the winner. From the experimenter's point of view this was also a more-less comparison task. To determine whether the 2½–4-year-old children in the experiment knew this, we surreptitiously replaced the original displays with three-item and four-item displays and asked which of these was the winner. Many of the older children were confused by this question and said that neither was the winner—an ob-

servation which in point of fact was correct. When asked to make the best possible choice, the children then went on to choose the display that honored the relation they were reinforced for during the expectancy training. Apparently the children did not immediately realize that it was all right to make a judgment of similarity, given the fact that neither of the new displays was identical to either of the original displays. Our variation in question format served to tell them that the transfer task called for a similarity judgment. My point here is that we started out with a task that was designed for young children and still we found that the task presented problems.

This example of the subtle ways in which a task can confound the assessment of those early cognitive abilities that are generally buried is not an isolated one. I have discussed others elsewhere (Gelman, 1978), and for me they are very sobering. They make it clear that in many cases, it takes more than a decision to look for early cognitive abilities. It is often exceedingly difficult to know how to design tasks so that they will be suitable for use with young children. I believe this derives in part from the fact that many of the preschoolers' cognitive abilities are fragile and as such are only evident under restricted conditions—at least compared with the conditions under which older children can apply their knowledge. This brings me to my next point.

Some might take the recent demonstrations of early cognitive abilities to mean that preschoolers are miniature adults as far as their cognitions are concerned. This is not what I want people to conclude, and should they so conclude it would not be in the best interests of either those who study cognitive development or the child. The fact remains that despite the recent demonstration of some complex cognitive abilities, young children fail a wide range of tasks that seem so simple for older children. I believe that many of the best insights into the nature of development will come from understanding exactly what conditions interfere with the use and accessibility of those capacities the young child does possess. These insights may also be of the greatest educational relevance. However, these insights can only come after we have uncovered the basic capacities that make cognitive growth a possibility.

What I do want people to realize is that we have been much too inclined to reach conclusions about what preschoolers cannot do, compared with what their older cohorts can do on a variety of tasks. We must cease to approach young children with only those tasks that are designed for older children. The time has come for us to turn our attention to what young children can do as well as to what they cannot do. Without a good description of what young children do know, it's going to be exceedingly difficult, if not impossible, to chart their course as they travel the path of cognitive development. What's worse, we run the serious risk of making unwarranted statements about the nature of preschool curricula. I have had people tell me that there is no point in teaching young children about numbers, since preschoolers cannot conserve numbers. This, I submit, is a non sequitur. The conservation task is but one index of numerical knowledge, and it is beginning to look like it is an index of a rather sophisticated knowledge.

My message is quite straightforward. We should study preschoolers in their own right and give up treating them as foils against which to describe the accomplishments of middle childhood. We have made some progress in recent years, but there is still plenty of room for those who are willing to take on the mind of the young child.

REFERENCE NOTES

1. Flavell, J. H., Shipstead, S. G., & Croft, K. *What young children think you see when their eyes are closed.*
Unpublished manuscript, Stanford University, 1978.
2. Carey, S. *The child's concept of animal.* Paper presented at the meeting of the Psychonomic Society, San Antonio, Texas, November 1978.

REFERENCES

Brown, A. L. The construction of temporal succession by preoperational children. In A. D. Pick (Ed.), *Minnesota symposium on child psychology* (Vol. 10). Minneapolis: University of Minnesota Press, 1976.

Bullock, M., & Gelman, R. Numerical reasoning in young children: The ordering principle. *Child Development,* 1977, *48,* 427–434.

Bullock, M., & Gelman, R. Preschool children's assumptions about cause and effect: Temporal ordering. *Child Development,* 1979, *50,* 89–96.

Carey, S. The child as word learner. In M. Halle, J. Bresnan, & G. A. Miller (Eds.), *Linguistic theory and psychological reality.* Cambridge, Mass.: Massachusetts Institute of Technology Press, 1978.

Fodor, J. A. Some reflections on L. S. Vygotsky's *Thought and language. Cognition,* 1972, *1,* 83–95.

Gelman, R. Logical capacity of very young children: Number invariance rules. *Child Development,* 1972, *43,* 75–90.

Gelman, R. Cognitive development. In L. W. Porter & M. R. Rosenzweig (Eds.), *Annual review of psychology* (Vol. 29). Palo Alto, Calif.: Annual Reviews, 1978.

Gelman, R., & Gallistel, C. R. *The child's understanding of number.* Cambridge, Mass.: Harvard University Press, 1978.

Gelman, R., & Shatz, M. Appropriate speech adjustments: The operation of conversational constraints on talk to two-year-olds. In M. Lewis & L. A. Rosenblum (Eds.), *Interaction, con-*

versation, and the development of language. New York: Wiley, 1977.

Glucksberg, S., Krauss, R. M., & Weisberg, R. Referential communication in nursery school children: Method and some preliminary findings. *Journal of Experimental Child Psychology,* 1966, *3,* 333–342.

Keil, F. *The role of ontological categories in a theory of semantic and conceptual development.* Unpublished doctoral dissertation, University of Pennsylvania, 1977.

Kun, A. Evidence for preschoolers' understanding of causal direction in extended causal sequences. *Child Development,* 1978, *49,* 218–222.

Lempers, J. D., Flavell, E. R., & Flavell, J. H. The development in very young children of tacit knowledge concerning visual perception. *Genetic Psychology Monographs,* 1977, *95,* 3–53.

Mandler, J. M. Categorical and schematic organization. In C. R. Puff (Ed.), *Memory, organization, and structure.* New York: Academic Press, in press.

Mansfield, A. F. Semantic organization in the young child: Evidence for the development of semantic feature systems. *Journal of Experimental Child Psychology,* 1977, *23,* 57–77.

Markman, E. M., & Siebert, J. Classes and collections: Internal organization and resulting holistic properties. *Cognitive Psychology,* 1976, *8,* 561–577.

Nelson, K. How young children represent knowledge of their world in and out of language: A preliminary report. In R. Siegler (Ed.), *Children's thinking: What develops?* Hillsdale, N.J.: Erlbaum, 1978.

Piaget, J. *The language and thought of the child.* London: Routledge & Kegan Paul, 1955.

Piaget, J., & Inhelder, B. *The child's conception of space.* London: Routledge & Kegan Paul, 1956.

Rosch, E., Mervis, C. B., Gray, W. D., Johnson, D. M., & Boyes-Braem, P. Basic objects in natural categories. *Cognitive Psychology,* 1976, *8,* 382–439.

Shatz, M. The relationship between cognitive processes and the development of communication skills. In C. B. Keasey (Ed.), *Nebraska symposium on motivation* (Vol. 26). Lincoln: University of Nebraska Press, 1978.

Shatz, M., & Gelman, R. The development of communication skills: Modifications in the speech of young children as a function of listener. *Monographs of the Society for Research in Child Development,* 1973, *38*(2, Serial No. 152).

Siegler, R. S. The origins of scientific reasoning. In R. S. Siegler (Ed.), *Children's thinking: What develops?* Hillsdale, N.J.: Erlbaum, 1978.

Trabasso, T. R. Representation, memory and reasoning: How do we make transitive inferences. In A. D. Pick (Ed.), *Minnesota symposium on child psychology* (Vol. 9). Minneapolis: University of Minnesota Press, 1975.

Early Childhood Education and Intervention
Establishing an American Tradition

RICHARD A. WEINBERG

The International Year of the Child provides us a rare opportunity to acknowledge the role that American psychology has played in understanding and enhancing the development of children. It is particularly in the area of early childhood education that we have seen the impact of psychology on an educational enterprise. Because so much of the learning experience in the so-called formative years affects development in major domains of behavior—perceptual-cognitive, language, social, and affective—it is no surprise that early education practices have been shaped by the accumulated scientific knowledge base of developmental psychology.

Like many other national enterprises, early childhood education in America has been a melting pot of ideas and influences. A unique tapestry of early education practices was created by professionals in the preschool community during the 1940s and 1950s; the fabric was woven from permissive interpretations of Freudian psychology, the thinking of European educators like Pestalozzi, Froebel, Maria Montessori, and Susan Isaacs, and the influences of our own pioneers—John Dewey, Arnold Gesell, and Erik Erikson.

The modal nursery school program in the 1950s could be characterized as providing good child care and opportunities for middle-class children to socialize

with their peers in a warm, supportive environment. The emphases were on nurturing social growth and fostering mental health. Nursery school attendance was an option available to children from families who could afford such luxuries.

The Coming of the Revolution

A revolution in American early childhood education (Hodges & Smith, Note 1) occurred in the late 1950s and early years of the succeeding decade, precipitated by a number of social, political, and economic factors, as well as major discoveries about the psychological development of children. The hurling of *Sputnik* into the skies fostered a national self-consciousness about falling behind in the race to conquer the frontiers of space. Blame was placed on our educational system. The next generation of scientists and technicians were sitting in classrooms studying ''Autumn'' and Greek mythology. Almost overnight, a curriculum revolution penetrated all levels of American schooling.

Shifting the spotlight on the classroom occurred at about the same time that psychologists uncovered the importance of the preschool years for a child's cognitive development (Bloom, 1964). Jean Piaget's systematic observations of his own children and his work in genetic epistemology fostered a collective awareness among psychologists of the young child as an active learner. This view of the child as a participant in the learning process was confirmed by Jerome Bru-

From *American Psychologist*, Vol. 34. No. 10, pp. 912–916. Copyright 1979 by the American Psychological Association. Reprinted by permission.

ner's (1961) studies of thinking and learning at Harvard. Children attending the typical "prerevolutionary" nursery school were certainly exposed to cognitive activities, and preschool classrooms were strewn with books, arts and crafts, trucks, dolls, and other toys "appropriate" for young children. But the work of Piaget and Bruner, among others, nourished the creative minds of the educators who evolved a new kind of early education. The emphases of these programs were on structuring learning experiences and providing appropriate stimulation to foster and enhance the cognitive growth of young children. Hope stirred that by matching the appropriate curriculum activities to the child's cognitive level, one could in fact accelerate the building of a child's cognitive structure. These programs heralded a new age of enlightenment about the enigmas of early childhood.

James McVicker Hunt's book *Intelligence and Experience,* published in 1961, also stressed the importance of adequate environmental stimulation for children's development. This popular volume reinforced a vast technology rooted in the behaviorist learning tradition. The behavioral technology was expanded to provide teachers with classroom management skills and parents with intervention strategies for coping effectively with daily child-rearing situations. At the preschool level, Bereiter and Engelmann (1966) introduced a curriculum that structured classroom language and cognitive experiences based on such techniques. In brief, a wide variety of experimental early childhood programs emerged, reflecting the diversity of theoretical lenses that psychologists and curriculum builders used to view the development of the young child and the nature of early educational interventions.

The discovery of young children as a treasured national resource also resulted in a burgeoning industry committed to stimulating and accelerating children's development. Revised baby and child care books and grocery store journals

bombarded parents with a dizzying array of how-to activities. Some books guided parents in Pygmalion-like efforts to transform their children into geniuses. Adults could play a more active role in increasing their children's IQ and could be provided with new reason for experiencing guilt as inadequate parents. No home with a newborn infant was complete without an automated crib mobile that provided appropriate perceptual stimulation. Grandparents were urged to buy creative toys for their grandchildren because these objects contributed to their development. Toilet training became a science—One wonders how many M&Ms have been administered in the nation's bathrooms as rewards to toddlers who have performed successfully. Overnight, the television program *Sesame Street* became an early childhood educator responsible for millions of pupils.

Getting a Head Start

What characterized the zeitgeist at the time these changes in early childhood education were taking place? In the early 1960s our national awareness was focused on the individual citizen's civil rights. Our concerns were reflected in part in Lyndon Johnson's War on Poverty and various programs offered through the Office of Economic Opportunity. Project Head Start, perhaps one of the most influential and massive federal social experiments in our history, was introduced as a preschool intervention effort. Since 1965, Head Start has provided a multifaceted educational program enriched with a broad spectrum of health care and social services to thousands of economically disadvantaged children. The impetus for Head Start was rooted in a commitment to the physical and psychological welfare of the nation's poor and was built on the assumption that if disadvantaged children (an at-risk population) were provided with an opportunity to develop learning readiness skills prior to their initiation to the formal public

31

school system, they would more easily adapt to the educational system and experience academic success. The crusaders for Head Start believed that such an intervention would alter the poverty cycle by ultimately providing disadvantaged children increased educational and occupational opportunities.

Head Start mushroomed from a brief summer intervention to a comprehensive preschool educational experience, representing an array of conceptual models and involving the active participation of parents as well as professionals in the implementation and governance of the programs. From its inception as a federally sponsored program, Project Head Start has been vulnerable, subject to endless controversy and misunderstanding (Zigler, 1978). The early reviews of Head Start's effectiveness as an intervention program were negative. In addressing Head Start's accountability, evaluators primarily focused on the question of whether children who experienced the program demonstrated greater gains on cognitive and personality measures than did comparison children who had not experienced a Head Start intervention (Zigler, 1976). Dozens of studies and research reports found that participating children did manifest significant gains on measures of cognitive ability, self-esteem, and school achievement. However, it became fashionable to assert the *failure* of Head Start because the gains were not maintained once the children had spent two or three years in elementary school. This so-called "fade-out phenomenon" was translated to mean that no long-term benefits accrue from experiencing a one-year Head Start program.

The Wolff and Stein (1966) report and the Westinghouse (1969) evaluation were among the bases for these early conclusions about Head Start's impact; scholars have continued to question the success or failure of the Head Start endeavor. Some, like Jensen (1969), have questioned the value of compensatory education programs in general and have rekindled interest in the nature-nurture controversy and the malleability of intellectual abilities. Others, like Lazar, Palmer, Zigler, and additional members of the Consortium for Longitudinal Studies, have mustered evidence to support long-term, lasting effects of Head Start models on the performance of school-aged children (Lazar, Hubbell, Murray, Rosche, & Royce, 1977).

It is beyond the scope of this essay to explore the complex issues and controversy that have surrounded the evaluation of Head Start programs and other early intervention efforts. Yet one must assert with the advantage of hindsight that the task of evaluating the effects of preschool intervention programs was approached naively. Many early childhood professionals were struck by the awesome problem of how to measure the impact of an intervention, particularly in light of vast conceptual differences among program models even within one project such as Head Start. The need for an expanded evaluation technology to meet the demands of the early childhood community became clear. It is unfortunate that measurement experts, test developers, evaluation specialists, and social policymakers did not collaborate with early education personnel in generating appropriate evaluation strategies during the initial development of intervention programs such as Head Start, when goals were being established and implemented. Some of the methodological blunders that characterized evaluations of early intervention programs might have been avoided or at least minimized. Such coordinated evaluation planning has occurred for some programs in recent years.

Head Start has been a fertile spawning ground for alternative models of early intervention, psychoeducational remediation, and preschool education (White, Day, Freeman, Hantman, & Messenger, 1973). The Head Start Planned Variation Project affirmed the importance of individualizing preschool programs to meet the needs of a specific community. In order to take advantage of their unique resources and to respond optimally to the demands of their constituency, early childhood educators in a community should select the particular educational model that has the best fit. One would hope that gone forever are the days when a canned early childhood program was purchased and served up to a population of preschoolers without being modified to meet the tastes of its consumers.

As a wellspring of new federal intervention programs, Head Start paved the way for funding Home Bound, Parent and Child Centers, and Follow Through, a program established with the belief that there should be continuity between the Head Start intervention and the subsequent experience of kindergarten and the primary grades of elementary school. Edward Zigler (1978) noted, "We can never inoculate children in one year against the ravages of deprivation; there must be continuity. It is crucial that the school follow the Head Start effort with a dovetailed second intervention that builds upon the gains of Head Start" (pp. 5–6).

The emphasis on human rights that ascended as a national priority during the 1960s resulted in early intervention programs aimed at indigent populations. The climate of the times also stimulated a reconsideration of the social and economic positions of men and women in our society. The changing role of mothers who joined the nation's work force was a catalyst for the child day-care movement. The socialization of little boys and girls has also come to reflect shifting roles and values.

The study of sex differences by psychologists has helped alter our thinking about sex role stereotypes. The perception of little girls as "sugar and spice and everything nice" who play with dolls and become either teachers or nurses has been challenged by a view that gender should not determine one's vocational choices, interests, or toys (Tavris & Offir, 1977). Moving women from the kitchen and car pool to the ex-

ecutive's office and operating room (as doctors) has resulted in new patterns of parenting but has also directly influenced the goals and curricula of many contemporary early education programs.

Looking Forward

A brief overview of some major forces that have shaped trends and issues in early childhood education and intervention during recent years has been presented. The cadre of professionals, including psychologists, working in early education is heterogeneous, representing diverse disciplines, alternative theoretical perspectives, and varied priorities for policy and action. One might turn to fantasy and wonder how other observers, given their orientations and biases, would chronicle the evolution of early childhood education and intervention programs in contemporary America.

Keeping one eye on the past and present and the other focused on the future, psychologists must continue to contribute to the early education enterprise. Let me share some reflections that might help give direction to these efforts:

1. It is critical that we keep our fingers on the sociopolitical and economic pulse of our culturally diverse society. Early childhood education programs must reflect the beliefs and values of communities; the goals of a program must be congruent with the mission of the cultural group to which the young child is being assimilated.

2. The increased sensitivity of the psychoeducational community to individual differences in children's cognitive styles, learning patterns, and motivational variables must be translated into early education programs tailored to meet the multiple needs of particular children. The move toward studying the differential effects of alternative models of early education on varying groups of young children should facilitate individualized programming and provide parents with an appropriate range of educa-

tional options from which to choose.

3. Appreciating the continuity of development throughout the life span, we must encourage attempts to study the longitudinal impact of early childhood interventions. We must also align the goals of programs for infants, preschoolers, and early elementary school-aged pupils so that such programs become components of an integrated, consistent plan for educating young children.

4. We cannot continue to abuse intelligence tests by relying on IQs as the major dependent variable in outcome evaluations of early education interventions. Efforts must be concentrated on developing an array of reliable and valid measures of social competence that provide more comprehensive indices of the impact of early intervention on children's psychological development in the social and emotional domains as well as the perceptual–cognitive sphere.

5. The legislative mandate of Public Law 94-142, aimed at providing least restrictive educational environments for handicapped children, will increasingly affect programming at the preschool level. The tasks of identifying at-risk populations, screening children with special needs, and developing educational plans should be targeted as RD&D priorities by more psychologists within clinical, school, and measurement subspecialties. Accurate assessment techniques and appropriate formative evaluation procedures are essential for implementing effective early intervention programs for children with identifiable learning dysfunctions or other special needs.

6. An expanding data base (see Clarke & Clarke, 1976) should temper our notion that early childhood is the quintessential development period for acquiring social competencies. It is possible for some children deprived of appropriate early experiences to catch up if provided with educational opportunities at later points in their development. This does not mean that we should diminish our commitment to early childhood education, but we should not assume that early deprivation inevitably results in psychological and educational deficits.

7. Despite our general lack of training in the use of television as an educational medium, we need to reconsider the potential that television has as a key positive socializing agent, bringing cognitive and social experiences to young children and their families.

8. We must recognize that early childhood education is a cooperative venture that has attracted the participation of parents, professionals from numerous disciplines (e.g., health care, social work, educational administration), and paraprofessionals. These participants often lack knowledge of human development and skill in working with young children. We must encourage in-service programs, continuing education, and other training endeavors that better prepare individuals for their varying roles in early education. The Child Development Associate Consortium offers a unique model for credentialing individuals who have acquired and demonstrated essential competencies in the field of early childhood education. The thousands of individuals who have received training as early childhood educators through preservice college programs, Head Start supplementary training programs, or on-the-job experience should routinely update their knowledge and expertise. Mainstreaming young handicapped children in regular preschool programs, for example, requires a clear understanding of the psychoeducational needs of special populations and an awareness of the problems associated with mainstreaming preschoolers.

9. Psychologists who have the inclination and talent should increase their involvement in the policymaking process at state and national levels. We have seen that action in the political arena determines funding priorities and in turn affects the nature of both early childhood education programs and professional training models. As advocates for young children, psychologists can also facilitate activities of federal agencies such as the

Administration for Children, Youth, and Families and organizations such as the Children's Defense Fund.

10. Finally, we must be aware of the effects of changes in early childhood education on other social institutions. In what ways are the American family's expectations about their young children's development influenced by the posture of the early childhood community and the nature of educational interventions? How have elementary school curricula been modified to mesh with the variety of educational programs that have emerged at the preschool level?

Contributions of developmental and educational psychologists to establishing an American tradition of early childhood education and intervention programs demonstrate the impact that psychology can have in fostering the welfare of young children—our nation's most valuable resource and the legacy of our American heritage.

REFERENCE NOTE

1. Hodges, W. L., & Smith, L. *Retrospect and prospect in early childhood and special education.* Paper presented at the meeting of the American Psychological Association, Toronto, August 1978.

REFERENCES

Bereiter, C., & Engelmann, S. *Teaching disadvantaged children in the preschool.* Englewood Cliffs, N.J.: Prentice-Hall, 1966.

Bloom, B. S. *Stability and change in human characteristics.* New York: Wiley, 1964.

Bruner, J. *The process of education.* Cambridge, Mass.: Harvard University Press, 1961.

Clarke, A. M., & Clarke, A. D. B. (Eds.). *Early experience: Myth and evidence.* London: Open Books, 1976.

Hunt, J. McV. *Intelligence and experience.* New York: Ronald Press, 1961.

Jensen, A. How much can we boost IQ and scholastic achievement? *Harvard Educational Review,* 1969, *39,* 1–123.

Lazar, I., Hubbell, V., Murray, H., Rosche, M., & Royce, J. *The persistence of preschool effects: A long-term follow-up of fourteen infant and preschool experiments* (Summary report of the Consortium on Developmental Continuity, Education Commission of the States, Grant 18-76-07843). Washington, D.C.: U.S. Department of Health, Education, and Welfare, 1977.

Tavris, C., & Offir, C. *The longest war: Sex differences in perspective.* New York: Harcourt Brace Jovanovich, 1977.

Westinghouse Learning Corporation, Ohio University. *The impact of Head Start: An evaluation of the effects of Head Start on children's cognitive and affective development.* Washington, D.C.: U.S. Office of Economic Opportunity, 1969.

White, S. H., Day, M. C., Freeman, P. K., Hantman, S. A., & Messenger, K. P. *Federal programs for young children: Review and recommendations* (Vols. 1–4). Washington, D.C.: U.S. Department of Health, Education, and Welfare, 1973.

Wolff, M., & Stein, A. *Factors influencing the recruitment of children into the Head Start Program, summer 1965: A case study of six centers in New York City (Study II).* New York: Yeshiva University, 1966.

Zigler, E. F. Head Start: Not a program but an evolving concept. In J. D. Andrews (Ed.), *Early childhood education: It's an art? It's a science?* Washington, D.C.: National Association for the Education of Young Children, 1976.

Zigler, E. F. America's Head Start Program: An agenda for its second decade. *Young Children,* 1978, *33,* 4–11.

Kindergarten Goals and Contemporary Education

THOMAS DANIELS YAWKEY
STEVEN B. SILVERN

Get the child ready for first grade. Teach reading and mathematics readiness. Socialize the child.

These typical goals for traditional kindergarten programs have perpetuated the notion that kindergarten is a place where children learn finger plays, sing songs, ride bikes, and piddle in the sandbox.

Each of these goals and activities is isolationist. Each encourages only one aspect of the child's development and ignores others. All are anchored in the belief that five-year-old children are not capable of more sophisticated educational involvement. The belief conflicts with the findings of Bloom, who states:

> Since our estimate suggests about 17 percent of the growth takes place between ages 4 and 6, we could hypothesize that kindergarten could have far-reaching consequences on the child's general learning pattern [1:100].

In brief, Bloom contends that a fifth of the child's growth occurs within only two years, or 3 percent, of the child's entire life (1).

As long as traditional goals are in effect, this phenomenal growth is undirected and haphazard. New goals must be developed to help the child attain his potential in growth and learning. Traditionalists defend their goals against new objectives by arguing that the child is entitled to the "right to be five." Defenders of contemporary goals retort that

we must let the child "develop to his full potential." These educators insist:

> It is not the job of kindergarten to get children ready for first grade, nor is kindergarten a readiness period for school work in an isolated area such as reading [2:45].

Hunt, Deutsch, Gagné, and other educators contend that children can learn at an earlier age than was formerly considered possible, but goals must be structured to aid the child in his cognitive, affective, social, and psychomotor development (3). Contemporary kindergarten goals must be integrated into one comprehensive curriculum and not promoted singly in various unidimensional curriculums. After all, the child develops as an integrated whole and is not made up of single aspects juxtaposed in a tiny body.

Experiences that call for activity are essential to the child's cognitive, affective, social, and psychomotor growth. With the goals proposed here, the child will still play in the sandbox, for play is fundamental, but contemporary goals will help the teacher direct play to build children's concepts—add to their understanding of volume, mass, and surface area—deepen their sense of self-worth, enhance their creative ability, and give them opportunities to share, cooperate, and help as well as develop coordination of large and small muscles.

Play-directed goals of contemporary kindergarten programs differ from those of traditional programs. Hymes contends:

> Growth and development whether physical, in-

Reprinted from *The Elementary School Journal*, Vol. 77 (1976). By permission of The University of Chicago Press © 1976. Copyright is held by The University of Chicago. Dr. Thomas Daniels Yawkey, Associate Professor, Early Childhood Education, The Pennsylvania State University.

tellectual or emotional requires a very active interplay between the child and the world around him [4:41].

Contemporary kindergarten goals do not dictate teaching method. One can establish contemporary goals in any pedagogy desired: kindergarten programs may be based on various points of view concerning child development (5).

Let's examine a number of contemporary goals appropriate for kindergarten.

Cognitive or intellectual goals

1. *Contemporary kindergarten goals stress growth and development and are foundations for content skills.*

The foundation and the content areas such as reading, mathematics, social studies, science, the arts, and related skills are cultivated through programs to develop concepts (6). The programs offer planned activities to develop skills built into key content ideas. Key content ideas, or root learnings, are derived from academic disciplines, which are repositories of man's accumulated knowledge about his world. Among the academic disciplines from which key content ideas may be drawn are linguistics, mathematics, and the social and the physical sciences. Content ideas—which are building blocks for thinking, perceiving, and remembering—are developed as a part of the child's cognitive functions. Bruner, Oliver, and Greenfield (7), Piaget (8), and Hunt (9) note that the child's thought processes change as the child grows older. Changes in thought processes indicate that the child's concepts and understandings are developing. Changes in thought can be accounted for by the child's interaction with his environment. Therefore, if concepts are to develop, the child must be involved in experiences and activities. Concepts are formed through involvement in language, mathematics, social studies and other key content areas.

When language is based on experience, words come alive, for they are part of a real adventure. Later, children can retell their experiences while the teacher writes the story. For example, five-year-old children learning about circuses see pictures of circus people and go to a circus. Through these basic experiences the kindergarten teacher can develop additional key ideas for the children by teaching related aspects of circus life such as group cooperation and animal care. Through other experiences, the teacher can develop additional root learnings in reading such as left-to-right and top-to-bottom progression.

In mathematics, as in language, concept development must be structured in and through experiences. At kindergarten snack time, children live number concepts when they match one cracker and one napkin with each child. Later, this root learning of matching (or corresponding) can be associated with number symbols, *0* to *10* or more. Still later, the children can count out toys, construction paper, scissors. Thus, other root learnings can be developed by associating language labels with action.

Concept development can be built into other content areas—social studies, science, the arts. Each area must be interwoven into the fabric that constitutes the cognitive growth of the child. Each concept may be thought of as a thread that strengthens the entire cloth. Concepts that are omitted may lead to flaws in the material. Content concepts are essential to the child's sound growth and development.

2. *Contemporary kindergarten goals stress growth and development, and are foundations for process skills.*

The child learns process skills as well as content skills. According to Welling and Welling (10), of National Education Program Associates, process skills are associated with problem-solving, observing, inquiring, generalizing, experimenting, discovering, classifying, verifying, and quantifying. Hildebrand's list of process skills includes decision-making, dealing with observable conflict, and creating (11).

The process skills, then, are procedures for observing the environment, for incorporating new information, for applying observations and information to solutions, and arriving at conclusions. Process skills are mastered through the child's interaction with the environment. Manipulating and exploring the world provide a foundation for cognitive structure. This structure "is a process of evolution by stages from sensorimotor activities through concrete operations to formal operations" (12: 12). A kindergarten program that provides experiences in problem-solving, communicating, decision-making, and creating provides for the total development of young children. Process skills allow the young child to examine, build, and grow toward a cognitive structure, lessening the possibilities of failure and frustration. The child masters process skills in conjunction with product or content skills.

Process skills may easily be developed through the child's play. During water play the child gets ready to place a toy boat into a pan of water. Before he lowers the boat, the teacher may ask the child, "Will the toy boat float, or will it sink?" The child is being asked to make a prediction. After a prediction is made as to whether the boat will float or sink, the child tests his prediction by placing the boat into the water. The session can continue with the child gathering several objects, predicting whether they will float or sink, testing each prediction, classifying objects into those that float and those that do not, and finally making a generalization about floating objects. This kind of practice, which uses process skills, may be applied to many other learning experiences such as sandbox play, swinging, climbing, playing on a see-saw, or standing still. The number and the variety of experiences are important if the child is to develop concepts, but practice is also important in developing the process skills if they are to be used without prompting by a teacher. Finally, process and product skills help children develop interest in and appreciation for their environment.

Affective Goals

1. *Contemporary kindergarten goals facilitate the building of positive self-concepts.*

According to Leeper and associates (13), children's awareness of differences in social class seems to emerge and develop in the intermediate grades or earlier. Children's awareness of self, however, probably develops from birth onward. The child's first expression of feelings seems to be linked to physical characteristics of the body. Taunts can contribute to feelings of anxiety, resentment, shame, guilt, and hostility in the child. Self-concept is determined by the child's physical, mental, and affective characteristics and feedback from adults and peers. The view that young children hold of themselves determines how they feel about themselves. The earlier children have positive experiences in connection with their body and their environment, the earlier they begin to build a positive image.

Children are explorers, setting off to study the unknown, groping for new information to replace old notions. The concept that young children have of themselves determines what they find. Children who feel that they are loved, that they are worthwhile and have contributions to make, invariably explore the environment and learn without fear. Children who know that they have adult support build positive self-concepts that eventually lead to independence. A negative self-concept places an unseen tether on children in the form of anxiety (14) and emotional blackmail (15). In exploring, these children limit themselves to safe areas. Children who restrict themselves to safe areas limit their growth potential. Self-concept, then, is important in determining what children say, do, and consequently think about themselves and others. The school must encourage children's feelings of self-importance, their sense of trust and their skills in dealing with the expectations of home and kindergarten.

To develop positive experiences in

kindergarten, the teacher accepts and believes in each child. The teacher shows support and trust. She works to establish a warm relationship: she calls the child by name; she uses eye contact; she gives encouragement through her facial expressions and through gestures such as a pat on the shoulder that show sympathy and understanding, and through frequent and meaningful conversations with each child.

Positive self-concepts can be built through instruction that recognizes the child's talents and accepts and rewards the child's knowledge and accomplishments.

Positive self-concepts can be reinforced by creating a classroom atmosphere in which communication between the five-year-old and the kindergarten teacher is open. The teacher must help the children understand, label, and accept feelings. A few simple words can help: "It's okay to feel sad when you lose something you love. It is the way you should feel." Or, "I know you are angry at me, but you must understand that. . . ."

Children can express and channel feelings through art. Molding clay, drawing, carving, fingerpainting, physical education activities—including vigorous exercises and games—music accompanied by singing, moving, and clapping and dramatic play and storytelling, all encourage children to express their feelings.

Psychomotor Goals

1. *Contemporary kindergarten goals build gross-muscle, fine-muscle, and eye-hand coordination.*

Children who have learning difficulties may also have problems with movement (16). Much of the growth and the development of the young child depends on gross-motor and perceptual-motor movement (16). Piaget, Hunt, and Kephart do not see development as an automatic unfolding, but as a process delayed or accelerated by experiences in the child's environment (16). Butler (17)

found a positive relationship between young children's intelligence and perceptual motor ability and between their achievement and perceptual motor ability. The curriculum should emphasize gross-muscle development, eye-hand coordination, balance, and rest or relaxation to perfect the child's abilities to walk, run, skip, jump, and climb. Gross-motor development and eye-hand coordination through children's play are important for another reason. By providing freedom to explore and move through play, early educators supply children with ingredients for success with symbolic learning. Kindergarten programs that emphasize gross-muscle development and eye-hand coordination on the playground, and the control associated with sedentary activities in the classroom, must be reexamined in the light of research of the late 1960's and 1970's. Because large- and small-muscle development and eye-hand coordination are essential to young children's learning, the entire kindergarten program must provide opportunities and encourage motor growth.

Gross-motor skills are learned, developed, and strengthened in active play outdoors and indoors. Large blocks, an old mattress to jump on, swings, slides, climbing apparatus, walking forward and backward on a balance beam (or on a narrow rail), running, and riding bicycles, all provide opportunities for children to build large muscles. All these activities require some form of lifting, walking, running, jumping and climbing.

Fine-motor skills also demand attention in kindergarten. Small muscles are strengthened through basic activities such as visual attention, grasping, and releasing, the use of straws and paper cups at snack time, and hammering and sawing egg cartons and orange crates. Large quantities of dough can be pounded, squeezed, pinched, and slapped. Toys and materials with levers, handles, or pulleys stimulate fine-muscle development. A sandbox with durable accessories of various types, especially things that can be filled, offers children myriad opportunities for psychomotor development.

Hand-eye coordination and fine-motor skills are interrelated and developed by tying shoestrings, buttoning jackets and sweaters, cutting with scissors, building with unit blocks, making letters, and tearing and crumbling paper. Fine-motor skills are also developed through water play, soap painting, fingerpainting, the use of clay and other gooey and smeary materials.

Gross and fine-motor development must get attention in the classroom and on the playground.

2. *Contemporary kindergarten goals teach health and safety.*

Health and safety are important aspects of the psychomotor growth of young children. In the area of health, from the moment of conception to birth and from birth onward, children are affected by what feeds their bodies. A diet that lacks protein foods such as milk, eggs, cheese, meat, fish, and poultry affects the development of a child's brain in ways that make him less able to learn. Malnutrition occurs in families that cannot afford essential foods and in families that lack knowledge of nutrition. Research studies have shown that when health needs cannot be met, children cannot develop to their full potential (18). For this reason, supplemental meals as well as dental and medical care are essential parts of contemporary kindergarten programs.

The safety and the physical welfare of young children are as important as nutrition and health care. Parents and teachers will be wise to continue the age-old admonitions, "Don't cross the street" and "Don't ride with strangers." Parents and teachers will be wise to supplement the warnings with lessons on safety and first aid. The technology of today makes it increasingly dangerous to be a child. The lure of what is seen on television must be countered by knowledge of safety rules and sense.

Even in learning environments that abound in learning materials, children's psychomotor and cognitive growth can be limited by accidents, illness, and disease. Dry shoes to replace wet ones, an extra sweater when a child seems cold, and safety rules for daily activities, all contribute to the children's well-being. Goals for health and safety give children the feeling that an adult cares and is concerned about them. A corollary: "The more complicated a society, the greater the need for the fundamental knowledge—how to live with others, for others, with self, for self" (19:165). The teacher, working with the children, can help them understand, establish, and maintain limits within which they all are able to operate. To let children learn by trial and error—to give no guidance at all—is a hazardous path for contemporary teachers to take in building psychomotor development. Teaching health and safety is probably one of the best means of helping children become aware of themselves and the world around them. Kindergarteners can benefit from study units on body structures and processes. Units might be designed to create awareness and understanding of sense organs, the development of teeth, the growth in height and weight. Skills of body care and grooming are important. Five-year-olds might be able to use lessons on proper care of clothing, clothing suitable for the environment, and suggestions on keeping hair clean and well groomed.

Social Goals

1. *Contemporary kindergarten goals provide for the development of social concepts and group experience.*

Social concepts and the ability to participate in groups are learned. According to Havighurst, these objectives of social learning belong in the school curricula (19). Young children learn to establish their roles as individuals in our culture. Socialization helps children to grow, to become aware, to become familiar with what people around them expect, and to know what they can expect from other people. Socialization in all forms of school activity is learning to get along with other children, playing with toys, and getting acquainted with the family, the community, and the kindergarten. These group experiences nurture the affective development of the young kindergarten child. With these basic experiences, children are more likely to become active members of society rather than mere observers. Children need the help of teachers—and parents—to develop satisfying relationships. Through adult guidance children build social concepts and group experiences.

In building social skills, teachers can take advantage of the great energy of the five-year-old, who generally prefers to play with one or two children in a group setting. The teacher can use the small-group setting to teach equality and individual rights, which are essential for group experiences and social contacts. The child's group must follow social rules as practical principles, not as teachers' orders to be obeyed. Among these rules are taking turns, listening when someone is speaking, and respecting personal ownership. "Sharing time" and active classroom discussions can help children make positive observations about others in the group. Letting the children talk about things they enjoy and experiences they have had is another method of developing social goals. Verbal sharing may encourage shy children and help keep attention on the needs and the interests of others.

The child must be given opportunities to interact with people outside his own peer groups. The child's social growth can be supported by planned experiences and direct contact with school personnel and the school environment, and trips to points of interest in the community. Role-playing of situations in the child's own home and family also broadens skills. To live, work, and play with children who have different skin color, capacities, and experiences is important in social development. Teaching social goals, like teaching other developmental goals, takes skilled guidance, thoughtful interpretations of observed experiences, and careful planning of active experiences.

2. *Contemporary kindergarten goals teach responsibility and self-discipline.*

Self-discipline and a sense of responsibility are crucial to our democracy and basic to our society. They can be developed through social and group experiences. These goals can gradually be attained by children as they learn what behavior is acceptable to others and as they learn to make choices based on limited alternatives. Responsibility and self-discipline help the young child move toward independent thinking and prepare him for interacting with people.

For the five-year-old child, the classroom provides opportunity to learn responsibility. Daily routines of eating, sleeping, and cleaning up help the child learn competency in managing routine situations. The teacher can leave to the children the responsibility for watering plants, feeding fish, resetting chairs and other classroom duties. The child understands and develops responsibility when he is allowed to live and practice activities that require responsibility. The child develops responsibility more easily through responsible actions than through authoritative commands from an adult.

Every five-year-old must begin to learn self-discipline. Adults must expect self-discipline and set examples. Definite limits and expectations must be established, and it is essential for children to know what is expected of them as class members. Throughout the day the child should have many opportunities for choosing. Opportunities of this kind encourage children to develop and attain their own goals. There are many decisions kindergarten teachers make for the five-year-old child that he is more capable of making himself—decisions that in fact he needs to make to learn self-discipline.

The contemporary kindergarten program is aimed at opening the way for maximum growth for all five-year-old children. Intellectual, affective, psychomotor, and social areas of the developmental model do not function separately or independently, but rather as a whole.

Kindergarten goals for contemporary education are interrelated and designed to provide the most stimulating and the most healthful environment possible for the child. The goals stated here recognize the child's ability for early cognitive learning, yet they also recognize his need to learn through the playing-out of real situations. The goals emphasize the necessity of learnings for today's children as opposed to the learnings of children of merely a decade ago. Contemporary kindergarten goals emphasize the child's need to be a child—to be cared for, to feel secure, to feel warm and loved, to feel important, to feel capable. Education is past the point where one simply stated goal is sufficient to build a program for the kindergarten child. Several interrelated goals that reflect theories of development and accommodate the whole child must be incorporated into the kindergarten. The developmental goals are necessary if a kindergarten program is to truly provide an environment beneficial to the growth of the child.

REFERENCES

1. Benjamin Bloom. *Stability and Change in Human Characteristics*. New York, New York: John Wiley and Sons, 1964.

2. James L. Hymes. "The Goal of Kindergarten Education." *Kindergarten Education*. Washington. D.C.: American Association of Elementary-Kindergarten-Nursery Educators, National Education Association, 1965.

3. Thomas D. Yawkey and Gene Aronin. "World of Work and Early Childhood Education: Retrospect and Prospect." Unpublished study. College Park: University of Maryland, 1971.

4. James L. Hymes. *Teaching the Child under Six*. Columbus, Ohio: Charles Merrill, 1968.

5. Joe L. Frost. "Analyzing Early Childhood Education Programs: The Nature of Educational Objectives," *Educational Leadership, 28* (May, 1971), 796–801.

6. Millie Almy. "New Views on Intellectual Development in Early Education," *Intellectual Development: Another Look*. Washington, D.C.: Association for Supervision and Curriculum Development, National Education Association, 1964.

7. Jerome Bruner, Paul Oliver, and Patricia Greenfield. *Studies in Cognitive Growth*. New York, New York: John Wiley and Sons, 1967.

8. Jean Piaget. *Child's Conception of Number*. New York, New York: W.W. Norton and Company, 1970.

9. Joseph McVicker Hunt. *Intelligence and Experience*. New York, New York: Ronald Press, 1964.

10. Edward Welling and Marie Welling. *Expansion of Life: An Action Design for Title One*. Boston, Massachusetts: Department of Education of the Commonwealth of Massachusetts, 1971.

11. Verna Hildebrand. *Introduction to Early Childhood Education*. New York, New York: Macmillan Company, 1971.

12. Thomas C. O'Brien and Bernard Shapiro. "Problem-Solving and Development of Cognitive Structure," *Arithmetic Teacher, 16* (January, 1969), 11–15.

13. Sarah Lou Leeper and others. *Good Schools for Young Children*. New York, New York: Macmillan Company, 1968.

14. Benjamin P. Frost. "Anxiety and Educational Achievement," *British Journal of Educational Psychology, 38* (November, 1968), 293–301.

15. Moshe D. Caspi. "Emotional Blackmail," *The Record, 70* (January, 1969), 279–96.

16. John E. Forpy. "Motor Perceptual Development," *Physical Educator, 28* (March, 1971), 11–12.

17. Anne Butler. *Current Research in Early Childhood Education: A Compilation and Analysis for Program Planners*. Washington, D.C.: American Association of Elementary-Kindergarten-Nursery Educators, National Education Association, 1970.

18. Harold G. Kopp. "Curriculum: Cognition and Content," *The Volta Review, 70* (Spring, 1968), 372–516.

19. Robert J. Havighurst. "Moral Character and Religious Education," *Religious Education, 51* (March, 1956), 165–67.

The Concept Readiness and Several Applications*

E. KUNO BELLER

The first part of this article will deal with a review of the concept of readiness and a proposed formulation, the second part with the application of this formulation to recent research on cognitive processes and the teaching of cognitive operations. The third part will deal with implications of research on emotional and motivational factors for readiness in disadvantaged children.

Reading, per se, is not discussed in this article. Learning, language development and training, and certain disturbances of readiness are presented. A major question to be answered by the reader, therefore, would be: "Is this not information which should be interpreted to parents anxious to aid their children in mastering the reading process?"

From *The Reading Teacher*, Vol. 23, No. 8 (May 1970). Reprinted with permission of the International Reading Association and E. Kuno Beller.

*The discussion of applications is based in part on research carried out by the author with support from the Ford Foundation through a grant to the Philadelphia Council of Community Advancement and with the support from the Head Start Evaluation and Research Center at Temple University.

The Concept Readiness

Few concepts in education have been surrounded with more controversy than the concept readiness. Nevertheless, the question of whether the child is ready to learn and to be taught anything new in the cognitive, social or emotional realm remains a vital issue to many educators. Rousseau's (1964) viewpoint of two centuries ago, which is well reflected by his statement, "Regard all delays in teaching as so much time gained; it is already a great gain to have reached this stage without loss: let childhood ripen in children. On the other hand, are certain lessons unavoidable? If so, be careful not to administer them today, if they can safely be put off until tomorrow," has continued to the present day. Underlying Rousseau's concept of readiness was a concept of maturation. One of his major criticisms of education in his day was that educators did not wait for the necessary faculties to ripen in the child. He advised educators to make maximum use of sensory-motor functions which are well developed in the child and suggested a series of activities which the

43

child could carry out and which would go a long way in preparing him for more complex intellectual activities later on in his development. Rousseau's ideas were formalized into a pedagogic system by Pestalozzi (1967) and Montessori (1914). The elaboration of Rousseau's ideas of a sensory-motor phase of development as part of a cognitive development had to wait for the genius of Piaget two centuries later. It is important to keep in mind that, whereas Rousseau and his followers emphasized the concept of readiness, they labored hard to specify the activities which the young child was ready to carry out in preparation for later stages of development. Some of these specifications will be discussed in the context of Piaget.

A different school of readiness which bears some superficial resemblance to that of the thinkers discussed above is represented by Gesell and his associates. Gesell continued the tradition of Darwin, Galton, and Hall (Kessen, 1965) and was more interested in biological speculations about developmental changes in behavior than in the interactions of organism environment and experience and the effects of this interaction on development. He considered maturation as the basic principle for development and maturation was conceived as developmental change due to inner forces. Environmental factors may influence these developmental sequences but the basic course is laid down by biological factors (Gesell, 1954). So, we find Ilg and Ames (1964) of the Gesell Institute, who developed an elaborate battery of tests for school readiness, write:

"The need for accommodation of the environment to both age and individual differences becomes evident from the moment of the child's birth . . . as hard as the mother may try to impose a rigid schedule on some infants, she is not successful unless she responds to the individual demands . . . ", and " . . . the greatest single contribution which can be made towards guaranteeing that each individual child will get the most possible out of his school experience is to make certain that he starts that school experience at what is for him the "right" time. This should be the time when he is truly ready . . . " (1964, P. 6, 14)

For Ilg and Ames, true readiness is based on careful records of what children actually do under normal circumstances. Environmental factors such as ethnic background, social class or any other system of environmental influences are not given any systematic place in the determination of readiness. Biological speculations are offered in the place of psychological theory to account for developmental change. The same viewpoint is reflected by others who are much more concerned with education and curriculum than were Gesell and his associates, e.g. Hymes (1958). "As surely as the baby sat and crawled and stood and walked, always in his own good time, the power on which reading instruction can build will also develop. Maturation and living make this inevitable."*

At the opposite extreme, are statements such as those made by Watson earlier in the century: "Give me a dozen healthy infants, well-formed, and my own specified world to bring them up in and I'll guarantee to take any one at random and train him to become any type of specialist I might select—doctor, lawyer, artist, merchant-chief and yes, even beggar-man and thief, regardless of his talents, penchants, tendencies, abilities, vocations, and race of his ancestors," and more recently by Bruner (1960): "The foundations of any subject may be taught to anybody at any age in some form." Such statements provide useful information concerning attitudes underlying educational policies in a broad sense, but they hardly qualify as propositions of knowledge, especially in the empirical sense.

*For an informative discussion of the ambiguity surrounding the concept of maturation, the reader is referred to Tyler (1964). For an interesting discussion of the implications of the concept readiness with regard to the age at which a child can be taught cognitive skills, the reader is referred to an extensive review by W. Fowler (1962).

The concept readiness is too complex to lend itself to simplistic generalizations. Statements concerning readiness become more meaningful, in the sense of being testable in some ways, when the criteria of readiness are pinned down to specific activities or operations in such a way that their relationship to the rate of learning and level of achievement of new activities or operations can be ascertained and in some way predicted. Even more important for the concept of readiness to be meaningful is the requirement that the activities and operations which define readiness relate in some logical way to new activities and operations which are to be learned or to the educational method by means of which the new operations are to be taught. This approach to the problem of readiness poses greater difficulties, especially for studies dealing with developmental change in complex psychological processes.

Cognitive Factors In Readiness

Fruitful beginnings in this direction of the proposed formulation of readiness have recently appeared in the research literature. Gagne's (1961, 1962) research on the role of learning sets in the acquisition of knowledge, particularly his study of readiness for learning various steps in the hierarchical sequence of mathematical operations, meets some of the requirements which are being proposed in this paper for the study of readiness to learn complex cognitive operations. Gagne proposes a hierarchical system within which certain operations such as "counting," "addition," "subtraction," "multiplication," and "division" are the elementary steps which have to be mastered by an individual to be ready for an understanding and for the mastery of more complex steps such as the solving of equations.

Piaget's formulations of cognitive development have opened up new horizons for the establishment of successive criteria of readiness as a propensity to move from isolated, less coherent mental operations to increasingly more interrelated and complex cognitive operations. For example, in Piaget's (1952) system of sensory-motor development, vision, and prehension start out as isolated reflexes. The integration and eventually the dominance of vision over prehension not only moves a child to a higher level of development, but changes altogether the child's experience. Passive reflexity changes into voluntary and eventually into goal-directed behavior. This and other formations described in great detail by Piaget, lay the foundation for further intellectual development such as intentional cognition. At this point, Piaget shows how the next step in cognitive development depends heavily upon experience. While engaging in goal-directed behavior and encountering obstacles in the path towards the goal, the child develops notions of temporal sequence, causality, and the relationship between objects other than himself. Confrontation and interaction with peers forces the child to question the validity of his egocentric views and to revise them. Piaget shows how each stage in development makes a child ready for the next step. Most importantly for meanings of readiness, Piaget makes explicit the logic of developmental progression and shows how operations on one stage prepare the child for operations on the next stage. Piaget's concept of conservation is a case in point. He defines clearly the mental operations, e.g., decentration, multiple classification, and reversibility, which a child must be able to carry out so as to be ready for the operation of conservation, which requires the synthesis of these operations. Sigel (1969) has carried out a series of pioneer studies in this area. These investigators have trained children who could not conserve in the prerequisite operation of multiple classification, multiplicative relations, reversibility and seriation. They found that such training of prerequisite operations made the child more ready to carry out the operation of conservation.

45

It becomes clear that Piaget's system of cognitive development provides a meaningful model of progression in which mastery of certain operations meets the criteria of readiness which appear most meaningful to this writer. Research such as that carried out by Sigel and his associates promises to provide experimental verification of such criteria of readiness in cognitive development.

The discussion so far has been limited to a consideration of readiness in relation to the development of cognitive abilities and skills. The concept of "cognitive styles" does not refer to an ability or skill but rather to a disposition which may influence a child's readiness to benefit more from one type of instruction than from another. In other words, cognitive style may function as a readiness factor in the individualization of instruction. To illustrate such a relationship, the author will discuss a study which he has carried out recently (Beller, 1967). To begin with, a child may order the world he experiences or what he perceives in a variety of ways. One of the ways in which a child may accomplish this is by grouping or classification. There are different types of classification. Kagan, et al. (1963) and Sigel (1970) have referred to this process as "cognitive style" and have distinguished several different styles. They have developed first a set of pictures (Kagan, et al.) and later a set of objects (Sigel) to determine the preferred style of any individual. Sigel has distinguished three major styles: a descriptive-analytic or part-whole style; a contextual-relational style; and a categorical-inferential style. The term descriptive-analytic or part-whole cognitive style refers to the classification of objects in terms of their objective characteristics such as color, size, or form. The contextual-relational style refers to the classification of objects in terms of their functional use and relation to each other. The term categorical style refers to the classification of objects in terms of some inferred characteristics which are not directly observable.

It is assumed that children form such preferred dispositions or styles of experience early in their life and that these remain stable characteristics, in other words, offer an experiential typology. In a recent study (Beller, 1967), the author has investigated the possibility that methods of language training may correspond to one or another of these cognitive styles and that this common core might make a method of training more or less effective, depending upon its correspondence with the child's preferred style. Such a study was indicated because of the nature of certain types of language instruction. For example, phonetic training, the training of vocabulary and classification consist largely of teaching a child to associate letters or sounds with words, words with objects, words with words, and objects with objects. The association between words and between objects is achieved through the use of criteria for grouping objects as belonging together or as not belonging together. Moreover, objects can be associated in a variety of ways. This association may be based on a shared characteristic such as color, size, and shape which both objects have in common, on a functional relationship between two objects, or on an inferred characteristic shared by both objects. For example, if you consider a (building) block and a box, the two may be together because both share a common color such as brown, or because both start with a "b" (i.e., descriptive, part-whole style), because the block can be put into the box (i.e., relational style), or because both are toys or are made out of wood (categorical style). Thus, in the process of teaching phonetics, vocabulary, and further characteristics of objects which have become part of the child's vocabulary, the child learns to use certain categories for associating the reference objects, e.g., "block" and "box." The criteria of association correspond exactly to the cognitive styles described earlier, namely descriptive-analytic, relational, and categorical.

The relevance of this study for readiness was that it controlled experimentally the logical relationship between operational criteria of readiness, namely cognitive styles and the methods of language training. Readiness in this case was not conceived of as an ability, but rather as a disposition which might make it possible to individualize language instruction and thereby make language training more efficient. Specifically, by varying the correspondence between the child's preferred cognitive style and the method of language training, it was possible to determine the effects of the child's cognitive style (i.e., readiness) or learning (regardless of the method of teaching), the effect of method of language training on learning (regardless of the child's cognitive style), and thirdly, the interreacting effects on learning of both the child's cognitive style and the method with which he is being trained. The outcome of the study demonstrated that readiness in the form of cognitive style and teaching method affected learning or language acquisition both separately and in interaction with one another. Children with a dominantly descriptive style achieved better recognition memory of vocabulary regardless of the methods with which they were taught. Conversely, the descriptive method of language training produced better recognition memory regardless of the child's initial cognitive style. In contrast, children who had a predominantly relational style improved most in their associative memory regardless of the method with which they were taught. Again, the same applied to the relational method of training, regardless of the child's initial cognitive style. Finally, there was a consistent trend for children to achieve better recognition and associative memory wherever the method of training corresponded with the child's cognitive style or readiness. These findings emerged on a paired associate learning test which was especially constructed to evaluate the effects of cognitive styles (readiness, method of language training, and the interaction between the two).

Another set of findings in the study was obtained from the use and comparison of performance on the *Illinois Test of Psycholinguistic Abilities* before and after language training. A major finding relevant for readiness was that matching the child's cognitive style with the method of language training was clearly more effective than non-matching. The second major finding was found in a group of children who could not sufficiently verbalize to be classified with regard to cognitive styles. It was found that these children who were most backward in language development benefited generally more than other children from the functional-relational method of language training.

As indicated earlier, this study was discussed here to illustrate research on readiness in which it can be shown that a meaningful relationship exists between the operation of readiness and the method of instruction. A conclusion to be drawn from that study is that individualization of instruction has positive effects on language acquisition.

Emotional and Motivational Factors in Readiness

The interrelationship between readiness and method of teaching as well as the need for individualization of instruction can also be found in the case of non-cognitive factors such as emotion, motivation, and interpersonal relationships. With regard to the non-cognitive variables of readiness, it should be pointed out that it is often the non-cognitive aspects of teaching or educational methods which must be modified in order to maximize the effectiveness of instruction. In the case of the child who is not ready because of a lack of motivation to learn, it is, of course, indicated first to search for the causes which conflict with the motivation to learn or to be taught. When such factors cannot be found, or cannot be altered, special incentives, contingencies, and other non-cognitive factors are introduced into the teaching process to increase motivational readiness for learning. However, when the particular moti-

47

vational or emotional factors effecting readiness are unclear, then the theoretical or logical basis for introducing special techniques in the educational process remains also obscure. When that happens, the procedure is similar to the use or prescription of drugs which bring about desired changes without an adequate understanding of the processes responsible for the change. Motivational and emotional factors in certain disturbances of readiness to learn, such as "underachievement" and "school phobia" are still too unclear to permit a logical relationship between readiness and individualization of instruction. However, this problem does not exist in all cases of emotional disturbances in readiness. For example, if the problem is one of low self-confidence on the part of the child which results in a poor reaction to the learning situation, it is possible to maximize opportunities for success so as to let the child gradually build up his self-confidence. The problem here is that in spite of the frequent use of the term "self", especially in relation to the disadvantaged child, it is often difficult to assess, let alone measure, self-image, and self-confidence.

Considerable progress has been made in the area of interpersonal relationships and their effect on readiness. It has been generally known that lower-class, deprived children approach the formal education situation and the educator with a great deal of fear and mistrust which in turn affects their readiness to learn and perform in this situation. This condition has a similar depressing effect as test anxiety on cognitive performance (Sarason, 1960). The author has carried out a study (Beller, 1968) in which, among other things, the effects of this initial apprehensiveness of the disadvantaged child on cognitive performance were investigated. The major purpose of this study was to evaluate the effect of timing of educational intervention in deprived, lower-class children. One group of children began school with nursery at four, a second group began schooling in kindergarten at five, and a third group en-

tered first grade without any prior preschool experience. These three groups have been compared in a longitudinal study on cognitive and motivational factors and on the interrelationship between these variables. The initial level of intellectual functioning was assessed at the outset for each group. In order to reduce the adverse effects of a new and unfamiliar situation, children were given an opportunity to become familiar with the school environment for several months before the initial testing was carried out. It was found that child's initial I.Q. score did not vary as a function of the time at which educational intervention was started. In other words, the level of intellectual achievement of nursery children, kindergarten children, and first graders in Get Set and ghetto schools as measured by several tests did not differ at the outset when they entered school. Because of uncontrollable circumstances, the same battery of tests had to be given to a group of children immediately after they entered school, that is, within the first three weeks after school entry. This group differed from the other two groups by having a significantly lower performance score on one of the tests; namely, the Stanford Binet tests. The inference was made that this deviant finding was due to heightened undissipated apprehensiveness over the new situation. This inference was tested subsequently by selecting a comparable group in the same classroom and giving them the same test several months after they entered the first grade. The new group performed significantly better than the group which was tested immediately after school entry.

The relevance of this study for readiness was twofold: first, a child's initial level of intellectual performance served as a base line for measuring the effectiveness of educational intervention; thus an artifically depressed initial base line could distort in a variety of ways the obtained change (from pre- to post-testing). Secondly, the emotional component of readiness greatly affected the child's intellectual performance. At least during the initial phase after entering school, the disadvantaged child is apprehensive and this tended to depress his performance. This initial apprehensiveness and its effect on the pre-test, the measure of readiness dissipated after a relatively short time and with it, the child's intellectual performance rose significantly. Thus, the logic of the relationship between emotional readiness and cognitive functioning was borne out: the apprehensiveness of the child in reaction to a new and strange situation, which represents threatening authority, produces generally inhibiting effects, which extends not only into interpersonal behavior, but also to the cognitve realm, at least insofar as performance is concerned.

The same study which yielded the finding described above explored in greater depth the effects of a child's mistrust towards the adult environment and the relationships of such mistrust with other motivational as well as cognitive factors. Mistrust of adults was defined in this study as conflict over turning to the adult for help and emotional support such as praise and affection. The term used for this measure was Dependency Conflict. A meaning of this conflict is that the child is conflicted over making use of the help and nurturing available to him from the adult environment. It is to be expected that such mistrust and conflict will affect behaviors of the child which are expected of him from the teacher. For example, it was found that a heightening of mistrust or dependency conflict in a child was associated with both lower motivation to achieve and with lower level of actual achievement. Parenthetically, it should be noted that measures of motivation to achieve and of actual achievement were obtained from entirely separate sources.

Since this finding was based on several hundred disadvantaged lower-class children enrolled in nursery, kindergarten, and first grade, and since the study extended throughout the entire school year, it would seem safe to conclude that mistrust of the teacher and conflict over turning to the teacher for help and emo-

tional support affects not only the child's readiness to perform but also his readiness to benefit from the educational experience. Whatever the causal relationship might be, it is clear from this set of findings that the disadvantaged child who is not ready to trust the educational situation and the adult educator is also handicapped in other ways, such as in his motivation to achieve and in his readiness to exhibit his abilities when asked to do so in a test situation. Moreover, these readiness factors influence a child not only at the moment of entrance into school, but appear to persist over time in some children as they continue their educational experience in school. This conclusion is not inconsistent with the findings reported earlier; namely, that as a group, children are more apprehensive when they enter a new situation than several months later, after they have had the opportunity to become familiar with the new situation.

Another finding in the same study is of interest. In comparisons of three groups of children by the end of the first grade, i.e., Group A which had been in school since nursery (three years); Group B, since kindergarten (for two years); and Group C, since first grade (for one year), it was found that length of time in school was associated with decreasing dependency conflict or mistrust of the educational environment. In other words, by the end of the first grade, the group of children who had been in school for only one year manifested the highest dependency conflict or mistrust of the teacher. The implications of this finding for readiness to benefit from educational experience and the meaning of the relationship between dependency, motivation to achieve and actual intellectual achievement have been discussed earlier. The child who mistrusts the helper and is conflicted over making use of the help available to him is less ready to benefit from the educational process. These findings offer an example of the role and interpersonal factors as an important part of readiness. A crucial next step for research in this area would be to investigate various modifications in the teaching process that might counteract and overcome the child's mistrust of the educational setting and his conflict over expressing his need for help and support in that situation. Such investigations would appear to be important, not only for the sake of facilitating cognitive development in the child, but also for socialization in other areas. For example, it was found that children who were high in dependency conflict also tended to have greater problems than other children in impulse control, particularly in the control of aggression. These continued problems may reflect a lack of readiness on the part of the child to respond to the socializing agent. Thus it would seem that the same forces, both internally and externally, which interfere with the child's readiness to respond to educational processes aimed at developing cognitive functioning also interfere with the child's readiness to respond to the socializing efforts of the educator on impulse control in general and on aggression in particular. However, it should be pointed out that the failure of socialization is often a two-way process. The teacher is no more "ready" to help the child cope with unacceptable impulses and behavior than the child is "ready" to respond favorably to attempts by the teacher to help him. This author has experienced considerable reluctance in a good many nursery and kindergarten teachers of disadvantaged children to recognize and permit the expression of even moderate aggression in the classroom. Thus, one is likely to find less overt expression of aggression in pre-school classes of the disadvantaged child than in pre-school classes of middle-class children. Of course, this does not result in socialization of the child's aggression and other undesirable behaviors; it simply keeps the undesirable behavior out of the classroom. The adult who does not permit the child to express undesirable behavior and does not help the child to cope differently with frustration and tension does not remove the instigation to such behavior but increases the child's mistrust

of himself and adult authority. In a broader sense, the teacher as a socializer has achieved a minor success and a major failure. When the same child who continues to live in the ghetto, under many frustrations, approaches adolescence, aggressive and other undesirable impulses come to the fore again, both in the classroom and away from the classroom. But at that point, the child is less ready to be socialized than he was in pre-school.

The author has not attempted to give specific suggestions to school personnel in dealing with communication with parents. It is hoped that the concepts and research findings presented will be shared with parents in a meaningful way. This is impossible until adults working with children understand the concepts and are able, therefore, to help guide parents in the understanding of children and how they learn.

REFERENCES

Beller, E. K. Cognitive styles and methods of language training. Paper presented at the American Educational Research Association, New York, February, 1967.

Beller, E. K. The evaluation of effects of early educational intervention on intellectual and social development of lower-class, disadvantaged children. Paper presented at a colloquium for Head Start, Washington, D.C., October 9, 1968.

Bruner, J. S. *The process of education.* (Part 4) Cambridge: Harvard University Press, 1960. P. 12.

Fowler, W. Cognitive learning in infancy and childhood. *Psychological Bulletin*, 1962, 59, ,116–152.

Gagne, R. M., and Paradise, N. E. Abilities and learning sets in knowledge acquisition. *Psychological Monographs*, 1961, 75 (14), 1–23.

Gagne, R. M., Major, J. R., Garstens, H. L., and Paradise, N. E. Factors in acquiring knowledge of a mathemati-

cal task. *Psychological Monographs*, 1962, *76* (7), 1–21.

Gesell, A. The ontogenesis of infant behavior. In L. Carmichael (Ed.) *Manual of child psychology*. New York: John Wiley & Sons, Inc., 1954. Pp. 355–356.

Hymes, J. L., Jr. *Before the child reads*. Evanston, Illinois: Row, Peterson & Co., 1958. P. 28.

Ilg, F. L., and Ames, L. B. *School readiness behavior test used at the Gesell institute*. New York: Harper & Row, 1964. P. 6, 14.

Kagan, J., Moss, H. A., and Sigel, I. E. The psychological significance of styles of conceptualization. *Monograph of the Society for Research in Child Development*, 1968, *28* (2).

Kessen, W. *The child*. New York: John Wiley & Sons, Inc., 1965.

Montessori, M. *Dr. Montessori's own handbook*. New York: Frederick H. Stokes Co., 1914.

Heafford, R. M. *Pestalozzi*. London: Methuen & Co., Ltd., 1967.

Piaget, J. *The origins of intelligence in children*. New York: International University Press, 1952.

Rousseau, J. J. *Emile ou de l'education*. Paris: Farnier Freres, 1964, P. 83.

Sarason, S. B., *et al. Anxiety in elementary school children*. New York: John Wiley & Sons, Inc., 1960.

Sigel, I. E. The Piagetian system and the world of education. In D. Elkind and J. H. Flavell (Eds.) *Studies in cognitive development: essays in honor of Jean Piaget*. New York: Oxford University Press, 1969. Pp. 465–489.

Sigel, I. E., and Olmsted, P. Modification of classification, competence, and level of representation among lowerclass Negro kindergarten children. In H. A. Passow (Ed.) *Reaching the disadvantaged learner*. New York: Columbia Teachers College Press, 1970.

Tyler, F. T. Issues related to readiness to learn. In E. Hilgard (Ed.) *National Society for the Study of Education*, Part I. Chicago: University of Chicago Press, 1964. Pp. 210–239.

Readiness Training Implications from Research

EDWARD PARADIS
JOSEPH PETERSON

Each year teachers working with pre-reading and beginning reading pupils are faced with the problem of defining the starting point for initial reading instruction. Should pupils start with informal readiness activities? Should they start with a formal readiness program that is part of the basal reading series? Should

From *The Reading Teacher*, Vol. 28, No. 5 (February, 1975). Reprinted with permission of the International Reading Association and Edward Paradis and Joseph Peterson.

a supplemental readiness program be used? Should the teacher omit readiness and start with direct reading instruction? Or, is there some other alternative? In most cases, teachers answer the question by following the advice of the reading authorities who created the basal reader program in use in the school system. Teachers tend to use the structured program which was produced as a part of the basal series.

These series usually carry a recommendation that teachers select only the

51

readiness activities appropriate for their pupils. Unfortunately, experience suggests that a limited number of teachers actually diagnose each child's readiness skills. In other cases, all pupils progress as a group through the readiness program regardless of the background brought to school. Knowledge of individual differences leads one to expect that a few pupils will already have developed the skills which constitute the readiness program and therefore will not need the readiness training. Two studies cited below, however, support the notion that certain traditional readiness activities involving visual discrimination may be designed to teach skills that large numbers of pupils already possess. Whereas a third study of auditory discrimination skills indicates that the first phonics skill taught to youngsters is probably more difficult at least for disadvantaged pupils than subsequent skills in the hierarchy.

Discrimination Skills

Mitchell (1965) examined the visual discrimination skills of 118 lower socioeconomic kindergarten pupils who had received no formal readiness training. Twelve pages of visual discrimination exercises such as seeing likenesses and differences of pictures, designs, letters and words were selected from prereading exercises presented in a popular basal series. On ten of the pages dealing primarily with discrimination of letters and words, 85 percent of the pupils reached or exceeded a criterion of 75 percent correct responses. The two pages of exercises where the criterion of 75 percent was not met by 85 percent of the pupils dealt with discrimination of minimal differences of pictures. Thus, the majority of the untrained lower socioeconomic pupils who were assumed not to have basic readiness skills did indeed possess most of the visual discrimination skills this readiness program was intended to prepare. The investigator suggested that teachers be selective in determining which

visual discrimination training material to use.

In a similar study Paradis (1974) examined the visual discrimination skills of preschool and kindergarten children of middle socioeconomic status who had not received formal readiness training. A measuring instrument composed of visual discrimination exercises requiring the discrimination of pictures, letters, and words was constructed by selecting representative exercises from the prereading activities accompanying seven widely used basal reader series. The battery was administered to 128 preschool and 440 kindergarten children. Results indicated that 97 percent of the kindergarten pupils and 69 percent of the preschool children were successful on more than 80 percent of the items. Most children had developed the skill to discriminate pictures and letters but encountered moderate difficulty in discrimination of words.

The auditory discrimination skills of 101 lower socioeconomic kindergarten pupils who had received no formal readiness training were examined by Paradis (1968). Eight auditory discrimination prereading exercise pages dealing with rhyming sounds and initial consonant sounds were selected from a popular reading series. An exercise page was defined as easy for the group if 85 percent of the pupils met a criterion of 75 percent correct responses on the page. Results indicated that none of the eight exercise pages was easy for the group. The pupils were relatively more successful with the exercises dealing with rhyming sounds, with 59 percent of the subjects attaining the criterion for success, than with exercises dealing with initial consonant sounds, where 7 percent attained success. In general, all exercises were judged as difficult. The investigator concluded that children from lower socioeconomic backgrounds are likely to need instruction in order to perform auditory discrimination tasks. The data did not permit generalization to other socioeconomic groups.

Implications for Teaching

The literature on good teaching is replete with the suggestion that teachers try to meet individual needs by diagnostic measures. One might assume that with any given program suggested for use in the school, large numbers of pupils would need the training offered by the program. The studies cited above, however, suggest that most children completing kindergarten and entering first grade can successfully work typical visual discrimination exercises with discrimination of letter forms. For most children at the reading readiness stage, then, the first grade teacher needs to assume that diagnostic testing will yield results which show that the majority of her students have mastered this skill and do not need instruction in visual discrimination of letters. This obviously does not obviate the need to test and then teach the names or sounds of the letters if the program is based upon this knowledge.

The results of the children's ability to discriminate words and pictures are mixed. Middle socioeconomic status pupils tended to have relatively more problems with discrimination of word forms than with letters or pictures. The teacher will need to be prepared to offer instruction in this area. Pupils who exhibit the ability to discriminate pictures and letters but are deficient in word discrimination skills may be predisposed to problems in learning sight words and will likely benefit from practice discriminating among words with minimal differences. An example of this type of practice is the following exercise where the child is to indicate all words like the stimulus word:

meet; meet, meek, meet, meet

The results from the Mitchell study which indicate that lower socioeconomic status pupils have more problems in discrimination of pictorial stimuli does not necessarily mean that the pupils should be provided with additional work in this

area. Research done by Rosen (1966) and Wingert (1969) indicates that visual discrimination training with nonverbal stimuli such as pictures and geometric figures has little effect upon reading achievement. From the standpoint of teaching reading skills, then, it would appear that little is to be gained from visual discrimination exercises where pictures are the discriminated stimuli. In this case, the teacher should move to the next readiness skill in the plan and test to determine who needs what.

Although a large number of kindergarten and preschool children are successful with visual discrimination tasks, the same cannot be said for auditory discrimination. In particular, children from a lower socioeconomic background, when considered as a group, do not exhibit adequate skills to perform auditory discrimination skills successfully. They need opportunities to practice discrimination of both rhyming sounds and initial consonant sounds. Most reading programs call for children to learn beginning consonant sounds early in the reading program as an initial phonic skill. The teacher needs to be aware that discrimination of initial consonant sounds will probably be more difficult for her pupils than discrimination of rhyming sounds. Thus, more practice should be provided for auditory discrimination of initial consonants than rhymes. The standard exercises offered in the readiness programs seem to be both necessary for most children and appropriate enough to allow the learning of the skills. Testing should reveal which pupils do and do not need this training.

The three studies presented emphasize the need for teachers to assess each individual child's readiness skills. Following the assessment of skills, teachers should tailor programs to meet skill deficiencies. Teachers can expect children to enter school with better visual than auditory discrimination ability and should adjust instruction accordingly.

Some children will enter school possessing skills that have typically been developed during the readiness period. These advanced children should not begin initial reading instruction by working exercises designed to develop skills they already possess. The practice of having all children do all exercises has left many children in the classroom bored and unchallenged. A more productive use of time would occur if the advanced children were permitted to proceed to the next stage of reading instruction.

REFERENCES

Mitchell, Ronald W. Kindergarten Children's Responses to Selected Visual Discrimination Exercises in Reading Readiness Materials. Unpublished colloquium paper, University of Minnesota, Minneapolis, Minnesota, 1965.

Paradis, Edward E. Kindergarten Children's Responses to Selected Auditory Discrimination Exercises in Reading Readiness Materials. Unpublished colloquium paper, University of Minnesota, Minneapolis, Minnesota, 1968.

Paradis, Edward E. "The appropriateness of visual discrimination exercises in reading readiness materials." *Journal of Educational Research,* vol. 67 (1974), pp. 276-78.

Rosen, Carl. "An experimental study of visual perceptual training and reading achievement in first grade." *Perceptual and Motor Skills,* vol. 22 (1966), pp. 979-86.

Wingert, Robert C. "Evaluation of a readiness training program." *The Reading Teacher,* vol. 22, no. 4 (January, 1969), pp. 325-28.

Kindergarten—What Can It Be? What Should It Be?

LEONA M. FOERSTER

Authorities in early childhood education are, for the most part, in agreement that kindergarten shouldn't stress "readiness" activities for first grade except in the broad sense that whatever comes before "readies" the individual for what comes after. There are more valuable activities for kindergarten than workbooks and pencils and long periods of sitting at desks. Unfortunately, such activities come too soon for many young children when they enter the primary grades. On the other hand, kindergarten shouldn't be a "laissez faire" situation in which children are thrust into an environment and left to their own devices with little direct adult intervention.

What, then, should be the role of the kindergarten year in the total school program? Perhaps the basic goals for kindergarten can be sorted into four major categories of equal importance—cognitive, affective, psychomotor, and linguistic goals.

Concerning cognitive goals, educators no longer hold the notion of fixed intelligence that perceives intelligence as an innate and immutable trait. Instead, educational psychologists tell us that intelligence can be viewed as a set of developed skills, skills which are greatly affected by an individual's interaction

From *Elementary English,* Vol. 52, No. 1 (January, 1975). Copyright © 1975 by the National Council of Teachers of English. Reprinted by permission.

with the environment. To strengthen children's cognitive abilities, then, teachers plan experiences in which the child acts upon that environment and in turn is acted upon by it. In the kindergarten, we plan the environment so that the children's curiosity will be heightened. They have opportunities to manipulate a variety of materials, and to talk about experiences.

The teacher is placed in the role of guide and questioner who helps children build concepts and generalizations. This is a weighty task, indeed, as it is through building cognitive structures that the child is equipped to organize experiences to make sense out of an otherwise incoherent world. In essence, we begin teaching children how to think in kindergarten.

Also important are the affective goals for the kindergarten year, those dealing with the social and emotional life of the child. Young children are egocentric in thought and deed. Socialization of the child comes about through planned experiences in which children learn the give-and-take of daily living. They learn to value such behaviors as cooperation and sharing, and to become social beings. Free choice activities in kindergarten learning centers result in a great amount of social growth. The teacher is there to supply materials, to suggest alternatives, and guide children toward solving their own problems.

Closely related to social growth is the emotional growth of the child. Again, the teacher structures experiences which will enable children to understand and accept themselves as well as to build positive concepts of self and others. The teacher guides the children in learning to cope with their emotions and to tap these emotions for self-enhancement and to channel them in positive directions as children interact in the kindergarten environment.

The third major category of goals for the kindergarten year might be called psychomotor goals. Included are the motor skills which are so important for the total development of the child. Activities are planned which promote physical growth as well as control of large and small muscles. A variety of motor activities are included in the kindergarten program ranging from running, jumping, climbing and other large muscle motor skills to finger plays, painting, clay modeling, and using manipulative toys which promote coordination of small muscles. Not to be overlooked in this area are such necessities as learning to tie shoes, button and zip clothing, pour liquids, cut food and the like which are so important in the life of the young child and are closely related to the child's growth in independence and development of positive concepts of self.

Linguistic goals have been left for last deliberately because language is so crucial in the other areas previously mentioned. Language is the strand which runs through all kindergarten activities. For example, language and cognitive development go hand in hand. Psychologists tell us that there is pre-linguistic thinking of a sort. However, language allows us to manipulate our environment internally and frees us from our senses. But complex thinking demands complex language skills. Conversely, vocabulary is useless to the individual without comprehension of meanings of words which are used. Language determines not only how we think but what we think as well. This is called linguistic determinism. Language and culture, too, are closely related.

Goals in the affective domain also have a linguistic component. Language is what makes us human. It greatly affects our relationships with others. Language is the means through which we can express ourselves, make our thoughts and feelings known to others as well as review the thoughts and feelings of others. Because language and self-concept have a close relationship, it is essential that the teacher accepts the child's language, whether or not it is a different language or dialect, and build upon that language as a base to increase language power.

Even in the psychomotor domain, language plays a vital role. Skill development without language development would be highly inefficient. Thoughts and actions are united through language, and skills are improved through verbal and non-verbal communication.

Language, then, plays a dominant role in the kindergarten program. Since language skills are not taught or learned in a vacuum, the kindergarten program should offer children rich and varied experiences, particularly first-hand, perceptual experiences, in which language skills are developed. Listening and talking will be a part of the many structured and unstructured experiences which are provided. Cognitive, affective, and psychomotor goals are met as communication skills are increased. A well-rounded language program will include a variety of dramatic activities, as well as art, music, and literature experiences.

When children "fail" in school, frequently it is because their communication skills are not developed to a degree which enables them to meet grade level expectations. This places a great responsibility upon the kindergarten for initiating a strong program of language development. Particular attention should be given to the child who is "linguistically different," that is, who speaks a language or dialect other than standard English. The type of program initiated depends upon the specific needs of the children in the room.

Kindergarten, then is a year of language development during which important cognitive, affective, and psychomotor goals are met in a challenging environment. The kindergarten room is a learning laboratory in which the teacher plays many roles to facilitate learning. Since children learn to use language by using it, this environment for learning will not be a quiet place, but instead will reflect the busy hum of activity.

More than a year of "readiness' for formal schooling, kindergarten can and should be a place to which children are eager to come, where they are challenged, their needs are met, and in which each child is considered and allowed to participate in the planning of many kinds of experiences. Hardly a frill, kindergarten can and should make an important contribution to the total school program as well as a significant impact upon the life of each child in the program.

Letting Children Communicate: The Synthesis of Language Skills and Language

CELIA GENISHI

When a colleague asked me about the content of this paper, I said it was about combining language skills and language in early childhood classrooms. He then asked, "Aren't language skills and language redundant?" Since that's the reaction I anticipated, I smugly answered, "No, language skills are not the same as language," and went on to explain the point.

The purpose of this paper is to show that effective teachers, especially at the early childhood level, know that language and language skills are not identical. They plan activities that build on the language children already know and use. In the primary grades they also teach specific skills that will enable children to communicate orally and in writing. A short summary of recent research is included here to reflect present trends in teaching and evaluating language arts.

First, the difference between language and language skills. Linguists and students of language acquisition sometimes offer a simplified definition of *language* —a systematic way of relating sounds to meanings. Language in this sense is spoken. It is what children learn at an early age and use to communicate their needs, thoughts, and feelings. Language develops naturally without formal instruction in almost all children.

In classrooms children encounter lan-

guage in a variety of ways. They converse with each other or their teacher; they comment on their own actions; they write down their thoughts or have the teacher write them down. Teachers who view such activities as an important part of language arts use the child's own language as the "material" for learning. These teachers are often associated with *informal* or *nontraditional* approaches to teaching.

Language skills, on the other hand, usually stem from direct instruction. They include specified aspects of listening and speaking along with components of reading and writing, such as letter identification and knowledge of spelling patterns. These are bits and pieces of language as it is written or printed. Teaching these bits and pieces is important and appropriate to develop literacy, but too often the teaching of skills replaces the use of language in elementary language arts programs.

When this happens, the language arts curriculum consists primarily of workbook sheets, textbooks, and publishers' manuals. Teachers who rely on these materials are generally called *formal* or *traditional* in their orientation. They may assume that every child learns in an orderly sequence. The learner's ability to discriminate between sounds, forms, letters, and words precedes the efficient acquisition of other, more complex sequenced skills of reading and writing. The skills acquired can later be assessed with standardized achievement tests. Al-

From *Language Arts*, Vol. 56, No. 6 (September, 1979). Copyright © 1979 by the National Council of Teachers of English. Reprinted by permission.

though the analogy is trite, I view these skills as trees that the child may or may not group in a coherent way to form a forest, or language as a whole. Teachers help children to see the trees and the forest when their curriculum is a synthesis of skills lessons and spontaneous language.

Research on Traditional and Nontraditional Teaching

Observation in many early childhood or primary classrooms shows that teachers are busy cultivating trees. The call for improvement in "basic skills" is not just a matter for academic discussion. Curricula that emphasize skills are being implemented. Taxpayers who are parents of children in public schools demand their money's worth, and part of their money's worth is children's satisfactory performance on standardized tests.

In addition to public sentiment, some results of two recent large-scale studies support the implementation of skills-oriented curricula to raise children's achievement test scores in the basic skills, or certain components of language arts and mathematics. Although the directors of each study asked different research questions, both studies involved primary grade children and included a contrast between formal and informal or traditional and nontraditional teaching. Formal or traditional teachers directly taught skills. They used published curricula and made the decisions about how and when lessons took place. Informal or nontraditional teachers had less structured lessons and offered children more opportunities to choose their own activities.

The first of these studies was done in England (Bennett 1976). The researcher looked for a relationship between formal and informal styles of teaching and achievement. The overall question he asked was, "Do open (informal) classrooms work?" The general answer was, "No, children in traditional classrooms

with traditional teachers do better on a variety of tests."

The second study, called Project LONGSTEP (Chalupsky and Coles 1976), was done in the United States and was intended to determine the effectiveness of teaching innovations in public schools. The researchers defined *innovation* as features like team-teaching, the use of many different media, open architecture, teacher-made materials, individualized instruction, the use of paraprofessional aides, and so on. The standardized tests used to measure achievement were the California Test of Mental Maturity and the Comprehensive Test of Basic Skills.

The results showed that children in schools with many innovations had lower achievement scores than children in schools with a moderate amount of innovation. Children who scored very high were in the most traditional classrooms. They spent the most time on skills lessons, using textbooks and workbooks in class.

For people whose major goal is teaching children to attain high achievement scores, highly structured, teacher-directed lessons are clearly favored. Those with goals and objectives that are not measured by traditional tests, such as ability to formulate questions or willingness to accept responsibility, receive less guidance from research. This second group may be encouraged by some specific findings from the two studies. Bennett found that the primary children who made the greatest progress in language arts, even on traditional test measures, had teachers who *mixed* traditional techniques with informal methods that emphasized children's creativity and own forms of expression. He also briefly described the unique success of an informal teacher who had an informally structured curriculum at the same time that she emphasized the learning of language and math through a wide variety of activities.

Project LONGSTEP also supports synthesizing approaches or striking a balance between formal and informal teaching. The researchers called the balance "moderate innovation." They added that factors that they did not study may affect children's success. For example, some aspects of individualized instruction may not be easily observed. Outsiders may not see children working alone or using contracts, but the teacher may have her/his own ways of recording individual progress and making appropriate changes in children's activities. Where individual children are in their learning and where they should go next might be information the teacher stores in her/his own mind.

Synthesizing Language Skills and Language: Preschool through Grade One

These research findings may discourage teachers who believe that education in the language arts is not adequately measured by standardized tests. The persistence of curricula to teach skills and of standardized tests to measure achievement in those skills overshadows efforts to use and cultivate language. In the last part of this paper, I will describe activities of three teachers who persist in including language in their daily programs so that they combine characteristics of teachers who concentrate on skills with those who allow children to use language but avoid teaching skills. These activities are not "brand new"; but they are the teachers' own adaptations, and they have been found to work.

The first teacher's children are three- and four-year-olds who do not receive any formal instruction in language arts. Instead, they have constant opportunities to use language in the classroom. Occasionally there are special projects that involve writing down what children have experienced. One successful project is the "Me Book." A group of up to ten children begin it by accompanying the teacher to one child's home where the teacher takes photographs of the front door of the house, the child's bedroom, toys, members of the child's family, and pets, if any.

After the photographs are printed, they are mounted in a booklet, and each child talks about his/her photos, one at a time, while the teacher writes down what is said. The process is informal. Some children choose to talk about several photos at one sitting while others talk at length about one on one day and another a week later. The teacher believes that the experience is informative because children learn something about each other and also have opportunities to tell about their own worlds. For the children these are books that they "read" at any time during the year. For the teacher they are a source of information about what the child can express and what the child's interests are. They are also a personal and enjoyable introduction to the skills of reading and writing.

Another teacher who values children's language teaches kindergarteners in a public school. For her, art is the best vehicle to encourage the fluent use of language. What children represent in their art stems from their own experience or imagination, so they talk freely about their drawings and paintings. Since they are just beginning to write, the teacher writes down what they say. They may dictate simple descriptions such as, "Mom and me are having a birthday party, and it's summer," or more complex narratives.

During a social studies unit, which the teacher calls "I can be . . . ," one child draws a picture of a policeman, a police station, and a car. His caption reads:

I can be a policeman. He's going to catch somebody that's going too fast and he's going to give them a ticket. Then he's going to take them to the station and talk it over.

Other children draw and talk about becoming nurses, firemen, bionic men and women, or cheerleaders.

The language program at this teacher's school includes reading readiness workbooks and other commercial materials, and her children spend some time each day working on skills in a prereading series. Yet art, the language arts, and music—not skills lessons—dominate her own curriculum.

The role of teacher-as-synthesizer of language and language skills becomes especially clear in the primary grades. The public generally believes that first grade is a crucial year for children because it is the year they "really learn to read." At least they advance this learning process. A first grade teacher in her first year of teaching successfully combines content from the traditional textbook series that she is expected to use with experience-based methods.

Unlike her peers in the same school, the teacher thinks that a language experience approach is ideal for introducing children to reading. Like every other teacher, she also knows that her children will have to take standardized achievement tests at the end of the school year. Her solution is to teach formal lessons based on the textbook in addition to assigning informal work in "creating writing." Since the children rotate from center to center, she sometimes has children read to her from a basal reader and later helps them write or dictate original stories for their story collections. Each child maintains "My Story Book," which again is a combination of language from skills lessons and the child's own language.

Here are two contrasting excerpts from a child's book:

A Big Bug

A big bug was in the sun.
Linda met the big bug.
Good morning, big bug.
The big bug met Linda.

This example is similar to the controlled language of a basal reader. The teacher writes the sentences for the child and keeps a simple record of which words the child can read both in context and in isolation. She underlines these words twice. Words not recognized are not underlined, and words recognized only in isolation or in context are underlined once.

The other example is very different:

we r Goin to Park two
Pla in the Park and haf
a lunsh. box and arebue
is hape

This what the teachers calls a "Brave Story." She instructs the children to write their own stories and spell words in whatever way they can. This story is a child's version of, "We are going to the park to play in the park and have a lunchbox, and everybody is happy."

In this first-grade teacher's classroom, children know that there are correct spellings for words, yet they feel free enough to experiment with their own spellings and ideas. They also appear to enjoy reading, either from their basals or their story books. When I visited the classroom, almost all the children volunteered to read something to me. Whether they read fluently or not, they took pleasure in the activity. One indication that the teacher maintains the children's interest and satisfaction in their work is this sentence from a Brave Story, "This is a story I thank of by myself."

Conclusion

A student once told me that she didn't see the point of large-scale evaluative studies that tell us once more that direct teaching of skills produces higher test scores. She thought that if researchers spend time and money investigating current trends in public education, they should also try to tell classroom teachers "how to make things better."

In the large studies cited earlier, researchers acknowledged that despite the prevalence of commercial materials, individual teachers can "make things better." Preschoolers use language freely, and in the classroom I mentioned they are asked to use the abilities they have to describe aspects of their home environment. They see their teacher use reading and writing skills, and some of them begin to read along. The kindergarteners and first-graders, who are primarily black and Mexican-American, are using language informally while learning traditional skills with teachers who do not know about the studies described earlier. Yet these teachers' synthesis of language and language skills led to readiness and achievement scores at the appropriate grade level. The scores were equal to those of other children in the same school who spent more time on skills lessons but who may not have experienced the satisfaction of combining bits and pieces of language into whole creations of their own.

In order to educate children who are able to communicate effectively, to use language in various forms for different purposes, we need to teach the skills that are essential to reading and writing—and we need to let children communicate. Communication does not occur while they quietly complete worksheets. It occurs when children and adults talk to each other, attend to what others say or write, and express themselves freely. Teachers who provide opportunities for communicating are personally rewarded when they hear children's enthusiastic conversations or see their creations.

Unfortunately, these teachers do not always receive public rewards. Their children may not have high test scores so that administrators who value the highest scores do not praise them. Perhaps the next step for those committed to the synthesis of language skills and language is the further development of measures that assess how well a child uses language orally; how originally he or she formulates a question, description, or narrative; how clearly he or she puts thoughts into words; and how children develop such abilities over a period of years. If we can demonstrate that such nontraditional measures are as valid as traditional tests of basic skills, we can publicly reward teachers who synthesize language skills and language in their classrooms.

REFERENCES

Bennett, N. *Teaching Styles and Pupil Progress.* Cambridge, MA: Harvard University Press, 1976.

Chalupsky, A. B. and Coles, G. J. "Exploring the Impact of Educational Innovation: Overview of Project LONG-STEP." American Institute for Research. ERIC Document No. ED 132 191.

Graves, D. H. "Research Update: What's New May Not Be Good." *Language Arts* 54 (September 1977): 708–713

Paul, R. "Invented Spelling in Kindergarten." *Young Children* 31 (March 1976): 195–200.

Film:

"Oral Language Development: Views of Five Teachers." This film is one of a series produced for the California State Dept. of Education Right to Read Program. It is beautifully done to show how early childhood and elementary teachers lay the groundwork for reading by ensuring opportunities for spoken language. Available through Agency for Instructional Television, Box A, Bloomington, Indiana 47401.

Pre-Reading Instruction

- **Learning to read is too crucial to leave to chance . . .**
  Ethel M. King

- **. . . children are ready because of hereditary and maturational factors, but also because of the learning opportunities in their particular environment.**
  Dolores Durkin

- **. . . it is feasible to teach auditory analysis skills well in advance of reading instruction . . .**
  Jerome Rosner

- **I only hope that as early reading programs become more institutionalized, they don't become more institution like . . .**
  Walter H. MacGinitie

INTRODUCTION

Reading readiness is a concept whose origins trace back to the early part of this century. Over this time span, however, the meaning attached to readiness has changed greatly. Durkin discusses these changes, and draws three conclusions concerning readiness for reading.

Foulke follows by showing that reading readiness is not a function of chronological age but language readiness. The concept is not new, but her treatment is thorough and practical.

63

A comparison of direct and incidental pre-reading programs is made by King. She favors the direct methods, but acknowledges the importance of incidental learning.

Kirkland, Nevius, and Hoffman and Fillmer point out that reading is more than simply the sum total of independent perceptual abilities. Synthesizing information and abstracting meaning are also essential. These authors discuss methods of promoting these seemingly "right-brained" functions.

The discrete skills that compose pre-reading are described by Hardy and her colleagues, Montgomery, Rosner, and Stanchfield. These authors present evaluation suggestions as well as instructional methods.

A unique perspective on the acquisition of pre-reading skills is taken by Evvard. This vitally important event in a child's life is reported through the eyes of a grandmother who happens to be an educator.

One of the most underrated skills that is a prelude to reading is listening. Crowell and Au list a scale of questions that can add to the already beneficial activity of storytelling, while Schickedanz describes other means of upgrading this favorite instructional tool of kindergarten teachers. Tutolo provides further directions on structuring storytelling in order that children may extract meaning as well as pleasure from stories they are told.

The somewhat controversial topic of teaching reading in kindergarten is raised by the final four contributors, who address the when, how, and why of this issue. Although we do not support reading instruction in the kindergarten year, the comments of these authors are worth the attention of all early childhood educators, no matter what their orientation.

Reading Readiness

DOLORES DURKIN

To understand how "reading readiness" got into professional vocabularies and then into the school curriculum, it is necessary to go back to the 1920's. That decade is relevant because it was characterized by the beginning of so-called

From *The Reading Teacher*, Vol. 23, No. 6 (March 1970). Reprinted with permission of the International Reading Association and Dolores Durkin.

"scientific" measurements of human behavior. Among the results of what became almost a craze to measure everything was the appearance of school surveys. Of special relevance to reading readiness is a finding common to many of the survey reports which indicated that large numbers of children were failing first grade, most often because of insufficient achievement in reading.

Within a short time—this was still the 1920's—concern about the finding became as widespread as the finding itself, and for at least two reasons. Successful teaching of reading, then as now, was considered uniquely important among elementary school responsibilities. In addition, the failures that were occurring resulted in first-grade classrooms populated by many "over age" children. Behavior problems blossomed, and so did concern about why first graders were having difficulty learning to read.

Logically, it would seem, a study of reading problems—whether carried on in the 1920's or now—would look to such multiple and commonsense causes as overly large classes, inappropriate materials, inadequate teacher preparation, lack of motivation on the part of the children, and so on. However, in the study of beginning reading problems that went on in the 1920's and 1930's, the factor given singular attention is to be found in a pronouncement appearing with great frequency in the professional literature of that period: First graders are having difficulty learning to read because they were not ready when the instruction started. Why beginning reading problems were attributed so exclusively to a lack of readiness and, secondly, why delaying instruction was soon proposed as *the* solution, can be understood only when the psychological setting of the 1920's and 1930's is brought into focus.

Described briefly, and therefore incompletely, the 1920's and 1930's was a period in which the ideas of Arnold Gesell dominated. As a physician, Gesell was especially interested in children's physical and motor development. Resulting from his work and his prolific writing about it came the notion that these aspects of development "unfold in stages." Or, to put it another way, a young child grows and develops as a result of maturation, not learning. Acceptance of this point of view would suggest that if a child is unable to perform some particular motor task—crawling, for ex-

ample—it is because he has not yet reached that point or stage of development which allows him to crawl. Thus, he is unready. The solution? According to Gesell and his disciples it was to let time pass. That is, let additional maturity occur and then the child will be ready and he will be crawling.

Intellectual Skills Merged with Motor Skills

Had Gesell and his followers confined their descriptions and explanations to motor skills, there would be little reason to quarrel with them because much about a child's physical development does depend upon maturation and, therefore, the passing of time. However, this is not what happened. Instead, prominent educators were soon using Gesell's explanation of motor skills to explain the development of intellectual skills. In fact, nowhere was this highly questionable merger more apparent than in the field of reading.

When, in the 1920's, school surveys revealed that children were failing first grade because of insufficient achievement in reading, the one "explanation" to get attention was that these first graders had problems because they were not ready when school instruction began. The solution? Still following the Gesell school of thought about motor development, some very influential educators were soon advocating that reading instruction be postponed so that the passing of additional time would insure a readiness for it. And so was born the doctrine of postponement. This doctrine fostered the notion that a] getting children ready to read and b] teaching them to read occur at distinctly different times in the school curriculum.

Such a notion is reflected, of course, in the long entrenched practice of having a readiness program followed by a reading program. In fact, and not many years ago, it was very common to find the first six or eight weeks of first grade given

65

over to the goal of "readiness." This practice apparently assumed that a child could be "unready" for reading on, for example, Friday of the sixth week of school but quite "ready" on Monday of the seventh week. "What a week-end!" is one possible reaction to such an assumption. A less sarcastic and certainly more helpful response, however, is to think more carefully about what it means to help a child get ready to read and, secondly, what it means to teach him to read.

Traditional Interpretation of Reading Readiness

Readiness—whether applied to reading or some other kind of learning—is an unquestionably valid psychological concept with permanent relevance. However, what is considerably less permanent and always open to question is how it is interpreted. Applied to reading, the concept of readiness was for a long time interpreted to mean that children become ready as a result of maturation. Or, to phrase this traditional interpretation somewhat differently, readiness for learning to read was thought to constitute a certain maturational stage in the child's development. Because this interpretation came into existence at a time when great efforts were being made to be objective and quantitatively precise about every description of human behavior—these were the decades of the 1920's and 1930's—it was very natural for educators of that period to seek out a quantitative and precise description of the stage of development which they believed constituted readiness for reading. The end result was the proclamation that a mental age of about 6.5 years defines readiness.

How seriously this proclamation was taken by the man who had much to do with promoting it can be seen in a 1936 article. It was written by Carleton Washburne, then superintendent of the Winnetka, Illinois public schools and, more importantly, a leader of the Progressive Education Movement. In the article Washburne (1936, P. 127) noted: "Nowadays each first grade teacher in Winnetka has a chart showing when each of her children will be mentally six-and-a-half, and is careful to avoid any effort to get a child to read before he has reached this stage of mental growth."

Washburne's comments are useful now because, in capsule form, they portray the once widely held belief that *getting* ready to read and *being* ready occur at completely separate points on some time line. It was just such a belief, of course, that led to the practice of having a readiness program at one point in the child's school life and a reading program at some later date.

Another Interpretation

With the initial or traditional interpretation, readiness was viewed as a product; specifically, a product of maturation. Viewing readiness as a product is very defensible, but current knowledge indicates that it is the product of both maturation *and* learning. Within such a framework, readiness can be defined as various combinations of abilities which result from, or are the product of, nature and nurture interacting with each other.

A view of readiness which sees it as a product is defensible; yet, to view it only as a product is incomplete. What must be added is that dimension which brings into focus a relationship, a relationship between a child's particular abilities and the kind of learning opportunities made available to him. Within this framework readiness is still a product, but a product in relation to a given set of circumstances. Or, to use another's words, readiness is "the adequacy of existing capacity in relation to the demands of a given learning task" (Ausubel, 1959, P. 147).

This interpretation, if accepted, offers three important reminders to educators:

1. Readiness is not one thing. In fact, the variety of abilities, both in kind and amount, which add up to readiness suggests that a more accurately

descriptive term would be "readinesses"—awkward, to be sure, but also accurate.

2. Although what makes one child ready for reading might be different from what makes another ready, *both* are ready because of the interplay of nature and nurture. This is a recognition that children are ready because of hereditary and maturational factors, but also because of the learning opportunities in their particular environment.

3. Because readiness depends not only upon a child's abilities but also upon the kind of learning opportunities made available to him, it is possible for a child to be ready when one type of reading program is offered, but unready when other kinds are available.

This dependence of readiness upon the type and quality of instruction that will be offered also has some implications for assessing a child's readiness. What it highlights right away, for example, is the inadequacy of any attempt to assess it apart from the kind of reading instruction that will be available. In positive terms the implication is: If readiness is "the adequacy of existing capacity in relation to the demands of a given learning task," then the best and even only way to assess a child's readiness for reading is to give him varied opportunities to begin to read.

Providing Reading Opportunities

When should these learning opportunities be offered? In responding to such a query, it is of initial importance to remember that the practice of starting children to read in first grade and at the age of six is the result of convention, not of any evidence that there is something about six-year-old children which makes this a particularly productive time to start teaching reading. With such a reminder in the background, it seems appropriate to suggest—but with a little

reservation—that since kindergarten is the first level of public school education now offered, kindergarten is the time to learn about children's readiness by giving them varied and interesting opportunities to begin to read.

The "little reservation" is rooted in the knowledge that some kindergartens are now bombarding children with whole-class, drill-oriented instruction. Knowing that this unfortunate practice is spreading, it seems wise to repeat the recommendation: Give kindergarten children *varied* and *interesting opportunities* to begin to read.

The wording for such a recommendation was carefully selected. For example, the emphasis on "opportunities" is there because it implies that with some children in some kindergartens the opportunities might not "take." Acceptance of this is of basic importance. It frees the kindergarten teacher from thinking that every child *must* learn to read and so, in turn, also frees her from feeling any need "to put the pressure on." Today, unfortunately, some kindergarten teachers *are* "putting the pressure on" with their whole-class use of drill and workbooks. Predictably, in the years to come, there will be a reaction against this—a reaction which is not likely to make a distinction between a timing that might be just right, and a methodology that is all wrong.

The need for *varied* opportunities is emphasized because the easiest way to become a reader is probably different for different children. Consequently the "varied" refers to opportunities for learning to identify whole words, but also opportunities to learn to print and spell and, too, opportunities to begin to learn about letters and the sounds they record. The end result of such varied efforts would be insight into the readiness of the children and, too, very specific information about the way into reading that seems easiest for each child. Of course, another result is that some of these kindergarten children would be reading.

Probably the best way to clarify "kindergarten opportunities to learn to read" is to describe some. Through these few examples it should become apparent that readiness instruction and reading instruction are not always two different things.

In the kindergarten, because five-year-olds love nobody quite as much as they love themselves, reading opportunities of a whole-word identification type might begin with attention to the children's names. Since attendance-taking is a daily routine, it could also become a source of daily "practice" as children tuck their names into a card holder when they arrive and, later, read all the name cards—at first with much assistance from the teacher—to find out who is present and who is absent. Other opportunities to learn to read other words of interest—days of the week, months of the year, and so on—could be provided too. How the children respond to such opportunities and what they learn from them will offer a teacher much information about their readiness to read *via,* in this case, a whole-word approach.

Art projects can often be a vehicle for assessments because, in this case, they provide occasions for children to learn to print labels or even short captions for their pictures. Such activities have direct relevance for readiness assessment because some young children who have no interest in reading *per se* are found to be very interested in printing (Durkin, 1966). With this in mind, the kindergarten teacher who offers opportunities to learn to print is providing herself with the opportunity to identify children whose way into beginning reading ought to be through writing and spelling. In addition, however, she is also becoming aware of other children for whom the motor skill of writing is a formidable task.

Because many young children seem to enjoy playing with the sounds of language, it also makes sense to provide kindergarten opportunities for learning about letters and the sounds they record. For example, it might happen that the word *magnet* takes on special interest. Perhaps it was first introduced in a story,

and then simple experiments were done to show magnets, to demonstrate magnetism, and so on. The end result is that the word *magnet* is written many times for the children to see and thus—for some—to learn to read. With *magnet* written on the chalkboard, a teacher might one day say to the children, "You know some other words that start with the same letter. Who knows the name of this letter? . . . Who remembers some other words that start with an *m?*" Quickly, children like Martha and Michael proudly offer their names as examples. And then another child recalls the word *Monday.*

The end result is a list of *m* words, but also the teacher's opportunity to introduce letter-sound associations. In this case, for instance, the teacher might read the list, point out again that all the words begin with *m,* then repeat the words—this time asking the children to try to hear how they all begin with the same sound. A natural follow-up question would be, "Can you think of some other words that begin with the sound that you hear at the beginning of these words? Listen. I'll say them again and then maybe you can think of other words that begin with the same sound."

As a result of this plus other instances of attention to letters and sounds, a teacher has the chance to learn which children are unable to name letters and, what will be more common, which are unable to hear initial sounds in words. At the same time, however, she is also learning that other children know the names of many letters and even are successful in hearing and distinguishing among beginning sounds.

These very few illustrations of "kindergarten opportunities to learn to read" hardly describe a total program. However, they ought to be sufficient to exemplify the main points suggested. They have illustrated, for example, that the assessment of readiness and the teaching of reading can result from the very same situation. Thus, the teacher's use of the children's name in attendance-taking was

68

a chance for her to learn about their readiness to read whole words. In addition, though, for the children who were in fact "ready" it was the start of their learning to read—in this instance, children's names.

The few examples also ought to have shown that a single teaching procedure will be readiness instruction for some children, but reading instruction for others. For instance, the use that was made of the word *magnet* could result in beginning learning in phonics for some. Yet, for other less ready children, the teacher's questions about a particular group of words beginning with *m* would only be the first step in a series of steps which will finally result—perhaps during kindergarten—in the ability to hear and distinguish among initial sounds in words. For these latter children, the teacher was carrying on a type of readiness instruction. However, with the children who were very ready to grasp the connection between *m* and a certain sound, reading instruction was taking place.

In summary, then, three points seem particularly important:

1. Readiness for reading should not be viewed as comprising a single collection of abilities which will be the same for all children. Actually, what makes one child ready might be quite different from what makes another ready.

2. Whether or not a child *is* ready depends upon his particular abilities, but also upon the reading instruction that will be offered. This type of dependence means that readiness can be assessed only when a child is given varied opportunities to learn to read.

3. What a child is able to learn as a result of these opportunities offers very specific information about his readiness. With some children, a particular opportunity will result in reading ability and so, quite obviously, these children were ready. With others, however, the same op-

portunity will not "take," and so for them it is a type of readiness instruction. That the same teaching procedure can be reading instruction for some children and readiness instruction for others suggests serious flaws in school practices which seem to go out of their way to create an artificial separation between a readiness program and a reading program. A much more defensible way of working is to view readiness instruction as reading instruction in its early stages.

Acceptance of these views about readiness also entails acceptance of a variety of challenges for educators. Probably the major one has to do with the need for greater flexibility in the way schools handle beginning reading. Within the context of this view of readiness, for instance, there would be no room for thinking that there is one best age for starting reading; no room for thinking there is one best methodology and one best set of materials. Nor, certainly, is there a place for thinking that all children must accomplish the same learning at the same time.

Another and briefer way of stating these challenges is to insert the reminder that the important question for educators is not, "Are these children ready to learn to read?" but, rather, "Are we ready to teach them at a time, at a pace, and in a way that is just right for each child?"

REFERENCES

Ausubel, D. P. Viewpoints from related disciplines: human growth and development. *Teachers College Record,* 1959, *60,* 245–254.

Durkin, Dolores. *Children who read early.* New York: Teachers College Press, Columbia University, 1966.

Washburne, C. Ripeness. *Progressive Education,* 1936, *13,* 125–130.

How Early Should Language Development and Pre-Reading Experiences Be Started?

PATRICIA N. FOULKE

Educators should not use *age* as a criterion for language and pre-reading training but rather devise means to diagnose the *language level* of the child. It is possible to describe the stages of language development in general terms. However, by comparing "normal" and "abnormal" language development we have a more specific basis for establishing accurate diagnosis. This paper briefly lists the *stages of early language development, compares normal with abnormal language development,* and explores *characteristics of language impaired school age children.* The *skills necessary for reading* and the *level of language development* provide key information for the teacher. *Specific diagnosis* and *specific teaching examples* are provided at the end of the paper.

Early Language Development

The process of language development begins soon after birth as infants cry to express hunger, pain, or the need to exercise. Whether one believes that behavior is innate or learned, parental response reinforces the behavior of the infant. Infants begin to recognize facial expression, gestures, outstretched arms, physical closeness as well as parental dialect, inflection, intonation, rhythm, and mannerisms. Around the age of one month infants begin to react by one to two syllable babbling, cooing, and repetition of

From *Elementary English*, Vol. 51, No. 2 (February, 1974). © 1974 by the National Council of Teachers of English. Reprinted by permission.

tongue sounds. By eight months infants begin to play with sounds, and produce jargon (the special language a baby develops) that sounds like questions or commands, and to respond to negative language. By ten months the infant is associating sounds with objects, identifying family members by name, responding to games and imitating musical tones.

Listening skills develop between 12 and 24 months. The baby is developing auditory memory, can follow some simple instructions, and can point to parts of the body as named. Speaking skills are developing as he learns to imitate adult exclamations and acquires words. The child can ask for things and begins to use two word sentences around 21 months. Jargon begins to fade by two years of age.

A three year old has a vocabulary of 1200–1500 words, uses words to ask questions and to entertain others, recites rhymes, and may talk incessantly. At age four children use abstract structures such as prepositions, conjunctions, pronouns and articles. They may have 2000 words in their vocabularies and speak in long involved sentences. At five years they have 3000 words in their vocabularies, ask questions, use a variety of different speech parts, and have all of the basic elements and structure of adult language behavior.

Comparison of Normal with Abnormal Language Development

After exploring the sequence of normal language development it is helpful to study various language disorders. Children are not all at the same stage of development at the same age. A child with a language development lag or language disability needs to be handled differently from a child who has developed normally. Age should not be used as a criterion for language and pre-reading training. The *language level* of each child is the key to planning a language or reading program.

Delayed language development may be caused by hearing loss, mental retardation, neurological disorder, or various other medical conditions. Because a child must hear before discriminating, a hearing loss will affect speech development. The sounds made as well as the failure to develop listening skills may indicate a hearing loss. This may in turn affect social rapport and emotional behavior.

Mental retardation and/or neurological disorder may slow down or distort language development. Some children cannot connect sound and meaning. Some are unable to recombine the elements necessary in order to decode. Some children display telegraphic speech, leaving out most words other than nouns: John-car-store or Carrie-bus-airplane express meaning between child and parent.

A child with a neurological disorder may find it difficult to perceive, understand, or remember and may have bizarre or very peculiar behavior. Behavior problems such as hyperactivity, distractibility, short attention span, or catastrophic reactions (exaggerated emotional response to normal events) may affect language development. Mary may be able to attend for one minute provided she is not distracted by a truck outside.

Autistic children do not use gestures, jargon, nor do they seem to desire communication. Language development for these children appears to be on a very low level. Aphasic children are those who may have trouble receiving language, integrating it or expressing it. Poor articulation is one of the most obvious speech problems.

Characteristics of Language Impaired School Age Children

Who is the child with a language impairment? In every elementary classroom there may be several children who have not been able to learn language concepts. As small toddlers these children may have had difficulty with articulation, vocabulary development or syntactical patterns. Their first problems may have been encountered in a readiness program, or it may have been the first stages of reading that caused frustration and bewilderment.

Visually, such children may have poor discrimination of shapes, letters or words. John cannot tell the difference between a circle and a square or between $\times$ and $+$, $\triangle \triangledown$, or $[$ and $]$. He is not ready to be exposed to letters. He may transpose parts of words or letters. (b-d, p-q, saw-was, pat-tap, slit-silt are common mistakes.) He may attend to detail and be unable to relate the detail to the whole context. He may not notice the internal detail of words. He may not be able to remember a visual sequence. He may "read" from context cues or memorization.

Auditorially, the child may not be able to interpret what is heard, may not understand spoken words completely. The child may not be able to discriminate between phonemes and other environmental sounds. Tommy cannot tell the difference between a car and a truck outside unless he sees them. He may not be able to associate sounds with particular objects or experiences. He may respond inconsistently to sounds and be thought to be hard of hearing. He may be forced to attend to minute background noises that other children are able to screen out. He may have poor auditory memory for retaining the sequence of sounds or words.

The level of such a child's language conceptualization may be low. He may have reduced vocabulary. George finds words like wrist, elbow, ankle much more difficult than the obvious arm, leg, head concepts. He may confuse usage of

71

words. It may be difficult for him to organize sentences in proper order. He may have trouble holding in his mind a long sentence spoken to him until he has been able to comprehend it. He may not be able to express himself except in very simple language.

The child with a language impairment may be a child with specific problems that are easily spotted or problems that remain obscure until probed. His visual and auditory channels may seem to be intact and yet there are indications of discrepancies that are affecting his language performance. Susan is unable to progress beyond "telegraphic" speech although she seems to see and hear normally. With evaluation, an individual program planned for her, and the realization that she has the understanding and support of adults who want to help her, she can be helped.

Skills Needed for Reading

Many children encounter their first devastating frustrations when they are expected to read at age six with the rest of the class. Language training that coincides with the language level of the child at least provides a chance to succeed.

There are certain skills that are basic in order to begin the reading process. A child needs to be able to recognize the shapes of the letters of the alphabet as well as the sounds of most phonemes. The child must respond to the left-to-right linear progression of sentences. Following the teacher's hand as in developing and reading experience chart stories reinforces this pattern. The child needs to learn the sequence of parts of spoken words and to be equipped to recognize words using various cues: the total configuration of letters making up a word, the sounds represented by those letters and the kinds of meaning implied by context. The child needs to be able to reason and to think about what is read, to have developed a reasonable degree of both auditory and visual perception, and to be able to sustain attention for an adequate period of time. A child needs to be at ease with the spoken language, which can be especially difficult for a child from a bilingual home. And it is helpful for a child to be able to take some initiative and to have an outgoing attitude toward new experiences.

Diagnosis of the Level of Language Development

Diagnosis of the level of language development is the key for a child who does have delayed or abnormal language skills. The child who is "ready" to learn specific language concepts at the age of four or five is fortunate. Too many children begin programs with their peers only to meet frustration and failure. Early diagnosis at the age of four or five may identify children who are not ready so that they may be taught the skills they need before beginning reading.

Early diagnosis is being considered by many elementary schools in the country. Although there are several tests for language diagnosis available, methods are not well defined as yet. A number of new tests have been devised in the past year or two and are in the process of being evaluated. It is also possible to abstract sections of standardized tests and construct an individualized battery for informal testing in conjunction with teacher observation.

The first step in diagnosis is thinking about the areas of weakness in the child. The examiner's care in interpreting results may mean the difference between an accurate appraisal and a false estimate based entirely on test scores. Careful recording of the way a child works as well as evaluating the test answers provided may be the key to a future program. The examiner needs to consider carefully the areas for testing and the rationale for these choices; we should refrain, for example, from making assumptions about the child that may not be appropriate.

Whether the testing is done by the classroom teacher or by the school psychologist, care should be taken to set the stage so that the child can perform as well as possible. The choice of materials and presentation of test items should fit the child, especially if one that is hyperactive or has other behavior problems. The level of tolerance should be considered. Individual interests may be used as motivation.

Diagnosis should recur at frequent intervals to check levels of language performance. The language level of the child at the moment is crucial to the success of a program. Instruction should begin just below this level and continue to develop, building on concepts the child knows.

Specific Diagnosis (Based on ITPA)

1. Receptive process:

   a. Auditory reception: the ability to understand the meaning of what the child hears. Do boys play? Do chairs eat?
   b. Visual reception: the ability to understand the meaning of what he sees. See this? Find one here.

2. Integrative process:

   a. Auditory association: the ability to relate ideas that he hears. (complete analogy) A Daddy is big, a baby is. . . .
   b. Visual association: the ability to relate ideas that he sees.
   What goes with this?
   c. Auditory sequential memory: the ability to reproduce sequential stimuli from memory presented auditorially.
   Listen. Say 0-2-6.
   d. Visual sequential memory: the ability to reproduce sequences of figures presented visually.
   See these (sequence of picture). You make it like this.
   e. Auditory closure: the ability to identify from an incomplete auditory presentation.
   Listen. Who am I talking about? Da/y Bo/le
   f. Visual closure: the ability to identify from an incomplete visual presentation.
   Find all the dogs in here.
   g. Grammatic closure: the ability to automatically handle syntax and grammatic inflections.
   Here is a bed. Here are two . . .

3. Expressive process:

   a. Verbal expression: the ability to express concepts verbally.

   Tell me all about this. (label, color, shape, function, composition, major parts, numerosity).
   b. Manual expression: the ability to express ideas manually.
   Show me what to do with this.

General Teaching Techniques

Before planning specific lessons for a child consider general techniques that have been useful when working with a child who has a language disability.

1. Allow the child to learn through his/her best channel. Children may need visual clues such as a picture or watching lips closely. It may be helpful to slow down or break up a sentence so that they can decode one part before going on to the next.

2. Verbalization should be kept to a minimum. Explain directions as clearly and briefly as possible.

3. Plan the environment so that children are able to concentrate. A child will be able to concentrate more if not facing visual distractions or noise.

4. Structure the lesson so that he/she can succeed. Ask children to "think over" a wrong answer immediately and help them find the correct answer. Do not reinforce wrong answers. If they make many mistakes you may need to "recycle." Be prepared to "cue" the child, "model" the correct response, or reteach the concept.

5. Try to begin teaching just below his/her level and lead up as the child is able. The child probably wants to do well and to be challenged but not unduly frustrated.

6. Be flexible in your teaching. You may need to back up in the middle of a lesson and/or change your mind about the best approach or materials.

7. Make sure you are familiar with the materials and that they are all within reach before beginning to teach a lesson.

8. Sit close to a child. A hyperactive child will be better able to attend when within the same area as the teacher.

9. Praise a child for any efforts. Praise good behavior and ignore bad behavior when possible. "Catch" a child being good.

Specific Teaching Examples

Auditory reception

—Follow directions for an obstacle course or hop scotch.
—Identify animal sounds, environmental sounds or voices from a tape recording.
—Play "What will I take on my trip?"
—Match sounds made by bottles of water.

Visual reception

—Match categories in a pocket chart (animals, colors, shapes).
—Count Cuisenaire rods.
—Draw a picture of an object he has seen on a walk.
—Find an object in a picture.

Auditory association

—Classify objects that go together on a flannel board such as ball, bat, knife, fork.
—Problem solving—what would you do if?
—Associate an old experience with a similar new story told orally.
—Match objects that rhyme.

Visual association

—Find a shape that is different.
—Match a picture with a shadow on the wall.
—Match symbols in a game of "symbols" bingo.
—Find the part that is missing.

Auditory sequential memory

—Play "I'm going to New York and will take _____."
—Repeat tongue twisters in correct order.
—Retell events heard in a story in order.
—Repeat clapping sequence.

Visual sequential memory

—Place objects in order.
—Copy pattern of shapes.
—Reproduce peg board pattern.
—Place comic strip pictures in order.
—Draw a map of route to school.

Auditory closure

—Complete sentence heard orally.
—Provide beginning sound for color words heard orally.

Visual closure

—Identify object from partially exposed picture.
—Finish shape that has one part missing.
—Present one piece of puzzle at a time for child to complete.

Grammatic closure

—Complete statements. Here is a boy. Here are two _____
—Answer riddle in a complete sentence.
—Choral reading.

Verbal expression

—Show and tell.
—Tell his own story about his family.
—Place hand in Magic Box—tell about the object inside.

Manual expression

—Pantomime.
—Finger plays.
—Stunts such as crab walk, duck walk.

BIBLIOGRAPHY

Auditory Discrimination Test, Joseph M. Wepman, University of Chicago.—a test to determine a child's ability to recognize the differences that exist between phonemes.

First Grade Screening Test, American Guidance Service, Inc. Circle Pines, Minnesota, 55014.—a screening test to identify those children who will not make sufficient progress in First Grade.

Developmental Test of Visual Perception, Marianne Frostig, Consulting Psychologists Press, 577 College Ave., Palo Alto, Calif.—a test to establish a child's level of performance in each of five areas of visual perception.

Illinois Test of Psycholinguistic Abilities, Samuel Kirk, et al. University of Illinois.—a test to delineate areas of difficulty in communication.

Peabody Picture Vocabulary Test, Lloyd M. Dunn. American Guidance Service, Inc.—an individual test designed to provide an estimate of a child's verbal intelligence through measuring hearing vocabulary.

Peabody Individual Achievement Test, Lloyd M. Dunn. American Guidance Service, Inc.—a wide range screening measure of achievement.

Pre-Reading Screening Procedures, Beth H. Slingerland. Educators Publishing Service, Inc. 75 Moulton St., Cambridge, Mass. 02138.—a test to identify first grade academic needs.

Purdue Perceptual Motor Survey, Newell Kephart.

Wide Range Achievement Test, J. P. Jastek et al. Guidance Associates of Delaware, 45 Gilpen Ave., Wilmington, Delaware.—a general achievement test.

Prereading Programs: Direct Versus Incidental Teaching

ETHEL M. KING

Controversial issues raised in beginning reading instruction in the last decade have created a dilemma for those developing curriculum at the prereading level. On the one side, we find some early childhood educators mainly concerned with the cognitive development of young children and recommending highly structured prereading programs where specific skills are taught directly and systematically. This approach answers critics who claim that nothing substantive is taught in kindergarten. On the other side, we find educators concerned more with the social and emotional development of the young child and promoting an incidental approach to prereading in which skills are integrated with other activities and taught as needed. The overall development of the child is given the highest priority.

The term "prereading" is generally used to indicate that period of linguistic development just prior to being able to decode visual, verbal symbols. No sharp distinction between prereading and beginning reading is implied—rather, a very gradual transition from exposure to graphic symbols to learning to read a written message. Some claim that the skills needed are the same at the prereading level as later, differing only in degree.

Direct teaching is defined as "an organization of instruction specifying definite terms or skills to be taught at stated times and by a systematic method" (Good 1973). Direct teaching programs can be either a locally developed curriculum or a published program such as the "Direct Instruction System for Teaching Reading," known as DISTAR (Engelmann and Brunner 1976). This explicit program is based on a list of basic skills and concepts, an analysis of the tasks required for learning, a division of tasks into constituent parts, and an outline for teaching in an orderly, prescribed manner.

Incidental teaching, on the other hand, refers to "the teaching of certain skills only as the need for them occurs in con-

From *The Reading Teacher,* Vol. 31, No. 5 (February 1978). Reprinted with permission of the International Reading Association and Ethel M. King.

nection with other schoolwork or with the pupil's activities or interests'' (Good 1973). This more informal teaching of prereading skills occurs in programs planned around projects, units, themes, or activities. It is frequently associated with open education, which may occur in the self-contained classroom as well as open areas. The emphasis falls on planning the environment so that pupils can experiment, manipulate, inquire, and communicate freely in integrated learning experiences.

Some of the major characteristics of incidental and direct teaching are summarized in the chart at the top of the page.

During a recent survey of the research dealing with the relative effectiveness of direct versus incidental instruction in prereading, it became apparent that the majority of studies reported the direct approach to be more effective, especially with children who might be classed as low achievers. However, one large study indicated that a carefully sequenced, informal conceptual-language approach was superior to more traditional training using the prereading phase of a basal series.

Ten of these studies will be surveyed here.

Schoephoerster and others (1966) investigated two approaches to teaching prereading skills in several kindergartens: an informal, unstructured program compared to a scheduled, structured program. The instructional tasks deemed important by the teachers were all related to verbal symbols, auditory discrimination of phonemes, visual discrimination of graphemes, phoneme-grapheme correspondences, and the use of spoken context as a clue to the identification of words.

Teachers who stated a preference for an informal reading program formed the control group, using some activities and materials of their own design and some ideas adapted from the teacher's manuals of the formal group (which unfortunately confounds the results). They also fostered the development of skills when opportunities arose during other activities.

Teachers of the formal prereading group used a commercially prepared program which included a workbook and a teacher's guide. Because it was assumed that pupils in the formal program would not all be ready at the same time, nor proceed at the same rate, they were grouped for instruction according to three levels of academic potential.

To determine whether or not the kindergartners mastered the six major skills, A Prereading Inventory of Skills Basic to Beginning Reading (McKee and others 1962) was administered at the end of the year, in May. Overall, the group receiving formal instruction performed signifi-

Development of prereading skills

Direct teaching	Incidental teaching
Objectives projected into experiences.	Purposes arise out of experiences.
Emphasis on intellectual development.	Emphasis on psychological and social climate.
Analysis of knowledge and skills necessary.	Assessment of potential of children and environment.
Sequence of specific learning experiences.	Integrated learning experiences based on needs and interests.
Formal scheduling with definite time allocation.	Informal scheduling through large blocks of time.
Specific skills activities.	Skills embedded in interdisciplinary studies.
Objective evaluation.	Subjective evaluation.

cantly better than the group receiving informal training. While scores indicated a consistently higher trend for all ability levels within the formal group, these scores were only significant for the below average group. The authors concluded that children at all ability levels, but particularly those of lower ability, profit more from formal teaching.

While no attempt was made to assess the effect of the structured program on attitudes toward reading, no detrimental effects were observed.

A study conducted with four year olds (Karnes and others 1968) compared an incidental approach with a highly structured program aimed at language and cognitive development. Children who received direct instruction were superior in reading readiness and number readiness compared to those in a traditional nursery program. Similar positive evidence was found in social adjustment for school activities.

Much of the concern for prereading has been prompted by the need to provide more adequate learning opportunities for the socially and economically disadvantaged, especially to overcome the learning deficits common among these children. In a longitudinal study of disadvantaged children (Di Lorenzo and Salter 1968), all received instruction which emphasized language and cognitive development. However, when methods of reading instruction were varied among groups, those receiving direct teaching of reading skills in structured cognitive activities made significant gains.

In contrast, Prendergast (1969) compared three groups of upper middle-class children—in an unstructured nursery school program, a Montessori structured program, and a nonnursery school group. After seven months there were no significant differences among the groups, which seemed to indicate that four year olds from middle-class homes developed certain prereading competencies with or without nursery school experience.

Stanchfield (1971), in a comprehensive study including children from all social levels, investigated the effectiveness of teaching prereading skills in a sequential, developmental order. Six skill areas were emphasized: listening comprehension, auditory discrimination, visual discrimination, oral language, motor-perceptual development, and sound-symbol correspondence. The experimental program used elaborate lesson plans and a variety of materials, and inservice meetings were conducted weekly. The control groups followed the regular curriculum, where reading skills were taught incidentally. Seventeen matched pairs of schools provided a representative sample of ethnic and socioeconomic backgrounds and academic achievement. Children's subsequent scores on the Murphy-Durrell Reading Readiness Analysis showed significant differences favoring the structured, sequential program.

Kelley and Chen (1967) investigated whether or not formal reading instruction in kindergarten would both increase reading competency and favorably dispose children toward reading activities and school. While those receiving formal instruction excelled, it was found that attitudes towards reading were a function of intelligence or readiness levels and not the type of instruction.

A number of prereading skills have been identified as being related to success in learning to read. (Several studies were experimental, leading to the question of whether or not their findings would reappear if tested in the classroom.)

In two related studies, a comparison was made of the effectiveness of 1) direct versus incidental teaching on the development of prereading skills, and 2) a program that emphasized training with verbal symbols versus one that included a variety of stimuli.

The subjects were five year olds who attended kindergarten for half days. Each teacher had two classes, one in the morning and one in the afternoon. Therefore, it was possible to have each teacher teach both the experimental and the control programs, to minimize the teacher variable, counterbalancing for time of day. The first study ran for six months and the second, using the same design, ran for eight months the following year. In each case, teachers were provided with the equivalent amount of teaching materials, although the nature of the materials differed. For the direct instruction group, 20 major skill areas were identified and teaching activities suggested. Many materials were teacher designed, but each class was also provided with sets of cards, pocket charts, flannel and magnetic boards, and so on.

In the first study, with children from middle socioeconomic backgrounds, the experimental group received direct teaching for fifteen minutes daily, emphasizing verbal symbols in specific skill development. The control groups followed the traditional program, with incidental instruction. As measured on the Murphy-Durrell Reading Readiness Analysis, the direct instruction group was superior.

The second study, with children from upper-lower socioeconomic level homes, compared two types of direct instruction, one emphasizing verbal symbols, the second including many nonverbal symbols.

For example, in the nonverbal groups, children learned to discriminate among colors, shapes, and sizes. The verbal groups discriminated among letters and words. Although scheduled as direct teaching, all the activities were conducted informally and more in the spirit of a game.

The teachers were encouraged to individualize as much as possible. Low-achieving pupils might discriminate between two grossly different stimuli, average pupils from among three or four similar stimuli, and advanced pupils might be reading some words as they looked for similarities or differences. Again, the results for reading readiness were significant, favoring the group whose activities had been verbally oriented.

In both studies the hypotheses being tested were concealed from participants. However, parents and teachers reacted much more positively to the verbal programs, and the children in these programs were observed to be enthusiastic participants with positive attitudes.

In another large study (O'Donnell and Raymond 1972), kindergarten pupils and teachers were randomly assigned to two groups, one for a conceptual-language program and another for a basal reader approach. The classes varied only for twenty minutes each day for direct instruction. Children in basal reader classes received prereading instruction that included daily group activities followed by individual seatwork exercises. The conceptual-language approach consisted of many informal experiences designed to develop concepts and language. These children studied simple concepts of economics, geography, and science at varying levels of difficulty. Teachers informally but systematically presented 22 reading concepts to children who could profit from them; less able pupils were exposed to fewer.

After six months of instruction, the kindergartners were tested on visual and auditory discrimination, knowledge of letter names, reading readiness, and adjustment to school. Compared to the basal reader group, subjects in the conceptual-language classes were significantly higher on general readiness scores, and this difference was greatest among children of below average intelligence. No observable changes in the adjustment of the children were found.

The researchers acknowledged the importance of a constellation of prereading factors, including knowledge of letter forms and names, auditory and visual perception, breadth and depth of experiences, motor coordination, ability to follow directions, and listening. However, this study suggests they are best developed in experiences that give kindergartners opportunities to use language in situations free of expectancy. This conflicts with the findings of the other studies surveyed here, all of which indicated that direct reading instruction was more effective in giving kindergartners reading readiness skills.

In synthesizing the research findings and interpreting the implications for instruction at the prereading level, some of the basic skill areas have been identified. They will be presented now with an illustrative example for either curriculum development or instructional procedures. Certainly the list is not complete, but five main areas are: listening to stories read, picture reading, auditory discrimination, visual discrimination, and forming associations.

1. Listening to stories read. The emphasis is on interpretation of what is heard and on gaining familiarity with "book language."

   a. Listening for details: Answer guided factual questions.

   b. Listening for the main idea: Select the most important idea from several possibilities.

   c. Following a sequence of ideas: Discuss the order of events; follow directions.

   d. Comparing and contrasting: Discuss points of similarity; discuss points of difference.

   e. Drawing inferences: Predict the outcome.

   f. Listening critically: Discuss realism or fantasy; discuss fact or opinion; discuss plausible or absurd.

   g. Evaluating: State preferences and reasons.

2. Picture reading. The emphasis is on the interpretation of visual, nonverbal symbols.

   a. Reading for details: Answer guided factual questions.

   b. Reading for main idea: Compose a title for the picture.

   c. Following a sequence of ideas: Arrange a group of pictures in order.

   d. Classifying: Arrange pictures by groups.

   e. Reading for inferences: Discuss what might have happened before and after.

   f. Reading critically: Distinguish between fact (photograph) and opinion (illustration).

   g. Evaluating: Discuss which picture best represents the mood of a poem; discuss personal feelings about ideas depicted in pictures.

3. Auditory discrimination. The emphasis is on hearing similarities and differences of phonemes in words and sentences.

   a. Word discrimination: Listen for separate word entities in phrases and sentences.

   b. Phoneme discrimination: Identify separate sounds or combination of sounds within words; identify similarities and differences in phonemes in the order of initial, final, and medial positions.

   c. Auditory memory: Recognize words named; recognize sound(s) made by letter(s) named.

4. Visual discrimination. The emphasis is on seeing similarities and differences in graphemes, words, and sentences.

   a. Letter discrimination: Match capital letters; match lowercase letters; match capitals with corresponding lowercase letters.

   b. Knowledge of letter names: Learn incidentally with letter discrimination.

   c. Word discrimination: Match disimilar words; match similar words.

   d. Directionality: Develop appropriate eye movements on a printed page; follow a sequence of letters in words; recognize letter reversals.

   e. Sentence discrimination: Match sentences, phrases, and words in a duplicated copy of a language experience chart with the original.

   f. Visual memory: Recognize letters shown; recognize letters named; recognize printed words named; recognize printed words shown.

5. Forming associations. The emphasis is on relationships.

   a. Following directions: Aural—listen to directions in games, participate in cooperative play activities; reading pictures—follow instructions in recipes, experiments, and construction activities.

   b. Speech-to-print: Develop language experience charts.

   c. Phoneme-grapheme correspondence (two-way association): Sound-to-letter—match appropriate sound(s) (in context) to letters(s); letter-to-sound—match appropriate letter(s) (in context) to sound(s).

d. Phoneme-grapheme-morpheme correspondence (three-way association): Match appropriate pronunciation, picture, and visual form of word.

e. Combining letter knowledge with context clues: Identify words through oral context and initial letter(s).

Prereading program: direct versus incidental teaching. Surely this is not a dichotomy—we can achieve a blend. Learning to read is too crucial to leave to chance through an incidental approach, and research supports this conclusion, especially for children of lower ability and those from disadvantaged homes. On the other hand, direct teaching will be a misguided effort if it becomes so formal and prescriptive that bored or frustrated children lack the ability to see relationships and make applications. Teaching may be direct without rote learning. However, it is essential to provide an accurate knowledge base for the child to use in informal, playlike activities.

Dependency on published programs is suspect, for prereading skills are best promoted by teachers who can provide alternative strategies according to the observed needs of individual learners. For teachers who are not locked in to a set program, there will be incidental as well as direct teaching. And, we are not concerned with only the teacher's involvement, but also parents and other adults with whom the child interacts, for they too should contribute both directly and incidentally.

REFERENCES

Di Lorenzo, L.J. and R. Salter. "An Evaluative Study of Prekindergarten Programs for Educationally Disadvantaged Children: Follow-up and Replication." *Exceptional Children*, vol. 35 (October 1968), pp. 111–19.

Engelmann, Siegfried and Elaine C. Bruner. *DISTAR,* 2nd. ed. Chicago, Ill.: Science Research Associates, Inc., 1976.

Good, Carter V., Ed. *Dictionary of Education*, 3rd ed. New York, N.Y.: McGraw-Hill Book Company, 1973.

Karnes, M.B. and others. "Evaluation of Two Preschool Programs for Disadvantaged Children: A Traditional and a Highly Structured Experimental Preschool." *Exceptional Children*, vol. 34 (May 1968), pp. 667–76.

Kelley, Marjorie L. and Martin K. Chen. "An Experimental Study of Formal Reading Instruction at the Kindergarten Level." *The Journal of Educational Research*, vol. 60, no. 5 (January 1967), pp. 224–29.

McKee, Paul, M. Lucile Harrison and James Stroud. *A Pre-Reading Inventory of Skills Basic to Beginning Reading, Part 1.* Boston, Mass.: Houghton Mifflin, 1962.

Murphy, Helen A. and Donald D. Durrell. *Murphy-Durrell Reading Readiness Analysis.* New York, N.Y. Harcourt Brace Jovanovich.

O'Donnell, C. Michael and Dorothy Raymond. "Developing Reading Readiness in Kindergarten." *Elementary English,* vol. 44, no. 5 (May 1972), pp. 768–71.

Ogletree, Earl J. and Rosalee W. Dipasalegne. "Innercity Teachers Evaluate DISTAR." *The Reading Teacher,* vol. 28 no. 7 (April 1975), pp. 633–37.

Prendergast, R. "Pre-Reading Skills Developed in Montessori and Conventional Nursery Schools." *Elementary School Journal,* vol. 70 (December 1969), pp. 135–41.

Schoephoerster, Hugh, Richard Barnhart and Walter M. Loomer. "The Teaching of Prereading Skills in Kindergarten." *The Reading Teacher,* vol. 19, no. 5 (February 1966), pp. 352–57.

Stanchfield, Jo M. "The Development of Prereading Skills." *The Elementary School Journal,* vol. 71, no. 8 (May 1971), pp. 438–47.

A Piagetian Interpretation of Beginning Reading Instruction

ELEANOR R. KIRKLAND

To understand how a child learns to read, from a Piagetian point of view, one must be aware of the sequential stages of the child's developing intelligence and look at the thinking processes characteristic of these stages.

Piaget views the growth of the child's "structures of knowing" as beginning in early infancy and ending in adolescence, and believes that the stages of intellectual development follow each other not in strictly chronological order but in a sequential and orderly manner. These phases may be accelerated by manipulating the environment, but only up to a certain point. The environment is important only as a child is able to pay attention to it, and this ability depends on the degree of assimilation which has taken place. However, the greater the variety of experience children cope with, the greater their ability to cope.

Thanks to Piaget, we have a rationale and a sequence of typical experiences to help us better understand child learning, help correct children's inadequacies, and give them a more mature approach to learning. Most importantly, Piaget has encouraged us to stop imposing adult standards of logic on children's thinking. He insists that we move "out of ourselves" and our traditional levels of expectancy and take a good look at the child's logical thinking, which reflects the child's developmental progress.

The teachers of young children getting ready to read must understand what tasks are involved in reading. One must ascertain a child's stage of development, determine whether the child possesses the logical reasoning ability to perform the task, and then plan teaching strategies to allow the child to acquire the logical abilities necessary for the task. If the child does not display mature enough logic, then the teacher must set up an environment that will allow the child to learn the necessary logico-mathematical operations.

Necessary Skills

There are many skill areas, interrelated both in function and development, in which a child must reach a certain level of maturity before reading can begin. The three main categories are: first, organic development (sensory, for receiving information; perceptual, for understanding, organizing, and integrating information; and neuromuscular, for using information physically); second, social development (development of interpersonal relations); and third, symbolic development (concept formation, verbal language, visual language).

Assuming that the child has the necessary organic and social maturity—and keeping in mind that Furth and Wachs (1974) indicate that even some seven year olds are not yet physiologically mature enough for traditional school demands—it is in the area of symbolic development that Piaget's work takes on special meaning for the teaching of reading. Specifically, reading requires a level of cognitive maturity that enables the child to deal with a variety of rules, abstractions, and classifications of more or less "concrete" objects.

From *The Reading Teacher*, Vol. 31, No. 5 (February 1978). Reprinted with permission of the International Reading Teacher and Eleanor R. Kirkland.

These abilities include: directionality (ability to perceive and orient oneself to the top, bottom, sides, front, and back of an object); ability to perceive the distinguishing characteristics of small and capital letters, words, and pictures, and the ability to classify or recognize common characteristics of words, pictures, numerals, letters, etc.; ability to understand concepts presented in the text; ability to focus hearing upon and repeat phonemic sounds in words in order to associate these sounds with their visual counterparts in reading.

To the above, add the ability to focus listening upon verbal instructions of the teacher; general ability to focus attention upon the task at hand.

Many children are introduced to formal reading during the preoperational stage of development, approximately age two to seven. What are the implications of the development of language and thought at this stage for the learning/teaching of reading?

Preoperational Thinking

Throughout the early sensorimotor period, the child has been unable to use an image or word to represent an object or event not actually present. As the child moves into the preoperational stage of thought, s/he can differentiate a word from what it stands for (for example, use the sound "dog" for what it represents—a dog). Now, thought is lifted to an entirely new level.

Since thought comes before language, the latter is fitted on to thought that already exists. But once the child can use language, thought is extended over an immensely increased range.

Nevertheless, between two and five years of age, thinking tends to "center" on one striking feature of the situation. It is also irreversible in that the child is unable to move back mentally to the starting point from which the immediate thinking began. At this age, in Piagetian conservation tasks (which involve seeing objects in different transformations), a child can for example focus only on the length of a row of pennies and not also on its spatial relationships. Thus the "centering" child cannot be expected to learn rules and also to apply them.

Several characteristics of the child's thinking process may prevent this preoperational child from easily learning the alphabet and its phonemic representations: egocentrism, inability to follow transformations, limited concentration, and irreversibility of thinking.

By roughly three or four years of age, children have copied the adult model of language, but we must not overestimate their level of thought from the new maturity of their speech. We have a tendency to think they understand more than they do. One fundamental lesson for parents and teachers from Piaget is that while language is important, mere verbalization and verbal knowledge are of little value. Children can only see an event from their own viewpoint; they are unable to conceive the viewpoint of others.

As children are exposed to more social interaction and find other children's perceptions conflicting with their own, they begin to accommodate to others' egocentric thoughts. Children of five or seven will begin to seek verification for their thoughts as they must consider others' viewpoints (peer pressure). However, a child still dominated by egocentrism may not be very interested in learning to read other people's words and thoughts.

By seven or eight, children's thinking becomes more systematized; that is, their thought now conforms to certain rules and their thinking becomes more like what we adults call logical. The sequence and structure of actions in the mind, or the schemas now available, are altogether different in kind. The ability to reason and "understand" demands higher order schemas which permit a simultaneous grasp of the successive sequences of actions taking place in the mind. Most children of seven or eight years are aware of these sequences. They can see the part they themselves play in ordering their experiences and controlling their thoughts, and that they can use different schemas at will.

Piaget's observations led him to believe that it is schemas in the process of organization that children tend to repeat playfully and with seeming pleasure. Further, when such schemas have become organized, the apparent pleasure disappears and the schemas cease to be repeated unless they are combined to form new schemas or serve as a means to some end.

Learning, then, seems to start from the child, from the schemas already available to the child. Actions—such as exploring, discovering, using new ways to solve old problems—all have an intrinsic interest for the young child and are self-expanding. We must always bear in mind that there must not be too great a gap between the schemas available to the child and those demanded by the situation.

Elkind (1969) reported a study where the researchers showed kindergarten, first, second, and third grade children a card with 18 pictures pasted upon it in the shape of a triangle. The children's task was simply to name every picture on the card. The kindergarten children named the pictures according to the triangular pattern in which they were pasted. They began at the apex and worked around the three sides of the triangle. This same pattern was employed by the third graders and to some extent by second grade children. First grade children and some second graders, however, read the pictures across the triangle, from top to bottom and from left to right. Elkind concluded that these children were in the process of learning the top to bottom and left to right swing which is essential in reading English. Because they had not entirely mastered this swing, they spontaneously practised it, even where it was inappropriate.

Children of two to four years of age (preconceptual period) cannot reason inductively or deductively, but instead reason transductively, going from particular to particular without apparent logical connection. Transductive reasoning prevents children from forming true concepts because they cannot cope with general classes. They are unable to distinguish between "all" and "some".

In the succeeding concrete operational stage (generally around age six to eight), children have made considerable progress. They are able to classify more consistently and can give reasons for their actions and beliefs. Language too progresses rapidly and assists internalization of behaviour through representation, which acts to speed up the rate at which experience takes place. Yet thought at this stage is restricted in quality and effectiveness by two things. It is dominated by immediate perceptions—by the dominant aspect of what is attended to, and by the fact that the child is unable to keep in mind more than one relation at a time. These limitations have clear implications for those who deal with pre-school and lower primary school children.

When a six year old was asked, "What makes a car go?", he responded, "The wheels. The motor. The petrol. By the steering wheel." This set of explanations, although related to the movement of the car, does not constitute an ordered explanation. Piaget in his earlier works used the term "juxtaposition" to describe this phenomenon, which in effect involves an inability to see any relationship among the parts which constitute a whole.

Paradoxically, young children also engage in a type of reasoning (syncretic) in which they tend to connect a series of separate ideas into a confused whole and assign to quite different things a similarity which to an adult is illogical. The child reasoning syncretically perceives the whole but does not see the differences within it. For example, in word recognition, the child would have difficulty discriminating between *cat* and *cut*, *wash* and *wish*, *came* and *come*. These children focus on one aspect of a situation at the expense of the other.

They are unable to attend to differences among, things and to their similarities at the same time.

The schoolchild who is still preoperational also cannot attend to transformations from one state to another. Although these children can anticipate cause-effect relationships, they cannot think about all the steps in between.

Such "faulty" logical thinking is directly involved in difficulties during learning to read. We teach children letter-sound associations and then expect them to miraculously put the sounds together into a word and words into meaningful sentences. Instead, we must prepare them for logical thought.

Learning to attach a phonemic equivalent to a graphemic symbol can be taught to young children—they can memorize. Thus, the small child may know the letters *c, a,* and *t,* but letters are transformed by their surroundings (*cat*) and they then denote a different grapheme-phoneme relationship—the separate sounds of *c,a,*and *t* do not sound like *cat,* even if you "say it fast."

Children taught by memorizing the sound-symbol relationships only appear to have difficulty in comprehension. The preoperational child who is not able to perform analysis on transformed words would have difficulty producing the phonemic equivalent of, for example, the *a* in *mat, mate, mark.* That same preoperational child would have difficulty deciphering the "long a" sound in *great, grate, eight.*

Piaget emphasized that children must have a rather large conceptual base acquired from firsthand experience before words will have meaning for them. In classroom practice, this means all children must acquire experience by interacting with others and the environment, not merely memorize details.

The "centering" child, as mentioned before, can easily memorize rules but is usually unable to keep the rule in mind while applying it. Thus children from two to seven should not be expected to pursue a reading program based on naming the grapheme-phoneme correspondence at the same time they are putting letters together to form words and words together to form sentences with meaning. Decentration is crucial to successful reading comprehension.

In summary, the preoperational child can center on or pay attention to only one aspect of a situation at one time; s/he reasons not inductively or deductively, but transductively; s/he is not able to hold various attributes of a situation in mind at one time while searching for some common characteristic; and s/he reasons by proximity.

Reversing Thought

Reversibility of thought processes allows the child to follow an operation from its conclusion back to its beginning and vice versa. A preoperational child, who cannot reverse thought processes, should not be expected to convert graphemes to phonemes by memorizing the sound that goes with the symbol (in reading) and also validate his or her "knowing" by attaching the right grapheme to the phoneme (in writing). That takes reversibility in thinking.

When children are presented with both uppercase and lowercase letters, different type faces, manuscript and cursive writing, and variations in assigning phonemes to particular letters, the nonconserving, transductive, preoperational child (generally from two to seven years of age) may experience failure in beginning to read. This indicates that it takes "concrete stage" thinking to deal with parts and wholes of words, and to think about all the possibilities one letter of the alphabet might denote.

Thus, in order to deal with the transformed letters and hold rules of relationship in mind while synthesizing meaning, a child must be a conserver, a concrete thinker. Millie Almy found a rather high correlation between the ability to "conserve" concrete substances and beginning reading achievement. This indicates that the abilities to reverse thought and decenter perceptions, which underlie conservation, might be prerequisite to successful beginning reading instruction.

Taking some of the Piagetian tasks into consideration, reading requires representations (the evocation of vivid mental images). From the mechanical point of view: Discrimination of letters (*p* vs. *q*, *b* vs. *d*) and conservation of directions (left to right) require a well structured concept of space and awareness that the letters are also arranged linearly (for example, *saw* vs. *was*). The grouping of letters into words and sentences requires classificatory schema, and in addition, classifactory rules state when a capital letter is required, and that most of the time only an empty space is required between words.

As far as content is concerned, the child must have not only mental images of static unrelated objects but also the mobility of thought to coordinate the relationships among objects in space, time, and logic. For example, the passage "John went to the circus with his sister and father; there he saw elephants and clowns" involves space, time, classification, seriation, number, social knowledge, and physical knowledge.

One of the most important issues is whether language influences the development of thought or whether thought influences the development of language. This question has far-reaching consequences for planning programs for preschool and the lower primary grades in particular, for there is no dispute as to whether language influences the development of thought when the formal level is reached in the middle school years. Piaget's position is that up to the formal operational stage, the development of thought (logical structures) influences the development of language and not the other way around.

Granted that the evidence is running in favor of the precedence of thought, what does this imply for the teaching of language skills in the early years? Per-haps it implies what at first seems the extreme view of Furth and Wachs (1974), who assert that the message the child who begins school gets is, "Forget your intellect for a while, come and learn to read and write; in 5 or 7 years' time, if you are successful, your reading will catch up with the capacity of your intellect, which you are developing in spite of what we offer you."

Furth suggests postponing the teaching of reading in favor of providing opportunities to develop thinking. His argument runs as follows: "Young children (5–7) are capable of operative intelligent thinking well in advance of spoken language and 'light years' ahead of what they can read or write. . . . Piaget's work suggests that it is thinking that should be strengthened so that the child can use the verbal medium intelligently."

Furth recommends that reading be relegated to an elective activity, encouraged but never imposed, and that this postponement would have no serious effect on the child's eventual capacity to read. This hypothesis remains to be thoroughly tested, but Furth's emphasis on providing an environment for the encouragement of thinking certainly follows from Piaget.

There would certainly be reaction against such a proposal. Perhaps learning to read is that kind of skill which develops best if begun when the child is first ready, which usually means the early primary years. It may also be that there is merit in Furth's contention that not enough effort is spent in the early years to encourage thinking.

It is not unreasonable to expect (but also not proven) that children can make use of the same strategies used in acquiring language and thought in order to become skilled readers. In fact, the proposed similarity of process in reading and language may be an important tool for teachers. Remember that some important concepts about reading must be learned before reading begins. First children need to know what reading is—meaningful communication between writer and reader. Children should understand that what they say can be written down, and what can be written down, can be read by them. Second, children need to know what a word is. Why should we expect an illiterate youngster to know that "want to" is two words when s/he usually hears "Do you wanna help me?"

Of course, meaning is the final goal for beginners just as it is for skilled readers. If written material represents the living language of children, early concentration on the context of language as a cue to words may shorten the procedure. Apparently, use of the language experience method, in which stories dictated by children are the material of instruction for the first stages in reading, has some long-range positive effect. This agrees with Piaget's emphasis on children first having experiences with words, opportunity to interpret what they have experienced, and interaction with others and the environment.

There is evidence that language which represents the language systems of children is more comprehensible to them than syntactic patterns that are unlike children's language. For the first stages of reading, this means that stories children dictate from their own experiences will provide the best written materials for reading instruction. This is the essence of the language experience approach.

If a child is not succeeding with the activities generally expected of kindergarten and first grade children, the teacher well versed in Piagetian theory can take a careful look and see at what developmental level the child is operating. Teachers are becoming increasingly adept at prescriptive teaching—pinpointing a child's deficits and providing activities especially selected to help him or her overcome them. The teacher must provide many kinds of concrete experiences from which the child gradually learns to generalize, developing an abstract concept needed at that child's particular level of intellectual functioning.

We need a great deal more research in

order to know precisely what to teach when, and how best to fit our teaching to the individual child. But we are making progress and it is indicative of the genius of Piaget that his theories are finding applications in reading language instruction in early childhood education.

REFERENCES

Almy, Millie and others. *Young Children's Thinking: Studies of Some Aspects of Piaget's Theory.* New York, N.Y.: Columbia University, Teachers College Press, 1966.

Elkind, David and J. Flavell, Eds. *Studies in Cognitive Development.* New York, N.Y.: Oxford University Press, 1969.

Furth, Hans G. and Harry Wachs. *Piaget's Theory in Practice: Thinking Goes to School.* New York, N.Y.: Oxford University Press, 1974.

Kamii, C.K. "Preschool Education: Socio-emotional, Perceptual-motor and Cognitive Development." *Handbook on Formative and Summative Evaluation of Student Learning.* Benjamin S. Bloom and others, Eds. New York, N.Y.: McGraw-Hill, 1971.

Lavatelli, Celia Stendler. *Piaget's Theory Applied to an Early Childhood Curriculum.* Boston, Mass.: American Science and Engineering, Inc., 1970.

McNally, D. W. *Piaget. Education and Teaching.* Sydney, Australia: Hodder and Stoughton, 1973.

Pulaski, Mary Ann. *Understanding Piaget.* New York, N.Y.: Harper & Row, 1971.

Roberts, Kathleen Piegdon. "Piaget's Theory of Conservation and Reading Readiness." *The Reading Teacher,* vol. 30. no. 3 (December 1976), pp. 246–50.

Wadsworth, Barry J. *Piaget's Theory of Cognitive Development.* New York, N.Y.: David McKay Co., Inc., 1975.

Teaching for Logical Thinking is a Prereading Activity

JOHN R. NEVIUS, JR.

- Reading is limited by experience.
- Experience is limited by conceptual development.
- Concepts are dependent upon strategies involving thinking skills.

Starting from the position of adult knowledge, Piaget (1954) points out the profoundly different way that young children think from older persons: Reasoning does not reach a stage of logical abilities until about age seven or eight. Supportive evidence is available from Rowher (1970), Almy, Chittenden, and Miller (1966), and Furth (1970) which indicates that the general age span from seven to eleven is the time when a child becomes able to reason abstractly, as required in reading.

Such abstract thinking skills as predictions, guesses, confirmations and corrections are all important contributors to good reading, because they are required in forming a hypothesis—which from Goodman's (1967) point of view is a synthesis of skills that is essential for effective reading. Therefore, a basis for better reading may very well rest upon a prereading program which includes teaching for logical thought.

Siegel (1972) and Wohwill (1973) have shown that the development of logical thought advances on a broad horizontal front. Furthermore, concepts of logical thought can be taught appropriately when many experiences of a related nature are emphasized. For example,

Siegel provided children experiences in several related areas, notably grouping by color, form, structure, and relationship (such as "a hammer is used to pound nails"). The outcome was an increase in the children's understanding of classification. Wohwill was concerned with experiences that related to understanding conservation. His strategy was to provide children with opportunities to investigate and perform functions of measurement with length, volume, weight, and distance.

Most importantly, Siegel and Wohwill show that a horizontal emphasis allows a child to transfer problem solving skills from one learning experience to another of a similar nature. This transfer is our goal and is the reason we provide a wealth of interrelated activities: they provide opportunity for transfer of learning to occur. Goodman suggested that hypothesis formation is an important skill for young readers. A hypothesis is formed by making statements and drawing conclusions through investigation of many materials and forms of similar objects. Some activities that provide opportunities for the transfer of problem solving skills and thus the development of hypotheses are: patterning, comparing, classifying, and predicting. These can include art activities, cognitive activities, and psychomotor activities.

The following activities, familiar to most teachers, are proposed as ones that assist in learning how to develop hypotheses. Since young children learn by active manipulation and experience with materials, a range from simple to complex should be provided so children can find their own level of work.

From *The Reading Teacher*, Vol. 30, No. 6 (March 1977). Reprinted with permission from International Reading Association and John R. Nevius, Jr.

1. **Patterning** helps children become aware of repetition. Use activities that require auditory, visual, and tactile discrimination.

Teacher-directed activities:
   a. Have the children clap a sequence.
   b. Draw the children's attention to patterns of color, to the patterns that make up texture in clothing.
Student activities:
   c. Copy a colored pattern in crayon on a grid, or on peg board using colored pegs.
   d. Make an original pattern by glueing macaroni or pebbles on paper, or through repetition of numerals (draw, or use cut-outs).
   e. Create a pattern using objects with two properties (such as shape and color).

2. **Comparison** builds upon skills of observation as children create distinctions between objects, materials, and ideas, or note their similarities. Comparison tasks are not only prereading, but prenumber as well. They transfer to categorization and patterning.
   a. Compare objects in terms of size, texture, shape, color.
   b. Compare the growth rate of plants and animals.
   c. Weigh or measure objects and materials for mass, length, size, number.
   d. Compare degrees of cold or heat.
   e. Count objects (such as beads or small cubes) to determine amount compared to appearance of volume.
   f. Compare, match, group, or sort objects and materials on basis of certain features. (Teacher may call the child's attention to the significant feature or let the child decide which to use.)

3. **Classification** may be promoted through tasks which require children to make decisions by creating two or more groups of items or ideas. Through classification children may create inferences which lead to prediction or back to comparison; the teacher should guide this transfer.
   a. Classify by color, shape, structure.
   b. Classify by use.
   c. Arrange in three or more groups by some ascending or descending order.
   d. Create multiple categorizations that relate objects by two or more properties.
   e. Group by "alike" and "not alike."
   f. Group by properties like soft/hard, round/flat, thin/fat.

4. **Predictions** are made on the basis of prior learning and experience. Prediction teaches children how to pose questions before assigning answers.
   a. Test the effect of prediction, using magnets, scales, balances, water, and volume measurement.
   b. Use charts which ask how many of certain objects a child can pick up in one hand—for example, walnuts or almonds.
   c. Predict how long a sweet potato vine will grow when half a sweet potato is partially submerged in a jar of water. (Then compare with one already grown.)

5. **Hypotheses** are formed by making statements and drawing conclusions through investigating many materials and forms of similar objects. Ultimately the child determines logical consequences from predetermined clues.
   a. Make statements and draw conclusions concerning water, ice, steam, cooking, materials whose shape may be altered, sand or flour.
   b. Make statements about salted, spiced, and untreated meat products with respect to preservation.
   c. Investigate the tactile qualities of

sticky substances. How can the sticky property be changed? Try it.

d. Investigate the effect of heat, flame, and cold on various objects or substances.

Activities such as these are very familiar to teachers—in fact, it is their familiarity that makes them appropriate examples. The important thing is to build for transfer of information and problem solving skill. Logical thinking does not develop in a precise vertical line, but is developed when any activities of a broad general nature are presented to the child. In the classroom the presentation should appear unstructured but actually be carefully planned to provide a broad structure of experience. Careful arrangement of related activities can help the children achieve transfer.

Although there is no research that shows such activities will lead directly to improved reading, it does seem reasonable to suggest that facility with logical thinking is necessary before one can master the formal and rule content of reading. If this is indeed the case, then structuring the classroom to promote logical thought and teaching for the transfer of problem solving skills may be an overlooked aspect of prereading instruction.

REFERENCES

Almy, Millie, E. Chittenden and P. Miller. *Young Children's Thinking*. New York, N.Y.: Teachers College Press, 1966.

Furth, Hans G. *Piaget for Teachers*. Englewood Cliffs, N.J.: Prentice-Hall, 1970.

Goodman, Kenneth S. "Reading: A Psycholinguistic Guessing Game." *Journal of the Reading Specialist*, vol. 4 (May 1967), pp. 126–35.

Piaget, Jean. *The Construction of Reality in the Child*. New York, N.Y.: Basic Books, 1954.

Rowher, William D., Jr. On Attaining Goals of Early Childhood Education. Paper presented at OEO Conference on Research in Early Childhood Education, Washington, D.C., 1970.

Siegel, I. "The Development of Classificatory Skills in Young Children: A Training Program." *The Young Child*. Washington, D.C.: National Association for the Education of Young Children, 1972.

Wohwill, Joachim. "The Place of Structured Experience in Early Cognitive Development." *Revisiting Early Childhood Education*, Joe L. Frost, Ed. New York, N.Y.: Holt, Rinehart and Winston, 1973.

Thought, Language and Reading Readiness

STEVIE HOFFMAN
H. THOMPSON FILLMER

Societal pressure for increased academic achievement of children in elementary school has resulted in the earlier introduction of formal reading instruction in first grade and a highly academic orientation to the reading readiness program in kindergarten. This formality is particularly evident in early childhood programs designed to compensate for the limited preschool readiness experience of children from lower socioeconomic homes. Compensatory programs often emphasize a preplanned and highly structured approach to teaching language per se. The assumption is that if these children are provided intensive oral and written language experiences, both thinking and language skills will improve.

Such programs are based upon the view that language promotes thinking, as proposed by Vygotsky (1962). However, Carroll (1974) concluded from extensive research that language by itself has limited and sporadic influence on thought, and according to Piaget (1973), thought has its roots in action—language transmits only that which has been learned through concrete experiences. Thus, development of thought, especially in young children, stimulates language development, rather than the other way around.

Nevertheless, in formal language-development programs, five and six year olds are forced into language tasks unrelated to their own lives and before they have acquired experience in the sorts of problem solving essential to develop-

ment of the thinking processes necessary for reading. Unfortunately, children started in such a formal reading program before they are ready for the instruction may become disabled readers. (Dechant and Smith 1977, p. 112).

The timing of instruction is especially important in preventing reading disability. Reading disability too often is caused by starting the child in a planned reading program before he is ready. Such a child cannot handle the day-to-day learning tasks and finds himself farther and farther behind as time goes by. He becomes frustrated and develops antipathy towards reading. He actually learns *not to read*. This is quite different and far more serious than not learning to read.

Compensatory reading programs in later grades are often the result of premature reading skill instruction, but these programs also too often focus on skill demands that cannot be handled by the child who has learned *not* to read.

The problem, then, begins in a reading readiness curriculum based on the assumption that language produces thought rather than that thought produces language. These programs continue into reading skill activities that find support in that same view, then lead to compensatory programs still based on highly structured, abstract approaches to teaching language and reading skills, and end with the graduation of disabled readers.

In contrast, a readiness program based on problem solving allows young children to verbalize about experiences they have already had. Language is used as a vehicle for meaningful communication about what is known, and is developed naturally and efficiently.

This article therefore proposes a pro-

From *The Reading Teacher*, Vol. 33, No. 1 (December 1979). Reprinted with permission of the International Reading Association and Stevie Hoffman and H. Thompson Fillmer.

gram of concrete problem solving experiences and functional language development for prereading children, based on research in the areas of thought, language acquisition, and readiness for reading. The needed concepts and appropriate skills are shown in the Figure. The effectiveness of the curriculum design was substantiated in an original research effort with three to five year old, educationally handicapped migrant children (Hoffman 1972, Cage and others 1972).

Theoretical base

We believe there is merit in reconsidering the underlying rationale for a curriculum based on learning experiences that 1) involve problem solving concepts, 2) foster the developmental skills necessary for understanding these concepts, and 3) encourage the child to express what is known (functional language).

Waller (1977) did a comprehensive review of research investigations relevant to the role of preoperational and concrete thought in reading. Several of the studies reviewed (pp. 11–14) examined the correlation between conservation skills and reading readiness or reading performance in primary school children. Reading correlated most highly with conservation of number, and especially with seriation.

Recognizing that there are children who have learned to read prior to entering kindergarten, Briggs and Elkind (1973), examined the cognitive factors that might make the difference between readers and nonreaders in this age group. Again, high scores on conservation tasks appeared to be the determining factor in early readers' skill. In studies of perception, Elkind (1974) and his associates (Elkind and Deblinger 1969; Elkind, Horn and Schneider 1965; Elkind, Larson and Van Doorwick 1965) provided evidence that reading requires the kind of thinking called "operational"—Piaget's developmental stage of concrete operations.

It is important to note that Piaget and

his collaborators have made no reference in their research to any relationship between the development of thought and reading per se. It is, instead, Piagetian scholars who have interpreted Piaget's cognitive states of development as relevant to the reading process.

Along the same line, Furth and Wachs (1974) applied Piagetian concepts in their "School for Thinking," which uses specific classroom learning activities built around thinking activities. Furth and Wachs explain the skills kindergarten and first grade children need prior to engaging in academic learning activities. These skills are summarized as follows.

1. General movement thinking skills involve the use of large muscles in purposeful and knowing movement.
2. Discriminative movement thinking skills involve eye, lip-tongue, and finger movement, as in talking and writing, observing and reading.
3. Visual thinking skills involve the concepts of part-to-whole, figure-to-ground, and time perception.
4. Auditory thinking skills involve nonlanguage activities.
5. Hand thinking skills involve the concept of the hand drawing what can be seen, and verify through touch what vision thinks it sees.
6. Graphic thinking skills involve the match of movement and vision for accuracy and efficiency.
7. Logical thinking skills involve the child's comprehension of what she is doing and why.
8. Social thinking skills involve the relationship between logical operation and social cooperation in the intellectual and social understanding of a developing child.

These prerequisite skills of problem solving for young children are, according to Furth and Wachs (1974, p. 19), activities that begin "before language and [go] far beyond language," and where "if the language is used, it serves the purpose of communication and contributes to the thinking activity only in a most peripheral fashion." Although their experimental program was discontinued with qualitative results reported, they expressed conviction that a curriculum must "intentionally and purposefully emphasize the development of thinking

Prereading problem solving and thinking skills

Concepts to be learned	Developmental skills to be acquired
Classification concepts	
Everything can be sorted into like groups.	To group according to size, shape, color, other physical properties (taste, smell, feel, weight), number, living and nonliving things, use, roles
Some groups can be sorted into subgroups.	To group animals and people into male and female groups
	To group living things by age
	To group nonliving things into subgroups
Some groups have overlapping classifications.	To find common characteristics within two or more groups
Relational characteristics	
Every substance has relational characteristics.	To work with and understand relative size (big and small, tall and short, long and short), relative volume (more and less), relative weight (light and heavy), relative number (more and fewer), relative location (up and down, in and out, top and bottom, on and off, over and under, near and far, front and back), contrasting characteristics (hot and cold, dry and wet, fast and slow, soft and hard, noisy and quiet, open and closed, is and is not, with and without)
Seriation concepts	
Substances can be ordered.	To manipulate objects according to gradations of length, height, size, etc.
Spatial concepts	
Space is a collection of separate forms.	To recognize a square, circle, rectangle, triangle and "blob" as seen in objects.
	To manipulate shapes into various spaces
	To construct four basic shapes
Number concepts	
Numerical quantities are not dependent upon the size of the space occupied.	To match on a one-to-one basis
	To work with the idea of more, fewer, enough
	To recognize numerals and understand their relationship to the concept of number
Temporal concepts	
There is a causal relationship to events in time.	To work with the idea of what comes first, what comes after, if-then relationships, time as a factor in our lives
Conservation concepts	
Substance can change shape and still be the same amount.	To work with and understand the constancy of matter
Functional language concepts	
That which is learned through discovery can be expressed in oral language.	To acquire and use a vocabulary which tells what, how, and why

in the child,'' and that it must ''help develop a child whose intelligence and personality are sufficiently mature and articulated so that he becomes capable of reading-based learning . . . '' (pp. 272–75).

The research of the past decade investigating the relationship between reading and cognitive development is considerable; the reviews of literature, such as Waller's (1977), are equally comprehensive. There is indeed support for a Piagetian approach to prereading for young children. At a conference held at the University of Florida in the spring of 1978, Elkind provoked additional thoughts regarding curricula for primary grade children. He proposed that most instructional programs for these young learners are of a ''disabling'' nature—that a ''disabling curriculum'' creates the inability to learn and, in effect, promotes nonlearning in children eager to learn.

involvement with a learning environment created by the teacher) has direct relationship to thought, language and, subsequently, reading. Bruner (1966) would undoubtedly support experiences for children where they interact with their world in their own ways and in their own stage of cognitive development. Building concepts through concrete problem solving, using skills found in children at a particular stage of cognition, and exercising the child's functional language are, it appears, supported by Piaget's theory that thought precedes language in the young child's learning. Children's concrete problem solving ability and their ability to express the what, how, and why of their problem solving experiences can provide the classroom teacher the rationale for building an enabling curriculum for young learners.

Classroom practices

Based on research evidence, on Furth and Wach's prerequisites for learning activities, and on Elkind's warning against a ''disabling curriculum,'' we propose that young children be provided the opportunity to investigate and explore, to inquire and discover specific concrete concepts, and that teachers should insure that the concepts suggested (see Figure) are understood by the child prior to the formal introduction of reading strategies.

Teachers will recognize when the child has acquired the concepts by observing the child's skills and noting the functional language used by the child to describe what he or she knows through his or her own investigating and discovering efforts. Learning experiences must be planned so that children work with concrete, manipulative materials rather than artificial and abstract drawings or pictures. The process is one of children learning rather than of teachers teaching.

Each of these concepts with its requisite skills (learned by the child in active

REFERENCES

Briggs, C. and David Elkind. ''Cognitive Development in Early Readers.'' *Developmental Psychology,* vol. 9 (1973), pp. 279–80.

Bruner, Jerome. *Studies in Cognitive Growth.* New York, N.Y.: John Wiley and Sons, 1966.

Cage, Bob and others. *Migrant Early Childhood Education in Putnam County, Florida: An Evaluation.* Final Report to the Migrant Section, Florida Department of Education. Gainesville, Florida: Institute for Development of Human Resources, College of Education, University of Florida, 1972.

Carroll, John. ''The Potentials and Limitations of Print as a Medium of Instruction.'' *Media and Symbols: The Forms of Expression, Communications, and Education,* David R. Olson, Ed., pp. 151–79. Seventy-third Yearbook of the National Society for the Study of Education. Chicago, Ill.: University of Chicago Press, 1974.

Dechant, Emerald and Henry Smith.

Psychology in Teaching Reading, 2nd ed. Englewood Cliffs, N.J.: Prentice-Hall, 1977.

Elkind, David. The Curriculum Disabled Child. Paper presented at the University of Florida, Gainesville, May 15, 1978.

Elkind, David. "Reading, Logic, and Perception: An Approach to Reading Instruction." *Children and Adolescents: Interpretive Essays on Jean Piaget.* David Elkind, Ed. New York, N.Y.: Oxford University Press, 1974.

Elkind, David and Jo Ann Deblinger. "Perceptual Training and Reading Achievement in Disadvantaged Children." *Child Development,* vol. 40, no. 1 (March 1969), pp. 11–19.

Elkind, David, John Horn, and Gerrie Schneider. "Modified Word Recognition, Reading Achievement, and Perceptual Decentration." *Journal of Genetic Psychology,* vol. 107 (December 1965), pp. 235–51.

Elkind, David, Margaret Larson, and William Van Doorwick. "Perceptual Decentration Learning and Performance in Slow and Average Readers." *Journal of Educational Psychology,* vol. 56, no. 1 (February 1965), pp. 50–56.

Furth, Hans and Henry Wachs. *Thinking Goes to School: Piaget's Theory in Practice.* New York, N.Y.: Oxford University Press, 1974.

Hoffman, Stevie. *Threes, Fours, and Fives Together: A Curriculum Resource Guide for a Multi-Age Grouping of Preschool Migrant Children.* Report to the Migrant Section, Florida Department of Education. Gainesville, Florida: Institute for the Development of Human Resources, College of Education, University of Florida, 1972.

Piaget, Jean. *The Language and Thought of the Child.* New York, N.Y.: World Publishing Company, 1973.

Waller, T. Gary. *Think First, Read Later! Piagetian Prerequisites for Reading.* Newark, Del.: International Reading Association, 1977.

Vygotsky, Lev. *Thought and Language.* Cambridge, Mass.: The M.I.T. Press, 1962.

Development of Auditory and Visual Language Concepts and Relationship to Instructional Strategies in Kindergarten

MADELINE HARDY
R. G. STENNETT
P. C. SMYTHE

Beginning kindergarten children are faced with learning an array of concepts and terminology which are essential to the development of pre-reading and beginning reading skills. The language of instruction used in kindergarten is complicated and children may fail to acquire major concepts because they do not understand the language being used by the teacher in presenting them. For some kindergarten entrants concepts such as word, letter, sound, middle, long, and draw a line are familiar, but for others they may be completely new. Little is known of how the language concepts and terminology which support the earliest stages of learning to read are presented during kindergarten. Even less is known about which specific concepts and terms are most useful to young children in helping them to learn to read or in what order these should be presented.

In 1966 Jessie Reid explored the general level of understanding of reading and writing of Scottish five-year-olds, as reflected in the vocabulary available to them in talking about these tasks. The children had little precise notion of what reading involved and were unaware that written words were composed of letters which stand for sounds. Extending Reid's work with English five-year-olds, Downing (1970) confirmed that the concepts *word* and *sound* were poorly understood.

From *Elementary English*, Vol. 51, No. 4 (April, 1974). © 1974 by the National Council of Teachers of English. Reprinted by permission.

Clay (1966) found that children in their first year in school in New Zealand had difficulty differentiating letters and words, and Karpova (1955) discovered that Russian children from 3½ to 7 years could not divide a sentence into its word units. Two American studies investigated grade one children's knowledge of word boundaries and concluded that they lacked precise concepts regarding the nature of a word (Meltzer and Herse, 1969; Kingston, Wendell & Figa, 1972). A third study compared kindergarten children's concepts of word boundaries in speech and print and found that while few children could segment either speech or print conventionally, some could match visual segmentation with their incorrect auditory segmentation (Holden & MacGinitie, 1972). Johns (1972) found a significant relationship between the reading achievement of fourth grade children and their concept of reading and concluded that one of the factors in children's reading achievement is their understanding of the nature of the reading process.

The above studies indicate the present lack of information regarding the acquisition by young children of certain language and reading concepts. Some areas of auditory and visual language concepts remain unexplored, for example, auditory concepts dealing with similarity and difference and with temporal position, and visual concepts related to book parts, spatial relations and size. Since more precise developmental data are required for a more enlightened approach to the introduction of essential language and reading concepts to young children, we conducted a preliminary investigation of language and reading-related concepts as part of a broader study of developmental patterns in elemental reading skills (Stennett, Smythe, Hardy, Wilson & Thurlow, 1970). Although this study was conducted with both kindergarten and grade one children, we are focusing here on the kindergarten level where the first formal instruction in auditory and visual language concepts takes place.

First, we compiled an exhaustive inventory of auditory and visual language concepts used in pre-reading and beginning reading programs and of instructional terms used by kindergarten and primary teachers. Concepts and terms were identified both by means of an examination of reading readiness and beginning reading tests, various kinds of instructional materials for kindergarten and grade one, teachers' handbooks, professional books in the area of the teaching of beginning reading, and also through consultation with kindergarten and primary teachers and consultants. Fifty-seven concepts were isolated and a test or test item developed for each.

Test Construction and Administration

Questions such as the following formed the rationale for test development: Do young children understand terms such as *word, letter, sound, letter name?* In presenting the concept "difference," would the term *different, not the same* or *not alike* be most efficient? Do kindergarten children understand directions such as "go *across* the page," "put your finger *under* the picture of the dog," "find the *last* house on the street," "find the *long* word on the *page?*"

In the area of auditory language concepts the following seven categories were identified with appropriate tests: Alphabet Production, Word, Rhyme, Letter Name, Speech Sound, Similarity/Difference (Same, Not the Same; Alike,

Not Alike; Different), Temporal Position (First, Beginning, Middle, Last, End).

We devised seventeen subtests to test these seven auditory categories. With the exception of alphabet production, in which they were simply asked to say the alphabet, children indicated their response by either pressing or not pressing a button. Button pressing activated a battery-powered light which could be seen only by the examiner. Trained examiners presented standard test instructions, but actual test items were administered from tape. In the subtest "word," for example, the examiner said, "When we talk, we say words. I want you to listen to some things on the tape recorder. Some of them will be words and some will be other things. Whenever you hear a word, press the button." The examiner then played the tape which contained 20 items, 5 of them real words, and 15 buffer items made up of 5 letter names, 5 consonant sounds, and 5 consonant blends. Each child's responses were recorded by the examiner on a preprinted answer sheet. In the subtest "different" the examiner said, "We are going to listen to two words on the tape recorder. Sometimes the words will be different. Listen carefully and when you hear two words that are different, press the button." Four word pairs were then played from the tape, two different and two alike; e.g., to-in, at-at, is-is, it-are.

In the area of Visual Language Concepts, two main categories were identified, book-related and word-related concepts. *Book-related* concepts were subdivided into: Book Parts and Symbols (Cover, Title, Front, Back, Title of Page, Line, Word, Letter, Capital Letter) and Spatial Relations (Bottom, Top, Left Side, Right Side, Across the Page). *Word-related* concepts were subdivided into: Spatial Relations (Under, Over, Beside, Below, Above, On Top Of, Between, Space Between), Following Directions (Box Around, Circle Around, Underline, Through) Spatial Position (First, Last, Beginning, Middle, End), and Size (Little, Big, Long, Short).

Test materials used in the visual language concepts tests were, as much as possible, actual reading materials used in the schools. All book-related concepts were tested using the first reader of a standard basal reader series. The test format and procedure were simple. The examiner said, "Show me the *front* of the book," "Show me the *back* of the book," "Show me a *page* in the book," "*Turn a page* in the book," "Show me a *line* on this page." In testing word-related concepts, simple pictures and words and cut-out pictures were used. Using a cut-out of a baby and a picture sheet, children were asked to "Put the baby *under* the bird." "Put the baby *beside* the bird." "Put the baby *between* the truck and the chair." Using a marking pen, children were asked to "Make a *box around* the bird." "Draw a line *through* the house." Again, viewing a picture sheet, children were required to "Show me the *last* picture." "Show me a *space between* the pictures." Finally, children were asked to find the *beginning, middle,* and *end* of words and to point to a *long* word, *short* word, *big* word, *little* word. Examiners recorded their evaluation of the students' responses on a pre-printed answer sheet.

The same tests were administered individually three times during the kindergarten year—October, February and May. Approximately 30 to 40 minutes of testing time per subject were required to administer the tests in each area, auditory and visual. Three trials of the tests of visual language concepts were given. The tests of auditory and visual language concepts constituted two test batteries of the five administered to each subject at each testing period. Additional test batteries included the following tests: Concept of Letters, Letter Orientation, Letter Recognition, Letter Naming, Visual Template, Auditory Segmentation, Auditory Blending, Phoneme Span, Eye Movement and Motor Speed. Testing was carried out in fully equipped mobile testing units which were placed near the school buildings.

Instructional Inventory

In order to monitor kindergarten instruction in the various auditory and visual language concepts, an instructional inventory was developed, with the cooperation of the four teachers involved in the study. The inventory, which contained items related to all areas of the pre-reading and beginning reading programs, was completed by the teachers at the end of each month. During the hour required by each teacher for the completion of the inventory, one of the test administrators involved in the study took responsibility for her class. The teachers were asked to indicate, on a check list, concepts to which the children had been *exposed* during the month, not those which they had necessarily *mastered*.

Information given by the teachers was summarized cumulatively at the three testing intervals, making possible some comparison of instruction and mastery of the various concepts.

The subjects of the study were 60 kindergarten children, 30 boys and 30 girls, who were enrolled in three public schools in London, Canada. The schools were chosen to represent three different socioeconomic levels. With the help of the teachers, 20 children were chosen from each school to take part in the project. They ranged in age from 57 to 69 months at the beginning of the study. An attempt was made to select a middle or average group of children in each school. No children with obvious physical or emotional deficits were chosen, nor were children who could already read upon kindergarten entry included.

Auditory Language Concepts

Table 1 presents the results of the test of Auditory Language Concepts in terms of the percentage of children achieving 90% or greater accuracy in each of the three testing sessions. The results for each concept are arranged in order of success in the initial session and infor-

Table 1

Percent of Kindergarten Children With 90% or Greater Accuracy on Tests of Auditory Language Concepts and Percent of Children Exposed to the Concepts Instructionally

Subtest	Test Period		
	October	February	June˙
Alphabet Production	44(30)*	64(100)	75(100)
Letter Name	38(30)	54(100)	56(100)
Rhyme	13(30)	46(100)	62(100)
Similarity-Difference	13(0)	39(85)	40(90)
Temporal Position	8(10)	19(45)	20(65)
Word	5(35)	12(100)	14(100)
Speech Sound	2(0)	17(70)	5(100)

*Percent of children exposed to the concept instructionally is indicated in parentheses.

mation regarding the percentage of children exposed instructionally to each concept is indicated in parentheses.

Examination of the mastery figures, 90% or greater accuracy, for the seven subtests reveals that with the exception of Speech Sound, growth took place throughout the year in all areas. The children in the study entered kindergarten with relatively high mastery of the auditory concepts Letter Name, and Alphabet. Rhyme, Word, Speech Sound, Temporal Position and Similarity/Difference concepts were less well developed. Mastery of Alphabet Production appeared to occur in advance of instruction. Over 40% of kindergarten children entered school having learned to produce the alphabet, although by October only 30% had been taught to produce it.

Ability to identify Words, Letter Names, and Speech Sounds from an auditory presentation was variable, with Letter Names most easily identified at all testing periods, Words much less well recognized, and Speech Sounds poorly understood. By June all teachers had

used the term "sound of the letter", but only 5% mastery was achieved in Speech Sound.

In Table 2 the Auditory Language Concepts, Similarity-Difference and Temporal Position, are presented in terms of mean correct percent responses and instructional exposure. With entering kindergarten children, "alike" was better understood than "same" but by June no difference in mastery of these concepts appeared. Understanding of Difference concepts was clearly differentiated, with "different" more easily understood than either "not the same" or "not alike" in October and "different" and "not the same" remaining easier than "not alike" at the end of the year. Temporal Position concepts were poorly understood by kindergarten children in October, especially "middle", which alone remained poor by June. Instruction was given in all concepts with the excep-

Table 2

Mean Percent Correct Responses of Kindergarten Children on Tests of Auditory Language Concepts and Percent of Children Exposed to the Concepts Instructionally

Subtest	Test Period		
	October	February	June
Similarity-Difference			
Alike	58(0)*	92(65)	90(75)
Different	54(0)	72(100)	70(100)
Same	46(0)	88(100)	92(100)
Not the Same	41(0)	74(100)	70(100)
Not Alike	31(0)	62(65)	66(75)
Temporal Position			
Beginning	60(0)	66(100)	80(100)
End	56(0)	72(30)	84(65)
Last	44(30)	78(30)	80(75)
First	41(30)	58(75)	82(75)
Middle	25(0)	39(0)	40(10)

*Percent of children exposed to the concept instructionally is indicated in parentheses.

tion of "middle", which was presented to only 10% of the children.

Visual Language Concepts

Table 3 summarizes the results of the test of Visual Language Concepts in terms of percent correct responses and instructional exposure. As with Auditory Language Concepts, a growth trend was noted in all areas throughout the kindergarten year. Considering the two main areas tested, Book-Related Concepts and Word-Related Concepts, children apparently came to kindergarten better equipped to deal with concepts related to words, than those related to books, and this relationship remained throughout the first year in school, in spite of instructional procedures employed. Of the Book-Related Concepts, the children entering kindergarten in this study were better equipped in their knowledge of Spatial Relations than in Book Parts and Symbols. Of the Word-Related Concepts, where entering knowledge was higher, concepts related to Spatial Relations were best developed followed by those dealing with Following Directions, Spatial Position, and Size.

Only about 30% of the kindergarten children in the study could differentiate "left side" and "right side" of a book page in October, and knowledge of these spatial concepts remained poor throughout the year with less than 50% mastery in June. Instructionally, however, "left" and "right" had been introduced to all by June.

Mastery of book parts and symbols concepts was generally poor throughout the year. For "title", both of book and of page, only 25% mastery was achieved by June, though 25% had been exposed to the concept by February. "Line" (of print), also poorly understood throughout the year, was introduced late instructionally, but 70% had been exposed to "line" by the end of the year. Throughout the kindergarten year, "letter" was better understood than "word." Less

than 50% of beginning kindergarten children could identify a printed "word" but slightly more than 75% could identify a "letter." Instructionally, by February all subjects had observed words, both singly and in sentences, and all had observed letters both singly and in context and had manipulated letter cards and plastic letters in activities such as matching.

Spatial Relations concepts were relatively well mastered by the children entering kindergarten. Exceptions were "under" and "space between." Instruction, however, was begun early and mastery of all Spatial Relations concepts was high by February.

Considering that instruction in Following Directions concepts was somewhat delayed, mastery of them was fairly high, with "make a circle around" best understood, and "underline" poorly understood. More than 90% of entering kindergarten children could "make a circle around" a picture, in spite of the fact that only 40% of them had been formally exposed to the concept by February. Similarly, mastery of the concepts "underline" and "draw a line through" was in advance of instruction by the end of the year.

Of the Spatial Position concepts, "middle" was best understood visually by beginning kindergarten children but by the end of the year mastery of all five concepts was high. Instructionally, little stress was placed on "middle" throughout the year.

Mastery of all size concepts except "short word" was almost complete by the end of the year.

Implications

In the beginning reading and language areas it is obviously unwise to make assumptions about the concepts and terminology which children can understand upon entering school. In some instances the instructional language used by the teacher may be misunderstood and this may prevent the acquisition of important

Table 3
Percent Correct Responses of Kindergarten Children on Tests of Visual Language Concepts and Percent of Children Exposed to the Concepts Instructionally

BOOK-RELATED CONCEPTS

Book Parts and Symbols				Spatial Relations			
Item	Test Period			Item	Test Period		
	October	February	June		October	February	June
Front	84(10)*	95(100)	93(100)	Top	67(65)	80(100)	76(100)
Cover	82(30)	85(100)	93(100)	Bottom	64(65)	80(100)	86(100)
Back	80(70)	95(100)	93(100)	Across the Page	62(30)	76(40)	78(40)
Letter	77(0)	95(100)	93(100)	Right Side	31(0)	41(30)	43(100)
Word	46(0)	70(100)	76(100)	Left Side	28(0)	37(30)	47(100)
Capital Letter	41(0)	44(75)	59(75)				
Title of Book	31(30)	29(75)	26(75)				
Line	21(0)	29(0)	35(70)				
Title of Page	20(30)	24(75)	26(75)				
Mean Percent Correct on Total Subtest	54	63	66		50	63	66

WORD-RELATED CONCEPTS

Spatial Relations				Following Directions			
On Top Of	97(35)	98(100)	98(100)	Circle Around	92(0)	99(40)	97(70)
Over	95(35)	97(100)	98(100)	Through	74(0)	88(10)	72(10)
Beside	87(70)	92(100)	95(100)	Box Around	67(0)	88(0)	71(70)
Above	84(0)	92(75)	90(75)	Underline	51(0)	59(10)	83(10)
Below	75(70)	95(100)	90(100)				
Between	74(35)	86(100)	93(100)				
Space Between	61(70)	88(70)	88(70)				
Under	56(35)	80(100)	93(100)				
Mean Percent Correct on Total Subtest	79	91	93		71	84	83

Spatial Position				Size			
Middle	87(0)	93(40)	95(30)	Big Word	74(35)	80(70)	91(100)
Last	71(30)	92(75)	88(75)	Long Word	69(35)	81(70)	90(100)
First	64(65)	90(75)	93(100)	Little Word	57(0)	75(70)	93(100)
End	61(0)	86(40)	93(75)	Short Word	57(0)	64(70)	62(100)
Beginning	54(30)	89(100)	90(100)				
Mean Percent Correct on Total Subtest	67	88	92		64	75	84

*Percent of children exposed to the concept instructionally is indicated in parentheses.

concepts. In other situations mastery of concepts may have occurred prior to the start of instruction.

It is essential that the auditory and visual language concepts and terminology peculiar to a teaching program or strategy be identified by authors and publishers of such programs and provision made for their orderly and systematic acquisition within the program. Reading programs must also provide instruments for the assessment of the degree of mastery of language concepts of entering kindergarten children in order that teachers can capitalize, instructionally, upon concepts already mastered. In the case of the children in this study, for example, the "draw a circle around" response should be required in preference to "underline." Language terminology should be used consistently in beginning reading programs and the introduction of alternative terms delayed; e.g., "Alike" and "different" should be used deliberately in preference to "same," "not alike," and "not the same."

Great care should be taken in developing tests for use with young children, as the test instructions may be so complicated by unknown terminology that they prevent the demonstration of mastery of the concepts or skills being assessed.

Careful attention to and control of the instructional language used with young children should create a less confusing and more meaningful atmosphere for the orderly and sequential acquisition of beginning reading skills.

REFERENCES

Clay, M. "Emergent reading behaviour." Unpublished doctoral dissertation, University of Auckland, Auckland, New Zealand, 1966. (Reviewed by Samuel Weintraub in *The Reading Teacher*, 1968, *22*, 63–67.)

Downing, John. "Children's concepts of language in learning to read." *Educational Research*, 1970, *12*, 106–112.

Downing, John. "The development of linguistic concepts in children's thinking." Research in the *Teaching of English*, 1970, *4*, 5–19.

Holden, Marjorie H. & MacGinitie, Walter H. "Children's conceptions of word boundaries in speech and print." *Journal of Educational Psychology*, 1972, *63*, 551–557.

Johns, Jerry. "Children's concepts of reading and their reading achievement." *Journal of Reading Behavior*, 1972, *4*, 56–57.

Karpova, S. N. "Osoznanie slovesnogo sostava rechi rebenkom doshkol'nogo vozrasta." *Voprosy Psikhologii*, 1955, *4*, 43–55. (For an abstract in English see D. I. Slobin, Abstract of Soviet Studies in Child Language. In F. Smith & G. A. Miller (Eds.), *The Genesis of Language*. Cambridge, Mass.: M.I.T. Press, 1966.)

Kingston, Albert J., Weaver, Wendell W., & Figa, Leslie E. "Experiments in children's perceptions of words and word boundaries." *Twenty-First Yearbook of National Reading Conference*, 1972, 91–99.

Meltzer, Nancy S., & Herse, Robert. "The boundaries of written words as seen by first graders." *Journal of Reading Behavior*, 1969, *1*, 3–13.

Reid, Jessie F. "Learning to think about reading." *Educational Research*, 1966, *9*, 56–62.

Stennett, R. G., Smythe, P. C., Hardy, Madeline, Wilson, H. R. & Thurlow, Merle. "Developmental patterns in elemental reading skills: preliminary report." London Board of Education, London, Ontario, Canada, 1970 (mimeo).

Teaching Prereading Skills through Training in Pattern Recognition

DIANE MONTGOMERY

Preschool children can recognize and name complex three-dimensional patterns and their two-dimensional counterparts, cartoons, photographs, and sketches (Lewis and Goldberg, 1969). But many children have great difficulty in learning the written symbols (words) of these objects although they are put on carefully graded schemes in school.

In the teaching of reading there has always been the gap between the transfer from representational figures, such as pictures and line drawings of objects, to the letter symbols of words. For years teachers have hoped that those schemes which introduced pictures, drawings, and games involving recognition of the whole or various parts of stimulus materials would enhance reading subskills. Although the children's interest and attention were captured, there was no evidence that the skills being practiced had transfer value.

There seemed no alternative to the exasperating conclusion of Witty and Kopel (1936) that the only effective form of training for prereading skills was that which involved words. It seems clear, however, that the analysis of the letters of the alphabet in terms of a visual code which can be taught at the prereading level is a fruitful one and substantiated by the theoretical formulations of McLaughlin (1963), Bryant (1971), and Sutherland (1969).

The solution to the problem is contained in a synthesis of recent researches in perception:

From *The Reading Teacher*, Vol. 30, No. 6 (March, 1977). Reprinted with permission of the International Reading Association and Diane Montgomery.

1. The perception of a flash of light is not as simple as at first appears, for it has brightness, intensity, and duration—in other words, it is a patterned stimulus, not a single stimulus. A letter of the alphabet is thus a complex pattern of lines, edges, angles, and orientations.

2. Our brains contain analysers for both stationary and moving lines, edges, angles, and colours (Morrell, 1967).

3. Evidence from the study of illusions (Gregory, 1962) suggests that our perception is based upon heuristics—a hypothesis-testing approach to patterns, comparing results with previous experience.

4. Sutherland (1969) suggests that we quickly analyse combinations of lines, edges, and colour blocks in patterns until we recognise a consistent pattern. We then translate this pattern into a more abstract form of descriptive rules. According to his theory the word we see "is not the pattern on our retina but the series of hierarchical rules to which we match this pattern."

The problem here is, what rules are contained in letters and words that are not contained in drawings—rules that could be directly taught to children and that the children could directly transfer to letter recognition—for the critical review of the Frostig materials by Smith and Marx (1972) shows that there is no direct transfer of training from tasks that use drawings to word recognition.

The researches of Attneave and Arnoult (1956) are enlightening here. They showed that for any training effect to be obtained on perceptual material there must be "ecological validity," that is, the training sample must be drawn from the same population as that to which one wishes to generalise.

This means that we shall not get direct transfer of training to word recognition by showing pictures of objects, we must train on words and letters or word and letter-like forms. This accounts for the failure of the Frostig materials—they do not have ecological validity and so one must not expect direct transfer to reading. A major difficulty is, however, the concept of what is a "word population" but is not a word. Nonsense words could of course fulfill this criterion but they can be more confusing and difficult for a beginner than words themselves.

My subsequent research was devoted to finding satisfactory answers to these three questions: What are the rules? What is a word population? What is the significance of treating reading as a pattern recognition skill?

The research of Allan (1965) illustrated that the essence of a pattern recognition skill lay in paying attention to detail, not in isolation but in relation to the whole structure: "Nothing else is required, an innate, involuntary structuring process which is not intellectual does the rest."

In the present research, attention was first concentrated upon discovering the "rules," and it became clear that in the preschool period children learn, for example, that this is a cup:

and so are these:

But after entering school they are taught that this is d *d*, this is P *p*, this is q *q*, and this is b *b*.

Thus a dimension such as orientation becomes critical for letter recognition. Bryant (1971) confirms this. Since children often hypothesise a word from its initial letter (or last letter, if their eyes scan from right to left) and key structures such as overall length and shape, rules for this dimension are critical.

The problem for teachers is how best this can be taught, for the words one uses to describe these differences are not necessarily meaningful to the child—for example, befores, afters, aboves, belows. The problems of some children are increased if their ability to test hypotheses about perceptual input are limited, or if their memory for forms is poor.

An analysis of the letters of the alphabet was undertaken with the result that this simple cypher was found to be a code on four basic elements when Futura, the sans serif typeface used in many childrens' books, was scrutinised:

O dots   I short sticks

⌐ looped sticks | long sticks

With these structures, twenty-three out of twenty-six letters can be made. Using just dots and short and long sticks, sixteen out of twenty-six letters can be made, and it was this group which received attention since it contained the problem group:

b d q p

The group consisted of *a b d i j k l o p q t v w x y z*. These elements of construction did correspond to the elements of perception and use of them would allow samples of the word population to be adequately drawn. The children could manipulate the dots and sticks, a task well within the repertoire of a five-year old, and no complex explanations would be needed.

Further possible subgroupings were explored in this group:

Subgroup I, single elements:

O dots   I I I sticks

Subgroup II, double elements:

a) dots/stick   b)stick / stick

a b d   v t x

Subgroup III, triple elements:

a) long stick   b) short sticks

k   w z

Since more than two targets can be searched for at the same time (Gibson and Yonas, 1962) even by young children, the "dot and stick" input for

a

can be quickly matched against the parent population *a p q b d* or their abstract rules. If however the child has to find *p*, then more cues have to be remembered for the matching process.

1. "Double-element," dot and stick pattern will take subject to subgroup 2a.

2. "Long stick" will cause him to reject '*a*' and be left with *p q d b*.

3. "Below" will cause him to reject *d* and *b*.

4. "Stick before," will cause him to reject *q* and find *p*.

This implies that there are four abstract rules needed to code *p* (*b q* and *d*). On examination of the other letters it can be seen that at the most two rules are required to name them. This accounts for the difficulties children have with these letters for their memories are limited to

a span of four units *on average* at four and a half years (Wechsler, 1949). McLaughlin (1963) argues that the level of a child's intellectual operation is determined by his memory span, four units being necessary for preoperational performance, six units for concrete, and eight for formal operations. It is interesting to note that the threshold of four units is also a necessary basis for beginning reading.

A Visual Pattern Recognition Test for Prereading Skills and a series of training materials to teach the coding rules were constructed and tested on the basis of these principles. Three equivalent forms of the VPR test consisted of:

Subtest IA: Eight-page booklet of coloured dot patterns (5 minutes)
Subtest 1B: Five-page booklet of dot and stick patterns (5 minutes)
Practice sheet: Letter discrimination
Subtest 1C: Nonsense word discrimination test (2 minutes)
Subtest 1D: Selected words, discrimination test (3 minutes)

The training materials consisted of:

1. Two five-page booklets of coloured dot patterns
2. Two five-page booklets of black dots and sticks patterns
3. Four sets of nonsense word jigsaws and templates cut according to coding rules and based on Allan's findings (1965).

The children manipulated sticks and dots in response to the printed patterns.

The subsequent researches showed a significant improvement in the reading performance (word recognition) of the group of five year olds trained with the pattern recognition materials and a similar improvement was found in a replication study.

Since transfer of training can be shown to occur from the pattern recognition training materials to the reading performance measured by the teacher when the rules are taught in abstract fashion using controlled materials, then reading performance will be accelerated when relevant training materials are presented—

relevant in the sense that the dots and jigsaws relate to the words in the first readers of the reading scheme. Such materials have already been prepared and are being tried out with success.

The final form and presentation of the Visual Pattern Recognition test were established in a series of pilot studies prior to the main research, and in all, 146 children between the ages of 4 years 6 months and 5 years 6 months were tested (mean ages 5 years 0 months). From the test scores Perceptual Readinesss Quotients (PRQs) were derived, along with a thirty-point diagnostic schedule for analysing particular children's learning difficulties.

The children's reading performance (word recognition—WR) was assessed in the third week of school by their class teacher using flash cards to find how many of the words in the first reading books they could recognise. This was of course not always a highly reliable system because of attenuation problems, but did form part of the usual pattern of assessment and proved to be highly reliable with experienced teachers.

The training time for each subject was half an hour a week. The subjects were tested by the teacher on WR and by the researcher on VPR before and after the four weeks training. There were one experimental and two control groups. The second group acted as a control for the Hawthorne effect (beneficial effect of a new procedure per se) known to operate in such experiments. Results are indicated in the accompanying graph.

The children's performance on the pattern recognition test (PR) was scored and the two scores (WR and PR) tested to find the degree of correlation. A validity estimate such as this is found to be .53 (or 27 percent predictive capacity) for the Harrison-Stroud Reading Readiness Profiles.

The findings for VPR/WR were very interesting for they indicated a predictive capacity of well over 50 percent (r_s = .64*** for girls; r_s = .73*** for boys; N = 34) and in the replication study (r_s = .73*** for girls, N = 45). The correlations rise to over 72 percent when age is held constant and reach over 80 percent (.90) when the teacher is experienced in the teaching of reading. Social class and intelligence did not cause the scores to vary significantly.

One feature of the replication study was very marked—the correlation between PR/WR for boys (N = 42) was very slight (r_s = .14), quite different from previous findings. The explanation for this was found in the changed entry procedures to the classes which did not affect the girls but had a marked effect on the behaviour of the boys. In this study, ninety children were taken into the five reception classes all at once instead of the usual procedure of taking thirty to thirty-five at the beginning of each term. The boys took longer to adjust to the more formal methods of teaching which the teacher had to use at times with such a large group. Various groups of children were left more to their own devices than was usual, and the boys were not able to have as much individual attention as they normally need in order to settle, thus their performance on the tests was distractible, idiosyncratic, and impressionistic, they had not acquired the earliest learning skills and showed 12-25 errors on the tests and a high count on the diagnostic schedule (+10 items).

There was a highly significant improvement in the scores of the experimental group over the control groups (p <.01) and no significant differences between the two control groups. Girls' reading performance (WR) was significantly better than boys' (p <.05), a well-established finding in other researches. Similar findings were found with respect to the VPR scores. Total scores on the VPR test were normally distributed (N = 146). These were converted to Perceptual Readiness Quotients and it was found that the PRQ of boys was significantly lower than that of girls at the age of 5 years 0 months, showing a difference of nine PRQ points.

The Pattern Recognition Test battery with its three equivalent forms is a useful diagnostic tool to find the child's readiness quotient in comparison with others in the same class and allows a full diagnosis of thirty types of errors that the child may be making. Once this diagnosis has been made, a programme of training may be instituted using the materials according to the special diagnostic and training schedules. These techniques make for a more efficient and effective use of the teacher's time in teacher-child interaction and do not demand the attention of the teacher throughout the exercise. Teachers in one of the pilot studies gave training to matched groups of subjects as effectively as the experimenter so that there was no significant difference between their scores. Thus there is no doubt that with guidance a teacher can successfully use the scheme effectively.

The Pattern Recognition Tests may also be used as a prediction of reading readiness and reading performance in its early stages. Although correlational values have varied because of constant errors in the word recognition scores on specified occasions, the consistent value when these factors are taken into account is a coefficient of $+.73$ ($N = 75$, $p < .001$). When age is held constant this value rises to $r_s = +.85$. Teachers who are experienced in the teaching of reading cause the correlation to rise even higher because of their more accurate assessment of children's reading attainment in the early stages and their more systematic approach to the teaching of reading, ($r_s = .90$).

The early gains of the experimental groups were found to persist even after a six month interval and so the tentative conclusion is drawn that a useful set of basic tools for the teaching of reading has been constructed. These tools are concrete in nature and most suitable for children in the intellectual preoperational stage.

REFERENCES

Allan, M.D. "Training in Perceptual Skills." Paper presented to the British Association. *Advancement of Science,* vol. 4, (1965).

Attneave, F. "Transfer of Experience with Class Schemes to Identification Learning of Patterns and Shapes." *Journal of Experimental Psychology,* vol. 54, no. 2 (1957), pp. 81–88.

Attneave, F. and M.D. Arnoult. "The Quantitative Study of Shape and Pattern Perception." *Psychological Bulletin,* vol. 53, no. 6 (1956), pp. 452–71.

Bryant, P.E. "Cognitive Development." *British Medical Bulletin,* vol. 27, no. 3 (1971).

Gibson, E.J. *Principles of Perceptual Learning and Development.* New York, New York: Appleton Century Crofts, 1969.

Gibson, E.J., J. Gibson, A.D. Pick and H. Osser. "Developmental Study of the Discrimination of Letter-like Forms." *Journal of Comparative Physiological Psychology,* vol. 55 (1962), pp. 897–906.

Gibson, E. and A. Yonas. "A Develop-

Mean improvement in reading grades

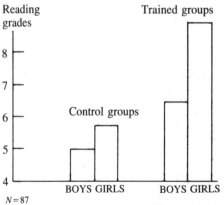

$N = 87$
(Grades from four onwards are actually different readers in a graded scheme.)

mental Study of Visual Behaviour." *Perception and Psychophysics*, vol. 1 (1962), pp. 169–71.

Gibson, J. "The Problem of Temporal Order in Stimulation and Perception." *Journal of Psychology*, vol. 62 (1966), pp. 141–49.

Gregory, R.L. *Eye and Brain*. London, England: George Weidenfold & Nicolson, Ltd., 1962.

Hershenson, L. "Development of Perception of Form." *Psychological Bulletin*, vol. 67 (1967).

Hershenson, L. "Visual Discrimination of the Human Newborn." *Dissertation Abstracts*, vol. 26 (1965), p. 1793.

Hubel, D.H. and T.N. Wiesel. "Receptive Fields, Binocular Interaction and Functional Architecture in the Cat's Visual Cortex." *Journal of Physiology*, vol. 160 (1962), pp. 105–54.

Lewis, M. and S. Goldberg. "The Acquisition and Violation of Expectancy: An Experimental Paradigm." *Journal of Experimental Child Psychology*, vol. 7 (1969), pp. 70–80.

McLaughlin, G.H. "Psycho-Logic: A Possible Alternative to Piaget's Formulation." *British Journal of Educational Psychology*, vol. 33 (1963), pp. 61–67.

Miller, G.A. "The Magical Number Seven, Plus or Minus Two: Some Limits on Our Capacity for Processing Information." *Psychological Review*, vol. 63, no. 2 (1956), pp. 81–97.

Morrell, F. "Electrical Signs of Sensory Coding." *The Neurosciences: A Study Program*. New York, N.Y.: Rockefeller University Press, 1967.

Pick, A.D. "Improvement of Visual and Tactual Form Discrimination." *Journal of Experimental Psychology*, vol. 69 (1965), pp. 331–39.

Smith, P.A. and R.W. Marx. "Some Cautions on the Use of the Frostig Test." *Journal of Learning Disabilities*, vol. 5, no. 6 (1972) pp. 357–62.

Sutherland, N.S. "Outlines of a Theory of Visual Pattern Recognition in Animals and Man." *Animal Discrimination Learning*, R.M. Gilbert and N.S. Sutherland, Eds. New York, N.Y. and London, England: Academic Press, 1969.

Weschler, D. *Weschler Intelligence Scale for Children*. New York, N.Y.: Psychological Corporation, 1949.

Wilcox, B.M. "Visual Preferences of Human Infants for Representations of the Human Face." *Journal of Experimental Child Psychology*, vol. 7 (1969), pp. 10–20.

Witty, P. and D. Kopel "Factors Associated with the Actiology of Reading Disability." *Journal of Educational Research*, vol. 29 (1936), pp. 449–59.

107

Auditory Analysis Training with Prereaders

JEROME ROSNER

The close relationship between children's primary grade reading achievement and their auditory perceptual skills continues to be recognized and documented (Wepman, 1964; Bateman, 1968; Zigmond, 1969; Rosner and Simon, 1971; Robinson, 1972). For example, I (1973) recently reported correlations between first graders' beginning-of-year auditory analysis skills and their end-of-year reading achievement subtest scores (Stanford Achievement Test, 1964) that range from .50 to .65, depending upon specific subtest. In addition to these correlational studies, there is one report in which I showed that the inclusion of auditory analysis training in a first grade reading program resulted in significantly better reading achievement for those children who received the training and whose entering auditory analysis skills had been substandard (1971).

The term "auditory analysis," as used here, refers to the resolution of spoken words into their phonemic elements. Hence, the goal of auditory analysis training is to teach the child a process for identifying the acoustical elements of the reading-spelling code as heard in the context of spoken language. As the goal is achieved, two basic concepts become accessible to the child: 1) certain phonemes differ when they are heard as isolated sounds in contrast to when they are heard in a spoken word—for example, the /b/ sound in isolation is not the same as the /b/ sound in the word "bat"; 2) the phonemic elements in a word have a specific temporal organization—that is,

the blended sounds of a spoken word occur in a precise sequence, from first phoneme to last.

It is obvious to most reading teachers that their students must have some competence in recognizing printed letters, both in isolation and in the context of a word, as well as in perceiving the spatial organization of letters in a printed word—that one letter is first, and that it is followed by others in a certain order. Indeed, teachers generally have little difficulty in familiarizing their students with the visual symbols to the level described above, nor do they lack methods for determining when these basic competencies have been acquired.

A similar competence in dealing with verbal sounds, though perhaps not so obvious, is equally important. As I stated elsewhere:

Learning to read, regardless of instructional system, requires the transformation of visual symbols into verbal language, be it audible or covert. . . . Ultimately, no matter what instructional system is used, the child must learn to associate the basic coding units of reading—the graphemes and their phonemes—if he is to be freed from the necessity of memorizing the visual construction and associated blended sounds of each word in his reading vocabulary. (1973, p. 60)

Relatively few programs are available for familiarizing children with phonemes to the level that can be achieved with letters, and few instruments are available for determining when adequate competence has been achieved. Testing a child's auditory discrimination skills, though useful, falls short of the criteria defined above.

The purpose of this study was to investigate the feasibility of teaching auditory analysis skills to prereaders—four-

From *The Reading Teacher*, Vol. 27, No. 4 (January 1974). Reprinted with permission of the International Reading Association and Jerome Rosner.

year-old preschool children—using the same training program that was used with older children in prior studies; a program that explicitly states the goals of instruction and provides valid tests to determine their attainment. As already noted, auditory analysis training has been shown to be effective with beginning readers. It was reasoned that it is desirable for children to learn auditory analysis skills prior to reading instruction, if only because they would then have more time to become familiar with the acoustical elements of the reading-spelling code before being expected to associate the sounds to printed symbols. The question of this study, then, was merely: to what extent can auditory analysis skills be taught to four-year-old children? Inasmuch as the children included in this study will not enter into a reading instruction program until they are in first grade, no attempt was made to assess the transfer effects of the training on reading achievement.

Method

Subjects. The subjects in this study were from two public schools. The preschool children (mean age in September = fifty months) were enrolled in an innercity public school (N = 26). One group of kindergarten children (mean age in September = sixty-four months) was enrolled in the same innercity school (N = 62). The other group of kindergarten children (mean age in September = sixty-three months) was enrolled in a school located in a middle class suburb of Pittsburgh, Pennsylvania (N = 57).

Procedure. The auditory analysis testing and training program used in this study is one component of the Perceptual Skills Curriculum (Rosner, 1972), a product of the Learning Research and Development Center at the University of Pittsburgh. The general goal of the auditory component of the Curriculum is to teach those skills in analyzing spoken words into their component parts—words

within phrases, then, syllables within words; ultimately, phonemes within increasingly complex contexts. The program is comprised of a number of inter-related behavioral objectives, instructional goals that are organized into levels and each level into a varying number of units, according to their relative difficulty. There is a criterion-referenced test for each objective, each test asking the question: "Can the child demonstrate mastery of this particular skill?" If he can, it indicates that he has also mastered all of the less difficult objectives in that particular sequence; he need not be tested in those. As such, the tests enable the teacher to "place" the child—determine how much he already knows, what yet remains to be learned and, especially important, what specific skill is to be learned next.

In addition to the tests, a number of teaching activities have been designed to aid the child in mastering each of the objectives. Thus, the teacher has available a variety of ways to teach the child the next objective within the hierarchical structure, and a test to determine when he has mastered it. The children are tested individually and each child receives an assignment based upon his own needs.

The auditory program consists of thirty-three objectives, organized into eight levels. The levels of the program are based on the complexity of the acoustical patterns with which the child must deal. The variables which affect complexity are: 1) the size of the unit of analysis (for example, word, syllable, single phoneme); 2) the complexity of the context in which the sound is embedded (part of a consonant blend versus a single consonant followed by a vowel); and 3) the relative position of the sound within the word (beginning, final, or medial).

Listed below are the terminal objectives for the eight levels:

Level A. Given a series of claps, ranging from one to four, reproduce the clapping pattern.

Level B. Given a spoken phrase of numerals, "write" the phrase, using a horizontal dash (drawn from left to right) to represent each numeral and "read" aloud any dash on request.

Level C. Given a series of spoken words followed by the same series from which one word has been omitted, state the omitted word. (For example, "Say *I see you.*"; Now say *I see.*"; "Which word did we forget to say that time?")

Level D. Given a spoken two-syllable compound word, restate the word omitting a designated syllable ("Say *cowboy.*"; "Now say it again, but don't say *boy.*"

Level E. Given a spoken three-syllable word, restate the word omitting a designated syllable. ("Say *carpenter.*"; "Now say it again, but don't say *car.*")

Level F. Given a spoken word, repeat the word omitting its initial consonant sound. ("Say *bat.*"; "Now say it again, but don't say /b/.")

Level G. Given a spoken word, substitute one beginning or ending sound for another. ("Say *meat.*"; "Now say it again, but instead of /t/, say /n/."; or "Instead of /m/, say /f/.")

Level H. Given a spoken word containing a consonant blend, substitute one consonant sound for another. "Say *slip.*"; "Now say it again, but instead of /s/, say /f/."; or "Instead of /l/, say /k/.")

The other objectives in each level define behaviors which have been shown to facilitate acquisition of the terminal behaviors described above. (A complete listing of objectives is available in Rosner, 1972.)

All of the children were initially tested in September, at the onset of the school year (T-1), in order to determine the number of objectives that they had already mastered. The curriculum was used throughout the year by the teachers of the innercity preschool group and the suburban kindergarten group as part of their regular classroom program. Final testing was conducted in May (T-2) of the same academic year. All testing at T-1 and T-2 was done by LRDC research assistants, not by the teachers. The reported scores indicate the number of objectives mastered within the auditory structure at each of the two testings. A score of:

3 indicates completion of Level A,
8 indicates completion of Level B,
12 indicates completion of level C,
17 indicates completion of Level D,
22 indicates completion of Level E,
25 indicates completion of Level F,
29 indicates completion of Level G,
33 indicates completion of Level H.

All three groups were tested at the beginning (T-1) and at the end (T-2) of the school year. The intent was to compare the auditory analysis skills of the innercity preschool group *at the end of their school year* with the skills that the older, innercity and suburban kindergarten control groups had shown *at the beginning of their school year*. If bias was present, it logically would be in favor of the two control groups in that their mean ages at the beginning of the school year (T-1) were approximately four to five months greater than the mean age of the experimental group at the end of their school year (T-2).

Results

The Table shows the mean number of objectives mastered by the one experimental *(Ex)* and the two control *(C)* groups at both T-1 and T-2, and the statistical differences between those means.

Comparisons between Group *Ex* and Innercity Group *C*. It is evident that greater changes occurred within the preschool group *(Ex)* than within the older kindergarten group *(C)*. At T-1, the mean number of objectives mastered by the *Ex* group was 2.72 (SD = 2.9), while the mean number of objectives mastered by the *C* group was 10.06 (SD = 5.9). The difference between these two means is highly significant (t = −6.99; df = 93; p < .001) in favor of group *C*. At T-2, the mean number of objectives mastered by group *Ex* was

Mean number of auditory objectives mastered by experimental (preschool) and the two control (kindergarten) groups

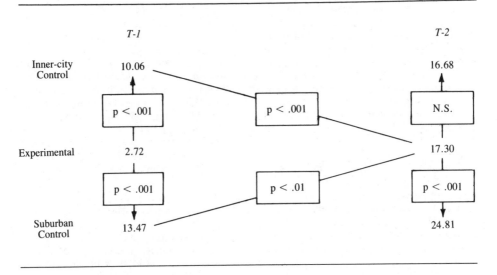

17.30 (SD = 3.0). In accordance with the design of this study, the T-2 mean was compared to the T-1 outcomes of the group C. In other words, the auditory skills of the trained (Ex) children (fifty-eight months of age) were compared with non-trained (C) children (sixty-two months of age) from the same neighborhood. The difference between these two means is once again significant (t = 5.59; df = 86; p < .001), but this time it is clearly in favor of the trained (Ex) group. A final comparison is possible between the T-2 measures of both the Ex and C groups. Despite the age difference between groups (Group C is approximately one year older), there is no significant statistical difference between these two means (T = 0.65; df = 86; p = ns); in fact, what advantage there is between means is with group Ex.

Comparisons between Group Ex and Suburban Group C. At T-1, the mean number of objectives mastered by group Ex (X = 2.72; SD = 2.9) was appreciably less than the mean number mastered by the suburban group C (X = 13.47;

SD = 7.7). The difference between these two means is highly significant (t = −7.90; df = 88; p < .001) in favor of group C. At T-2, the mean number of objectives mastered by group Ex was 17.30 (SD = 3.0). As described above, this was compared with the T-1 outcomes of group C (Recall that at T-2, group Ex was still four months younger than group C had been at T-1). As was the case with the innercity C group, the difference between these two means is again significant (t = 2.42; df = 81; p < .01) and again the favor now belongs to the younger Ex group. The third comparison, between the T-2 means of groups Ex and C, was also conducted. Here, the lead held by the older group (C) at T-1 is continued at T-2 (t = −6.23; df = 81; p < .001). This, however, is not surprising in that, as stated above, the suburban group C, once T-1 testing was completed, participated in the same training program as group Ex.

The data clearly indicate that for the children included in this study, auditory analysis skills can be taught to p30readers—at least as young as four-year-olds living in an innercity neighborhood.

The effects of the training with this group, as reflected in reading achievement, cannot yet be assessed; this information will not be available until the preschool group *(Ex)* completes first grade and participates in standardized achievement testing. However, the data from other studies, cited above, support optimistic projections.

Many children encounter difficulty in learning to read. There is evidence to suggest that at least one contributing problem is an insufficient familiarity with certain aspects of the phonemic elements of the reading-spelling code. This paper supports the argument that it is feasible to teach auditory analysis skills well in advance of reading instruction, thus dealing effectively with at least one aptitude that is closely related to reading achievement.

REFERENCES

Bateman, B. "The Efficacy of an Auditory and a Visual Method of First Grade Reading Instruction with Auditory and Visual Learners. *Perception and Reading.* Ed. H. K. Smith, vol. 12, part 4. Newark, Delaware: International Reading Association, 1968, pp. 105–112.

Robinson, H. M. "Visual and Auditory Modalities Related to Methods for Beginning Reading." *Reading Research Quarterly,* vol. 8. no. 3 (1972), pp. 7–39.

Rosner, J. *Phonic Analysis Training and Beginning Reading Skills.* Proceedings of the APA 79th Annual Convention, 1971, pp. 533–34. (Also LRDC Publication 1971/19).

Rosner, J. *The Development and Validation of an Individualized Perceptual Skills Curriculum.* Pittsburgh: Learning Research and Development Center, University of Pittsburgh, 1972. (Publication 1972/7).

Rosner, J. "Language Arts and Arithmetic Achievement, and Specifically Related Perceptual Skills." *American Educational Research Journal,* vol. 10, no. 1 (1973), pp. 59–68.

Rosner, J., and D. Simon. *The Auditory Analysis Test: An initial report.* Pittsburgh: Learning Research and Development Center, University of Pittsburgh, 1971. (Also published in the *Journal of Learning Disabilities,* 1971, 4 (7), pp. 384–92.

Stanford Achievement Test. New York: Harcourt, Brace, & World, 1964.

Wepman, J. "The Perceptual Basis for Learning." *Meeting Individual Differences.* H. Robinson, Ed. Supplementary Educational Monograph No. 94. Chicago: University of Chicago Press, 1964, pp. 25–33.

Zigmond, N. K. "Auditory Processes in Children with Learning Disabilities." *Learning Disabilities: Introduction to Education and Medical Management,* L. Tarnapoll, Ed. Springfield, Illinois: C. C. Thomas, 1969.

Development of Pre-Reading Skills in an Experimental Kindergarten Program

JO M. STANCHFIELD

Basic to the current approaches in teaching reading is the assumption that success in beginning reading is crucial and that reading programs in the primary grades must be organized to assure this success. Evidence of the importance of achievement in initial reading instruction is the large number of research studies designed to find more effective ways of teaching beginning reading.

Further evidence of the emphasis on early stages of reading is found in the relatively recent number of research projects in reading readiness. *Sesame Street,* through the powerful teaching medium of television, has greatly increased the interest of the nation in pre-reading skills. This innovative program accepts the premise that the pre-kindergarten years are a period of substantial and significant intellectual development (Palmer, 1969). It has adopted the techniques and approaches of commercial television to help preschoolers develop skills necessary to a successful start in formal reading instruction.

Recent Projects in Reading Readiness

An increasing number of authorities in early childhood education have recognized that children's education can, and should, begin long before the traditional age of five or six. Many recent studies in readiness have been conducted with children of three or four in a structured learning situation. In research reported

by Karnes in May, 1968, a traditional nursery school program was compared with a highly structured program focused on specific learning tasks designed to promote language and cognitive development. Four-year-olds were studied in order that follow-up evaluation could be coordinated with public schools in kindergarten. At the end of the experimental period, results of the Metropolitan Readiness Test showed superior performance by the experimental group in both reading readiness and numbers readiness. The University of Illinois researchers concluded that their findings illustrated the effectiveness of teaching specific content as well as school readiness.

A four-year study conducted in New York State by di Lorenzo and Salter (1968) studied the effectiveness of an academic year preschool program for the disadvantaged on a longitudinal basis, pre-kindergarten through second grade. The project encompassed eight school districts with a basic curriculum approach which emphasized language and cognitive development, but which varied in comprehensiveness and methods of reading readiness instruction. At the end of the first two years of the study, it was found that the pre-kindergarten experience had proven beneficial for the subjects and that the most effective pre-kindergarten programs were those with the most specific structured cognitive activities.

Much of the work in reading readiness has been done in the area of the culturally and economically deprived because these children lack the background with which middle or upper class children begin their formal education. Traditional preschool classes are not adequate to

From *The Reading Teacher*, Vol. 24, No. 8 (May 1971). Reprinted with permission of the International Reading Association and Jo M. Stanchfield.

prepare the disadvantaged child to compete with children of more privileged environments. Thus the gains achieved by disadvantaged children in structured reading readiness programs contrast significantly with results of a California study by Prendergast (1969), comparing the development of prereading skills in three groups of upper-middle class children; a conventional day nursery class, a Montessori preschool class, and a non-nursery school group. The conventional school offered common enrichment experiences, while the Montessori class provided a structured program to develop skills through the use of special methods and materials. At the end of seven months, children were compared on development of perceptual motor skills and receptive language. In most areas evaluated, no significant differences were found among the three groups. The researcher attributed this primarily to the fact that the upper-middle class environment encouraged the development of reading readiness skills without nursery school experience.

At the kindergarten level, investigators at the University of Iowa studied the effectiveness of the Frostig perceptual motor method in developing reading readiness among 108 disadvantaged kindergarten children. The findings of approximately eight months of training in sensorimotor and visual perceptual exercises were reported by Alley (1968) in *Exceptional Children*. Results, as measured by the *Marianne Frostig Developmental Test of Visual Perception* and *The Metropolitan Reading Readiness Test*, Form A, disclosed significant differences in favor of the experimental group.

The "nature vs. nurture" controversy was considered by Bernabei (1967) in developing a reading readiness program in the Bucks County, Pennsylvania, schools. Do children grow into readiness, or is this rather a function of training and experience? Bernabei saw no immediate resolution of the controversy and undertook an interim, eclectic approach—an Extended Reading Readiness

Program organized to cover a longer period of time than the standard kindergarten treatment. The program devised pupil learning experiences and developed materials related to a curriculum of readiness skills, including pre-reading and mathematics. An evaluation of the program after one year indicated significant differences in these skills between the interim class and the normal class.

Background and Objectives of the Research

Over the past seven years, the author has been engaged in research in the Los Angeles City Schools with approximately 500 first-grade children each year of varying ethnic and socio-economic backgrounds. The purpose of the research has been to experiment with a variety of materials and methods in teaching beginning reading to determine the effect upon the reading achievement of first-grade children. During these years, it has become increasingly apparent to the author, the teachers, and the administrators in the series of studies that there were certain pre-reading skills necessary for children to succeed in reading. Through experimentation it was found that many children were not able to acquire proficiency in the reading readiness skills in the time which could be allotted in the first grade. With this knowledge and with that from other reading readiness studies, the writer worked with teachers and administrators to develop a research design to teach these skills in a sequential, developmental order in six major areas: 1] listening for comprehension of content; 2] listening for auditory discrimination; 3] visual discrimination skills; 4] oral language skills; 5] motor-perceptual skills; 6] sound-symbol correspondence skills.

Through the process of grouping and the use of independent activities, the teacher taught specific lessons in the six areas to small groups of children. The skills of each lesson were developed in detail in the teacher's manual. These skills were taught and retaught, with sufficient practice periods, until an adequate level of proficiency was attained by the children. The objective of the study was to determine whether children taught pre-reading skills in a structured program would attain significantly higher scores on a standardized test of reading readiness skills than those children who had not been involved in such a program.

Procedures, Materials, Techniques

For the experimental program, seventeen schools were selected to provide a cross-section of socio-economic levels representing ethnic categories of black, Mexican-American, and other white children. Each experimental school was matched with a control school of similar ethnic origins, academic achievement, and socio-economic backgrounds. The teachers in both the experimental and control schools were randomly selected.

The teachers in the experimental program were given a teacher's guide for the reading readiness lessons and materials to implement their teaching. The specific pre-reading skills were taught in the language-arts block of time in the kindergarten program. During the fall semester of the school year, these teachers met each week after school at a designated school building to receive additional materials and to discuss the use of these materials. At these workshop-type meetings, the teachers also made certain kinds of instructional aids, such as puppets and flannelboard activities, from patterns provided for them. The teachers in the control schools followed the regular curriculum which they had been previously teaching.

The teaching philosophy of the program was established upon the premise that the skills in the reading process are the same on the pre-reading level as at the highest stage of reading development. The chief differences are those of degree and refinement. Therefore the materials and techniques used in the research were developed to parallel the

formal reading instruction which the children would receive as they progressed through the primary grades. Various materials were provided for the program.

In the teacher's manual, lesson plans were classified according to the six major areas of pre-reading skills, with the purpose of each lesson an emphasis upon improving one of these skills. Each lesson plan included six sections: 1] Purpose; 2] Preparation; 3] Presentation; 4] Evaluation in Terms of the Purpose; 5] Pupil Practice Materials; 6] Additional Experiences. "Preparation" included materials needed in the presentation of the lesson. "Evaluation" established a quick check of what the children learned in terms of the purpose of the lesson. "Pupil Practice Materials" provided independent follow-up exercises for reinforcement of the skills taught in the lesson. At the close of the lesson, "Additional Experiences" suggested activities related to the same skill as the one for which the specific plan was given.

Picture cards were used in a variety of ways: to stimulate imagination, to help in noting details, for picture reading, and for story telling. They served, too, as inspiration for painting, as motivation for dramatic play, and as stimulation for creative language, including stories dictated to the teacher.

The large flannelboard and pocket chart were big enough to be seen by a group of children. They were used by either the teacher or a child. The flannelboard held cut-outs of story characters, objects, letters, and numbers. The pocket chart served as another illustrative aid.

There were small flannelboards, pocket charts, and chalkboards for each child in a group. Small groups were formed on the basis of specific needs. By having individual manipulative materials for each child in the group, the teacher made sure that every child was involved in the activity and learning, and had instant feedback on individual progress.

Cut-outs of the characters and objects from a story were used on the large flannelboard to illustrate a story when telling or retelling it. Other cut-outs were used in teaching about 1] shape, size, and color; 2] sight-sound-symbol correspondence, and 3] numerals and simple number concepts.

Children are apt to lose much of their self-consciousness when they use hand puppets. They are intent upon manipulating the puppet appropriately and actually become the puppet character. In the experimental program, puppets were used to motivate oral language, both for retelling a story and for creating stories or conversation.

The books for this program were chosen primarily because of their universal appeal to four, five, and six-year-olds. Other criteria the books met were those of high literary quality, worthwhile illustrations, and appropriate format. The collection comprised a variety of categories, including Mother Goose, poetry, fairy or folk tales, animal stories, an ABC book, and song books.

Each phoneme box contained small objects, most of whose names began with one of the consonants. In the same box were a few objects whose names began with a different consonant. Children said the names of the objects and decided which ones started like a certain word from a preprimer.

An overview of the reading readiness program is shown in the following outline which lists the six major skills and the teaching techniques employed in developing them:

I. *Listening for comprehension of content.*

The ability to listen too often is taken for granted and therefore is seldom taught specifically. However, efficient listening must be learned and practiced. Because it is so important to speech, language, and reading, special attention was given to this area in the research program. The purpose of the lessons in this part of the experimental curriculum centered around listening for pleasure and relaxation, compre-

hending what someone read or said, memorizing, remembering, and following directions. The children listened to poems, songs, and recordings with an awareness of mood; they listened as the teacher read or told a story to answer directed questions or to recall and tell parts of the story; they listened to and followed simple, and later, more complex directions.

II. *Listening for auditory discrimination and development.*

As a prelude to the aural discrimination of words and word elements, the children had many directed listening experiences. After they learned to listen to the teacher, to each other, to music, and to sounds in their environment, the teacher began the development of the concepts of volume, pitch, direction, duration, sequence, accent, tempo, repetition and contrast, and distance. The teacher used a variety of recordings, tonal instruments, poems, jingles, and rhythms to develop these concepts.

III. *Visual discrimination and development.*

Observing and interpreting content. The interpretation of pictures and picture stories helped children to develop such skills as arranging items in sequence, making inferences, predicting outcomes, getting the main idea, and noting relevant details. Prior to this part of the program, the teachers organized school excursions and walking trips to give children opportunities to observe and become acquainted with the world beyond their immediate neighborhood. These firsthand experiences helped the children to understand concepts represented in the pictures and picture stories which otherwise might have had no meaning.

Visual imagery. Visual projection, or recognition of an object from its description, was developed through such techniques as having the children guess the answers to riddles about familiar objects, paint pictures from vivid descriptions, or illustrate stories. Visual memory was practiced by the children in a variety of simple exercises, such as describing objects or scenes from memory or by locating, with eyes shut, familiar objects in the room.

Visual discrimination. The children were taught to note gross likenesses and differences before they made finer discriminations. Picture-matching games and the comparing and contrasting of pictures, objects, and geometric forms were used to help the children make discriminations of size, shape, position, color, and small details. The development of these concepts laid a foundation for the further study of visual skills.

IV. *Oral language skills.*

The teachers provided experience in several areas related to oral expression: the ability to express ideas understandably to others; the ability to speak with the expression that conveys ideas, and with pleasing voice quality; the use of complete and well-structured sentences; the expansion of speaking and understanding vocabularies; the improvement of pronunciation and diction. Varied and stimulating opportunities were provided for practice in oral expression. These ranged from spontaneous discussion of personal experiences to participation in creative story telling, recitation of poems, or choral speaking.

V. *Motor-perceptual development.*

Through directed lessons, the children learned to coordinate vision and movement, to become aware of and to manipulate the parts of their bodies, and to perceive positions of objects in relation to themselves. They learned body control through exercises, games, dances, and the interpretation of music. Later, opportunities for the development of finer motor coordination were provided through activities in construction, cutting, pasting, tracing,

and coloring. Eventually the children were ready for paper and pencil exercises that further refined hand-eye coordination.

VI. *Sound-symbol correspondence.*

In the experimental classes, sound-symbol correspondence was developed on levels of increasing difficulty. Practice was given to reinforce the learning of the sounds of the alphabet letters. Aural and visual recognition, as well as letter discrimination, were stressed by association of pure letter sounds with the corresponding names and symbols, using objects and pictures. In the last step in the development of this skill, the children learned to write the various letters of the alphabet in manuscript form. The ability to count from one to ten was presented in the same sequence as letter recognition.

Results

The Murphy-Durrell Reading Readiness Analysis was given to the seventeen experimental classes and the seventeen control classes at the end of the school year. With the data from this standardized test, a three-way analysis of variance was performed with sex, experimental-control, and ethnic group as the main effects. The scores from the five tests of the Murphy-Durrell Analysis were studied separately and in total. When the F-test was significant, it was followed by t tests between the groups.

Table 1 shows that the experimental group achieved a higher score than was achieved by the control group in the total test and also in all of the individual parts of the test.

Table 2 indicates that the girls as a group achieved higher scores than the boys in the total test as well as in the individual parts of the test. However, this difference might have been due to chance in the first parts of the phoneme and letter names sections of the test.

Table 3 indicates that the children in the "other white" group scored higher on the total test and in all individual parts of the test than did the Mexican-American and the black children. While the Mexican-Americans achieved a higher over-all average than the black children, the latter group was slightly higher in both parts of the Letter Names Test.

Table 4 shows the means for the total test separated according to the three main effects: experimental-control, sex, and ethnic group. Table 5 gives the analysis of co-variance for these three main effects and their possible combinations. In this analysis, a test was made to see if the means shown in Tables 1, 2, 3, and 4 were significantly different. It was found that all three main effects showed significant differences.

The experimental groups achieved significantly higher scores than the control groups. The girls, as a group, achieved significantly better than the boys in the study. The "other white" group achieved significantly higher scores than the Mexican-American and the black groups. It should be pointed out that the experimental Mexican-American and black groups achieved considerably higher scores than the control group of "other white."

Table 5 also shows that combinations of the various possible groupings did not produce significant additional differences. That is, although the three main effects were significant, the interactions between the groups were not significant. Kindergarten children taught in a structured, sequential program with appropriate materials achieve significantly more than those in the regular curriculum.

Table 1   **Mean scores for experimental and control groups on** *Murphy-Durrell reading readiness analysis*

Group	Phonemes Test		Letter Names Test		Learning Rate Test	Total
	Part 1	Part 2	Part 1	Part 2		
Experimental	15.92	18.57	20.51	21.71	10.80	87.50
Control	11.98	12.62	14.24	16.66	7.54	63.05

Table 2   **Mean scores by sex on** *Murphy-Durrell reading readiness analysis*

Group	Phonemes Test		Letter Names Test		Learning Rate Test	Total
	Part 1	Part 2	Part 1	Part 2		
Boys	13.72*	14.84	17.00*	18.35	8.64	72.56
Girls	14.19*	16.35	17.75*	20.01	9.70	77.99

*Differences on Phonemes Test Part 1 and Letter Names Test Part 1 not statistically significant; i.e., could be due to chance.

Table 3   **Mean scores for ethnic groups on** *Murphy-Durrell reading readiness analysis*

Group	Phonemes Test		Letter Names Test		Learning Rate Test	Total
	Part 1	Part 2	Part 1	Part 2		
Black	13.19	14.43	16.78	18.62	8.20	71.21
Mexican-American	13.45	14.91	16.57	18.45	8.87	72.24
Other White	15.21	17.45	18.78	20.49	10.43	82.38

Table 4 **Means for total score on** *Murphy-Durrell reading readiness analysis*

	Black	Mexican-American	Other White
Boys	67.68	69.37	80.64
Girls	74.73	75.11	84.12
Total	71.21	72.24	82.38
	Black	Mexican-American	Other White
Experimental	82.68	84.57	95.27
Control	59.73	59.92	69.49
Total	71.21	72.24	82.38
	Boys	Girls	Total
Experimental	86.04	88.97	87.50
Control	59.09	67.00	63.05
Total	72.56	77.99	75.28

Table 5 **Analysis of co-variance for total scores on** *Murphy-Durrell reading readiness analysis*

Source of Variation	Sum of Squares	D. F.	Mean Square	F	P
Experimental-Control	205120.56	1	205120.56	315.28	0.00
Sex	10089.19	1	10089.19	15.51	0.00
Ethnic	34876.29	2	17438.14	26.80	0.00
Exp.-Con. X Sex	2122.16	1	2122.16	3.26	0.07
Exp.-Con. X Ethnic	464.45	2	232.22	0.36	0.70
Sex X Ethnic	764.55	2	382.27	0.59	0.56
Exp.-Con. X Sex X Ethnic	714.53	2	357.27	0.55	0.58

Note: Column P gives the probability of differences occurring by chance. Normally, if P is equal to or less than .05, one can say that it would not happen by chance; i.e., it is significant.

REFERENCES

Alley, G., *et al*. Reading readiness and the Frostig training program. *Exceptional Children*, 1968, *35*, 68.

Bernabei, R. An evaluation of the interim class: an extended readiness program. Unpublished research, Bucks County, Pennsylvania Public Schools, 1967.

Di Lorenzo, L. J., and Salter, R. An evaluative study of prekindergarten programs for educationally disadvantaged children: follow-up and replication. *Exceptional Children*, 1968, *35*, 111–119.

Karnes, M. B., *et al*. Evaluation of two preschool programs for disadvantaged children: a traditional and a highly structured experimental preschool. *Exceptional Children*, 1968, *34*, 667–676.

Palmer, E. L. Can television really teach? Preschoolers watch Sesame Street series. *American Education*, 1969, *5*, 2–6.

Prendergast, R. Pre-reading skills developed in Montessori and conventional nursery schools. *Elementary School Journal*, 1969, *70*, 135–141.

How Doth My Grandson Grow—
in Reading?

EVELYN C. EVVARD

Watching my grandson grow into reading has been a delightful and enlightening experience for this teacher of reading. I found that grandparents, even miles apart, can establish a close and tender relationship with grandchildren. The bond I wrought was in writing stories about Kevin's activities as his mother related them to me by telephone and letters. As a result, the mailman and the telephone have become vital and personal parts of Kevin's life. His community has expanded to far-away, and yet miraculously close-by, places.

This is an account of Kevin's growth into reading, comfortably challenging yet unhurried—a joy to mother, Kevin and grandmother. His natural curiosity about his world has been captured in stories for his benefit.

When my daughter wrote that she had bought her 18-month-old son a set of magnetic letters and numerals, I admonished her, "Why teach letters when there are so many more interesting and needy things an 18-month-old must learn?" Back came an observation for which I had no answer: "What difference is there in learning the names of letters than in learning the names of other things?"

The plastic colored letters and numerals were attached to the refrigerator. (Incidentally, Kevin separated the letters into their color groups long before he knew the names of the colors.) When Kevin pulled off a letter, his parents named it—nothing more. Six weeks

later, his mother noticed that every time Kevin touched the letter *o* he named it. Please note than an *o* is an *o* no matter how it is turned. This consistent shape was easy to remember visually. At 20 months, he voluntarily penned *o*'s all over a sheet of paper, naming them as he wrote. He spent an hour at his self-appointed task—despite the dictum that a child's attention span is naturally short. (I suspect that a child works or plays until he or she is tired, frustrated or no longer interested. What we may be seeing in short attention-spans may be the result of outside imposed tasks alien to the child's interest.) At 22 months, Kevin knew all the letters except *v* and *f*; and these he could identify if his mother said, "Bring me the *f*."

We know that learning is in spurts—that a learner can reach a plateau and then seem unable to go on. Kevin had reached his first plateau. Learning the alphabet became an end in itself. He now used this information in his own way. He read letters on billboards, traffic signs, magazines, the books his mother read to him. He obviously loved to name letters. I'm sure Kevin gained thereby a great deal of internal satisfaction: success brought its own reward. And if the letters on the billboards did not admonish him to buy X-product, they did contain a message: "There's an *o;* there's an *s*."

Knowing the letters opened up a wonderful world to Kevin. A large part of modern life was his to enjoy. I remember this small child, still in diapers, stooping over the names of states inscribed around a fountain, happily pointing to the letters and naming them. We teachers (both professionals and mothers) must recognize that for the young

Reprinted by permission of the author and the Association for Childhood Education International, 3615 Wisconsin Avenue NW, Washington, D.C. © 1979 by the Association.

child this learning of the letters is an end in itself. It is NOT AT THIS TIME a step in the sequence of learning to read. Small children learn the names of the letters as they learn the names of other things. We don't say to them when they learn a new word, "Now use it in a sentence." We're just happy they have added a new word to their vocabulary. They should—maybe must—be given the opportunity to enjoy their knowledge in *their* way.

Learning to read has a long preparation via listening and speaking, personal experiences, developing and storing concepts and percepts. One does not learn to read in a vacuum. Kevin has been going to the library story-hour since he was 18 months old. The first time, he stayed a few seconds. He soon began to listen and now often looks forward to his trip to the library.

I began writing stories for Kevin because I made him a pair of shorts with a pocket on them. Instead of putting a toy in the pocket, I wrote a story about pockets. That was an immediate success and spurred me on. Each story was only four pages long, including the title page. The challenge in writing these stories was in using six or seven words to tell of an experience of Kevin's and to include a climax. I used words in his vocabulary, which of course are common everyday words. Where did I get my subjects? From his mother's letters and phone calls. Soon there came stories of clothing, camping, household and play activities, swimming, bathing, his dog, his baby sister. Since few words were used, the stories gave his mother and Kevin an opportunity to talk about the subjects, thus furthering their interpersonal relationships.

Some of the stories were in question form. It was then that I realized that questions, in demanding an answer, involved the reader in the printed word. The message became personal. It also gave adult and child opportunity to explore the subject further. In the story CAN KEVIN—"Can Kevin sit? Yes. Can Kevin run? Yes. Can Kevin fly? O, no!"—you can see how this ending led to a further discussion of things that can fly. The books became his favorite stories. He "read" them to me many times, but it was either by rote or else he read into the pictures his own vocabulary and syntax. If I had any idea I could teach Kevin to read the few words of the stories, I was mistaken. He was not ready.

After Kevin knew his letters, his mother taught him the alphabet song. She pointed out that knowing the names of the letters before learning the alphabet helped him to remember because he already had a mental picture of the letters. I think that we, too often, try to teach without first developing the concepts that lie behind that which we would like children to learn. I remember making a picture recipe-book for Kevin's mother when *she* was a preschooler, only to realize, when she failed to respond as I had anticipated, that I had not taught her the concept that she was to look from left to right on a single line. Ah, me!

Kevin's mother developed many pre-reading concepts through word games she played with him. He learned that a group of letters made a word when she wrote on his chalkboard "Kevin is a boy" and then erased the last word and read "Kevin is a," continuing until all were erased. She also wrote the sentence and erased only the last letter, each time reading what remained. Kevin learned that letters represent sounds.

By the time he was three and one-half years old, Kevin was ready to fly to a higher plateau. While I was reading to him, he asked about a favorite word: "Which word is 'cat'?" After I showed him the word, he pointed out two more "cat" words on the page. Kevin let us know what he wanted to learn.

My next visit with Kevin was the time of the big jump. His mother found him trying to read a book, but there were too many words he did not know. We found a number of beginning-to-read books in the library. The first five books I read to Kevin, and then he read them to me. The next ten books *he* read, not only to himself, but to his nonreading playmate—asking help with unknown words. His is a sight vocabulary; but he has some knowledge of the sounds represented by the letters, garnered by watching children's programs on television.

Kevin reads numerals. When his mother was separating a stack of newsletters into zip codes, she handed some to him saying of the last two numbers: "Put the 55s in this pile and the 57s in that pile." When he tired of the game, he went away, mother making no fuss about finishing a job. That, of course, is an aspect of incidental learning: opportunities offered to participate and learn, the child indicating when the particular experience is ended.

There is much a parent or grandparent can do to teach perceptions. Children look, but do not see; hear, but do not listen. I can say the same of adults, of course. Perception is a learned behavior. Does learning the names of the letters at an early age help in becoming visually perceptive? If a child can see small differences in lines and curves (the difference between *c* and *e,* for instance), is he becoming more keenly aware of other differences in his environment? Are these aptitudes already present in early life, ready to be nurtured and expanded? We need to think about such questions, so that we can develop the potential abilities at the most opportune time.

Parents and grandparents are the teachers of concepts. One morning Kevin's father looked down at him and said: "Hi, down there." That lovely remark, lovingly given, became the subject of a story in which Kevin explored the concepts of tall and short, big and little.

Does helping a child become acquainted with his environment—our modern world is full of letters, words and numerals—increase his curiosity about his environment? If a child, in touching an item, is asking: "What is this?" and is given the answer, are we developing curiosity behavior? I have long thought that one vital aim of education should be the perpetuation of curiosity: without it, we would still be cave men. When Kevin became curious about geometric figures, about the middle position of things, stories were written.

Lest you think that Kevin, approaching four years of age, is a bookworm, he is not. He plays with other children; works with his mother and father in garden and kitchen. He plants bulbs and counts those appearing above ground. He plays with his toys, talking to himself a great deal. He swings, rides his tricycle, shoots baskets, climbs, slides. In all he is a lovable, typical almost-four-year-old—who can read.

Though we live miles apart, I know that I have shared in Kevin's intellectual and physical growth. I have given him stories of his childhood and he has given me a deeper understanding of one child.

Using a Scale of Questions to Improve Listening Comprehension

DORIS C. CROWELL
KATHRYN H. AU

It is a common practice for preschool and primary teachers to read stories aloud to children, but this activity is seldom used to its maximum potential as an opportunity for developing cognitive and linguistic skills. The research described here tested the validity of a set of guidelines for transforming the reading aloud of stories into a program for the systematic development of comprehension skills which the child later must use in learning to read for meaning. Although the first application of these skills is to stories which the teacher reads to the child, they appear to be readily transferable to stories which are read independently (Cunningham 1975).

If training in listening comprehension is to be of benefit, it must help the child become an active processor of story information. To be sure that the child is actively processing information, the teacher should ask questions about the content of the story. Although teachers often do ask questions, they are not presented as systematically as may be desirable. According to the proposed model, comprehension questions can be ordered in terms of level of difficulty. If teachers were aware of the types of questions which children find more difficult to answer, they would be able to structure lessons by ordering the questions they ask from easy to difficult. They would also be able to guide a child's thinking through several levels of comprehension by the sequence of questions they ask. They would gain diagnostic information about a given child's level of compre-

hension from his or her answers to different types of questions, and would be able to provide appropriate instruction so that the child could improve.

As the first step in designing this program for the systematic development of listening comprehension skills, it was necessary to devise and then test a model of story comprehension based on the ordering of different types of questions along a scale from easiest to most difficult. The different types of questions which were proposed were placed along a hypothetical continuum ranging from no comprehension, through various levels of literal comprehension, up to the highest levels of inferential comprehension. It was assumed that a child who answered a question correctly at any given level would also be able to answer correctly all the questions below that level. Similarly, a child who failed to answer a given question correctly should also be unable to answer any questions above that level (Weaver and Rutherford 1974; Wheat and Edmond 1975).

While the content of a given story may have an influence on the ease with which a specific question is answered, the ranking of questions proposed here would appear to hold for a large number of children's stories.

The questions were carefully formulated so that they would be applicable to a wide range of different stories and so that they would be as passage-dependent as possible. To illustrate the latter concern, consider the following two questions:
A) What happened first?
B) How did Billy feel when Johnny teased him?
While the first question gives no clues

From *Language Arts*, Vol. 56, No. 1 (January, 1979). © 1979 by the National Council of Teachers of English. Reprinted by permission.

about what the correct response might be, it is possible with the information contained in the second to guess correctly that Billy felt unhappy.

The following is a description of the five different types of questions, from easiest to most difficult, upon which the model of story comprehension is based. Questions at the first three levels are literal, while those at the last two levels are inferential.

Level 1. Questions at this, the lowest level of comprehension, are designed to elicit from children any details of the story that can be recalled. Correct responses might include the name of a character or the description of an event in the story. In the study, the questions used were, "What was this story about?" and "Tell me about the story." Children were considered to have answered correctly if they gave any detail from the story.

Level 2. Questions at level two require children to make a simple interpretation, usually at a feeling level, which they need not be able to explain or elaborate extensively. Children may be asked to classify a story character in a stereotypic manner, for example, tell why they like that character; or they may be asked to select a favorite incident from the story. The specific questions used in the study were, "Do you like the bear? Why?"

Level 3. Questions at this level deal with the interrelationships among details or the sequence of events. A complete summary of major events is not required, but the child must be able to present any three events in the correct order or give a cause and effect relationship. The child was asked, "What happened first? Then what happened? And then what?"

Level 4. Questions at level four require children to integrate the various elements in the story into a structure not necessarily given by the story itself. In order to respond correctly they must be able to make interpretations and inferences and support them with sound reasons. Questions at this level might also call for the child to summarize the story, give the main idea, or use facts within

the story to predict its outcome and provide justification for that prediction. The question used in the study was, "How did Skipper solve the bear's problem?" If no reply was elicited the child was asked, "What was the bear's problem?

Level 5. At the highest level of the scale, the questions are intended to reveal the child's understanding of the story beyond what is actually given in the text. Such questions may call for children to relate the story to other stories or events or to change their ideas on the basis of new information. Questions at level five may also require children to use their imagination or creativity, but with the content of the story as a starting point. Specifically, the questions asked were, "Tell me another way this story could have ended." and "What else could have happened at the end of the story?"

Children are believed to be able to answer questions independently at level one before they can answer questions at level two, and so on through level five. The sequence in which skills of listening comprehension are believed to develop does not vary, but always proceeds in order from one, or no comprehension, to five. The time required for the different levels of skill to emerge, however, is probably not equal; for example, it may take much longer to progress from level three to level four than to progress from level one to level two.

Although it is generally agreed that literal questions are more easily answered than inferential or interpretive questions (Davis 1969; Feinman 1972; Rystrom 1970), it does not appear that a previous attempt has been made to validate a scale in which different types of literal and inferential questions have been ordered according to difficulty.

Method

Subjects. The subjects were twenty-five kindergarteners enrolled in a laboratory school for part-Hawaiian children from low-income, urban families. The children speak Hawaiian Islands dialect, a nonstandard form of English. Their verbal IQ scores upon entering kindergarten are lower than average although their performance scores are generally within average limits. In addition, twenty-one second grade children from the same population were tested.

Materials. A story that none of the children had heard before, "The Bear that Took Skipper's Name" (Dunn 1976) was edited to meet the requirements of the study (see Appendix). The edited story was short enough to hold the children's attention, and it had suitable characters and plot. The readability level of the story was found to be 2.1, according to the Harris-Jacobson (1975) procedure, suggesting appropriate vocabulary and syntactic complexity.

Procedure. There were two experimenters, each of whom tested half the children. The children were taken individually to a quiet room where a tape recording of the story was played for them. Immediately following the story, the experimenter asked the child the five questions representing the five levels of listening comprehension. The questions were always asked in the same order, beginning with level one and concluding with level five. The reading of the questions and the child's responses were taped for later scoring.

The tapes of the children's responses to the questions were scored independently by both experimenters. A score of zero was given for an incorrect response and a score of one for a correct response. An inter-observer reliability coefficient of .89 was obtained.

Results

The responses of the kindergarten children were used to establish the scalability of the questions. When these responses were tabulated, the pattern of scores yielded a coefficient of reproducibility of .92. Thus, the skill levels as represented by type of question do constitute a consistently ordered scale, according to Guttman's criteria (Sax 1968), and the proposed scale of listening comprehension skills was shown to be valid (see Figure 1).

Figure 1

Percent of Kindergarten Children Answering Correctly at Each Question Level

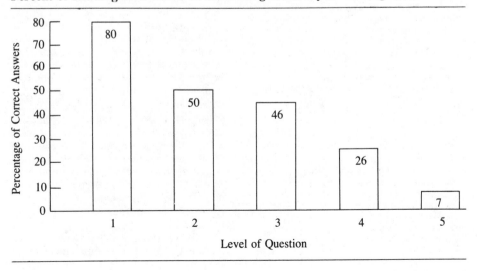

The scores obtained on the set of listening comprehension questions were also related to verbal IQ, as measured by the Wechsler Preschool and Primary Scale of Intelligence (WPPSI) for the kindergarten class. The Pearson correlation between these two sets of scores was .76 which was significant beyond the .001 level, suggesting a high level of correspondence between listening comprehension of stories and verbal ability.

It was also hypothesized that older children would have better skills in listening comprehension than younger children. To test this notion, the same procedure was used with the second grade children. As expected, older children were found to have a significantly higher degree of listening comprehension skill than younger children (second grade: $\overline{X} = 4.1$; kindergarten: $\overline{X} = 2.2$; $t = 5.44$, $p < .001$).

Individual Subject Protocols

Typical protocols of two kindergarten children, one who is functioning at an abstract, inferential level (Child 1) and one who is functioning at a literal level (Child 2) follow:

Child 1	Child 2
Question 1: What was this story about?	
The bear, the brown bear, the one that took things . . .	Skipper, I don't know.
Question 2: Did you like the bear? Why?	
(Yeah) because the bear got his own name.	Yes, because the thing stay wild.
Question 3: What happened first? Then what? Then what?	
The bear took the food and took Skipper's name and then everybody wants Skipper's name and then the bear went back and told Skipper.	Don't know.
Question 4: How did Skipper solve the bear's problem? What was the bear's problem?	
By giving him his own name. They wanted all the same name. They all wanted that name and the bear went back and told Skipper.	Toys. Q. I don't know.

Question 5: How else could this story have ended?

The bear could have been his pet.	Skipper wen give em his name. Q. I don't know.

The responses of Child 1 show clearly that he has comprehended the story at all levels reflected in the questions. Child 2, on the other hand, answered only the detail question satisfactorily. On the higher level questions, his responses were inappropriate or inaccurate.

Discussion

The scale of listening comprehension skills investigated in this study can serve as the basis for the development of a systematic program of listening comprehension. Knowledge of the different levels within the scale, as defined by different types of questions, can guide the teacher in diagnosing the level of comprehension of children and in planning lessons based on stories to be read aloud. While every child should be exposed to questions at all levels, the teacher can use questioning more systematically if questions are ordered according to level of difficulty. The series of questions presented here can be used diagnostically to determine the level of skill in listening comprehension of any given child. Once this diagnostic information is available, the teacher can provide appropriate instruction to help the child move to the next higher level of comprehension. By asking questions which are at the child's level or slightly beyond, the teacher can be more certain that the child will become an active processor of information; neither bored because the questions asked were too easy, nor discouraged because the questions are too difficult. In group instruction, the child who has adequate skills in listening comprehension is more likely to progress rapidly in reading comprehension, since he or she will have acquired a set of abilities that can be transferred to the reading task.

Although the scale provides useful guidelines for questioning, more work must be done before an adequate program of listening comprehension can be completed. One of the most important tasks will be to extend the list of questions, so that there will be a number of alternative questions at each level. With a greater number of questions available at each level, the teacher will be able to give each child more practice at the various levels of comprehension. Also, the greater the number of questions, the more likely it is that there will be questions at each level appropriate for any given story. When asking questions for diagnosis, the teacher will use ones comparable to those in the study. In active teaching situations, the information already discussed may be incorporated into the questions to guide the child to the next higher level of processing.

Another important task will be to review the stories which are most often read to young children in school in order to classify them according to the instructional purposes for which they may be best suited. For example, some stories have a very clear sequence of events, and therefore may be particularly useful in helping children to progress from level two to level three. Other stories have a central theme which is well supported throughout and would be helpful for children who are approaching level four. If a list were drawn up which would provide examples of stories appropriate for developing skill at the different levels of the scale, the teacher would find it much easier to provide systematic instruction in listening comprehension. Given a few examples, most experienced teachers will be able to think of several other similar stories which could also be used.

REFERENCES

Cunningham, P. M. "Transferring Comprehension from Listening to Reading." *Reading Teacher* 29 (1975): 169–172.

Davis, J. E. "The Ability of Intermediate Grade Pupils to Distinguish between Fact and Opinion." *Reading Teacher* 22 (1969): 419–422.

Dunn, L. M.; Chun, L.; Crowell, D. C.; and Alevy, L. *Peabody Early Experiences Kit*. Circle Pines, MN: American Guidance Service, Inc., 1976.

Feinman, L. "Meet Mr. Zee." *Elementary English* 49 (1972): 208–212.

Harris, A. J. and Sipay, E. R. *How to Increase Reading Ability*. 6th ed. New York: David McKay Co., Inc., 1975.

Rystrom, R. R. "Toward Defining Comprehension: A Second Report." *Journal of Reading Behavior* 2 (1970): 144–157.

Sax, G. *Empirical Foundations of Educational Research*. Englewood Cliffs, NJ: Prentice-Hall, Inc., 1968.

Weaver, S. W. and Rutherford, W. L. "The Hierarchy of Listening Skills." *Elementary English* 51 (1974): 1146–1150.

Wheat, T. E. and Edmond, R. M. "The Concept of Comprehension: An Analysis." *Journal of Reading* 18 (1975): 523–527.

APPENDIX

The Bear That Took Skipper's Name

Once there was a little boy named Skipper. He liked to go into the forest to watch the animals. He saw little squirrels gathering nuts. He also saw little rabbits eating lettuce. Skipper was so busy watching the little animals that he did not see the big bear hiding behind a tree. The little animals did not like the big bear. The bear took things that didn't belong to him. He ate their food. He always wanted what someone else had. All of a sudden, the big bear jumped in front of Skipper. "What do you have for me?" he asked. Skipper didn't have any food or any toys with him. He didn't think he had anything the bear would want. The bear was very angry. He shouted, "I want something that belongs to you." Finally, Skipper said, "I have my name. It is Skipper. I use it to let everyone know who I am. I answer when someone calls my name. You may have my name if you want it." The bear thought about the wonderful idea of having a name. He said, "I am going to take your name. Now my name is Skipper." The bear ran off to his home to tell his family that he had taken Skipper's name. Everyone in his family wanted Skipper's name. His father and mother took Skipper's name. His sisters and brothers took Skipper's name.

Soon the name Skipper, Skipper, Skipper was heard all over the forest. Everyone was all mixed up. None of the bears knew when to answer.

The big bear was angry. He went to find Skipper and told him what had happened. At first, Skipper did not know what to do. He thought and thought about it. Then he said to the bear, "You cannot all take the same name.

I'll help you think of a name just for you. Everyone should have his own name."

The name Skipper liked best was "Big Max." Big bear liked it too, so he said, "I will take the name Big Max." He went back to the other bears and helped each of them to find a different name. Big Max was so pleased to have his own name. His own name made him special.

Attention: Necessary Aspect of Listening

DANIEL TUTOLO

Recent studies have revealed that children improve with age in ability to focus attention and resist distraction while listening (Doyle 1973). Yet little has been written about how the teacher can help children focus attention on the listening task, thus minimizing distraction. While many children learn this easily in instructional settings, others find it difficult and therefore "giving directions" and "providing oral information" are regarded by teachers as serious instructional problems. This article will clarify the attention process and indicate how it relates to oral learning (listening).

Sensory inputs which bombard the ear in most classrooms often result in information overload and can limit effective teaching and learning. During the 1960s we learned that a quiet classroom is not necessarily an effective classroom. During the 1970s we are learning that noisy (busy) classrooms are not necessarily effective either unless children are on target with their listening.

Sensory input enters the ear and is processed and coded. From the input the listener selects relevant information for further processing and rejects those distractions which do not contribute to effective communication. There are several message characteristics which must be understood during the attention-listening process if we are to help children become efficient listeners.

Spatial Location. Where is the sound coming from? Tomorrow ask your children to close their eyes and listen to the sounds outside the building. After a short period of time, ask them to focus on sounds within the building but outside the classroom. Follow this with instructions to focus on sounds within the room. Finally, with eyes still closed, ask the children to listen for sounds within their bodies. Suggest to the children the ease with which this was done when they focused attention on one source and filtered out all other extraneous sources (Morton 1977).

Frequency Spectra. How often do sounds occur? Once again ask the children to close their eyes and begin by tapping a pencil on the desk in rhythm. After a few seconds increase the cadence so that the difference is evident. Have the children raise their hands when the sound changes.

Loudness. How intense is the sound that reaches the ear? Go to the back of the room so that children cannot see

From Language Arts, Vol. 56, No. 1 (January, 1979). © 1979 by the National Council of Teachers of English. Reprinted by permission.

you. Clap your hands together with enough intensity so that all children can hear. Increase the intensity and ask children to raise their hands when they hear a difference. Do this until all children are successful.

Semantic Continuity. What is the message? Of the four kinds of auditory input—spatial location, frequency spectra, loudness, and semantic continuity—the last is far and away the most important in instruction in attention-listening. While the first three depend exclusively on auditory discrimination the latter is a cognitive process. Semantic continuity assumes the other three; it is the essence of listening often referred to in the literature as auding. Here is a way to develop this capacity.

Read three English sentences in this manner:
   The boy ran home.
   He was in a hurry.
   Mother was waiting.
Follow this with three nonsense utterances of about the same length:
   Glib aly ni rox
   Ve hox reder sonex
   Le morax condo.
Point out to the group how easy it is to hear the differences and how meaning or understanding can be attached to only the former set of sentences.

I have attempted to show thus far that sensory input comes to the ear in four broad categories and that these sensory inputs must be coded by the listener. Next I will show that only certain inputs are selected for further processing—those that are pertinent to message construction and understanding.

The key to this understanding is pertinence. Intuitively teachers have routinely minimized distractions and asked children to attend to something important. Unfortunately it is not well understood that what is pertinent to the teacher may not be pertinent to the listener. The teacher may want the learner to focus on one category (semantic continuity) while the learner may focus on other inputs (spatial location, frequency spectra or loudness of other sounds) often regarded by the teacher as distractions. Sometimes information overload will influence this process negatively from the point of view of the teacher. Children may focus on the car honking in the distance and filter out the teacher's words. The student must regard the teacher's words as pertinent and capable of meeting the listener's needs, or communication between teacher and listener will not take place.

A variation of Norman's selection and attention model on the following page should make this clear (Norman 1968, p. 526).

Probably the best way to teach children to select important input for close attention is to keep teacher talk down to a defensible minimum. Decide in advance what you want children to listen for. Lundsteen's list of listening skills, reproduced in part below, can be helpful in this regard (Lundsteen 1971, p. 52).

General Listening Skills

 1. To remember significant details accurately.
 2. To remember simple sequences of words and ideas.
 3. To follow oral directions.
 4. To understand denotative meanings of words.
 5. To understand meanings of words from spoken context.
 6. To listen, to answer, and to formulate simple questions.
 7. To paraphrase a spoken message.
 8. To understand connotative meanings of words.
 9. To identify main ideas and to summarize (the who, what, when, where, why).
10. To listen for implications of significant details.
11. To listen for implications of main ideas.

Setting Purposes

Essential to attention-listening instruction is the notion of purposes set by the teacher for the listening process. Wait until room noises and distractions are minimized and set the stage for listening in this way. "I'm going to read a paragraph from your social studies book. Be able to tell me the important or main idea after I've finished." In this way the teacher creates a mind set for listening. Ausubel (1960) and others have referred to this as an "advance organizer." The advance organizer helps to set the purpose for listening and increases the probability that the listener will be on task.

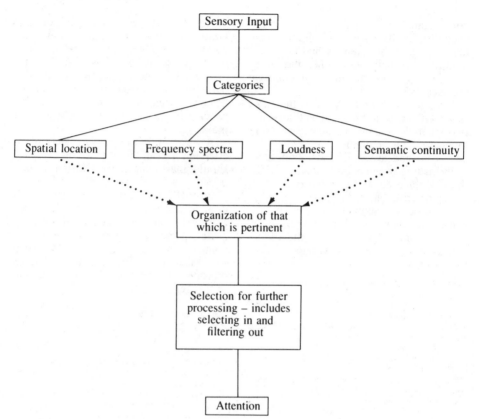

While we are not sure whether the use of advance organizers improves comprehension during listening, they do encourage the teacher to think ahead before giving directions and to keep the directions to a minimum. The listener has a task in mind before the message is received. All other sounds are considered appropriately as distractions and should be avoided by the listener.

Attention is crucial to good listening. Children can be taught to attend to important teacher messages but the teacher must understand the constraints within which he or she operates. If semantic continuity is important to you, then create an atmosphere where other distractions are minimized. Set purposes for the listening by providing an advance organizer. Keep words to a minimum and ask children to select from the message only those inputs which are helpful to solving the problem.

The route to improved listening is an understanding teacher who knows how attention is obtained and kept.

REFERENCES

Ausubel, David P. "The Use of Advanced Organizers in the Learning and Retention of Meaningful Verbal Learning." *Journal of Educational Psychology* 51 (1960): 267–72.

Doyle, Anna-Beth. "Listening to Distraction: A Developmental Study of Selective Attention." *Journal of Ex-

perimental Child Psychology 15 (1973): 100–115.

Lundsteen, Sara W. *Listening: Its Impact on Reading and the Other Language Arts.* Urbana, IL: National Council of Teachers of English, 1971.

Morton, Beatrice K. "Listening: First Steps in Developmental Drama." *English Journal* 66 (1977): 68–73.

Norman, Donald A. "Toward a Theory of Memory and Attention." *Psychological Review* 75 (1968): 522–536.

"Please Read That Story Again!"

Exploring Relationships Between Story Reading and Learning to Read

JUDITH A. SCHICKEDANZ

In searching for explanations for why some children learn to read without apparent difficulty early in elementary school while others do not, reading researchers have looked at children's experiences at home, prior to school entrance. A common finding in this research has been that children who learn to read easily in school are the same children whose parents have read to them at home (Durkin 1966; Sakamoto 1977; Sheldon and Carrillo 1952; Sutton 1964). Because the evidence from this research is correlational, we cannot be certain whether it is the story reading itself or some other associated factor that helps these children learn to read. Nevertheless, reading to young children is often recommended as a critical experience, and parents and teachers alike are encouraged to read to children as often as they can (Department of Education and Science 1975; Durkin 1970).

Surprisingly though, parents and

teachers rarely ask *why* they should read to children. Perhaps the question never arises because it makes such good sense that reading to children should be related to later reading ability. It is important, however, to know why reading to children makes a difference because unless we can answer this question, we have little to guide us in determining how best to read to young children, or in deciding what additional experiences we might provide to help children learn to read.

In this article, some of the common explanations for the effects of story reading will be discussed, and an alternative explanation, along with implications for classroom practices, will be presented.

COMMON THEORETICAL EXPLANATIONS

Several theoretical explanations for the observed relationship between extensive story reading at home and later reading achievement can be found, including:

• **Identification and social-learning modeling:** Children are thought to adopt behaviors of the parent because they

Reprinted by permission from YOUNG CHILDREN, Vol. 33, No. 5 (July 1978), pp. 48–55. Copyright © 1978, National Association for the Education of Young Children, 1834 Connecticut Avenue N.W., Washington, D.C. 20009.

wish to become like the parent. If parents read in the presence of their children, their children are likely to try to read, too (Elkind 1974; Gordon 1976).

● **Direct reinforcement:** Children are thought to receive many reinforcements in the reading situation (e.g., attention, physical contact, verbal praise). Because of this positive reinforcement children are thought to approach reading situations as a way to maintain reinforcement obtained there. In time, the reading situation itself would become reinforcing. Helping children learn to "love" books or to develop an "enjoyment" of books as preparation for later reading instruction seems to be based in part on this explanation (Durkin 1970; Flood 1977).

● **Emotional security and confidence:** The warmth of the story reading situation, as well as the generally positive affective climate created by parents when they read to their children, is thought to support the child's emotional well-being, and to build his or her confidence. Therefore, children approach the reading situation because they have developed good feelings about reading and are not afraid of it (Department of Education and Science 1975).

● **Language development:** The reading process is viewed here as basically a language-prediction process. The language learned from the stories themselves, as well as from discussions of the stories with parents, is assumed to make it easier for children to learn to read (Durkin 1970; Flood 1977; Smith 1977; Olson 1977).

● **Book knowledge and knowledge of reading:** Children are thought to gain basic understandings such as "books have beginnings and endings," "print is read from left to right," "when one reads, one says what is printed in the book," etc. (Durkin 1970).

INADEQUACY OF COMMON EXPLANATIONS

Most of the common explanations for why reading to children should be beneficial are based on, or are at least consistent with, a learning theory model of learning. Specifically, the first three explanations stress the importance of motivation and reinforcement derived *externally* from the learning act itself. In addition, they assume that story reading serves as *preparation for* instruction in reading that is to occur at some later time, not that it is itself a situation in which actual instruction can and does occur.

This "readiness" view of story reading is consistent with a learning theory model: Learning is viewed as linear or additive, accruing slowly, bit by bit through the establishment of "associations" or "bonds." In a learning theory model, the story reading situation would probably not even be suspected as a possible source of actual reading skills, because it would be viewed as too complex, disorganized, and unstructured for such learning to occur. It is not surprising, therefore, that benefits from the experience have been assumed by many to be ones that render the child receptive to and motivated for actual reading instruction that will take place *later* in school.

The language explanation assumes that reading is primarily a language process. While there is wide support for this view, even its most ardent advocates do not say language is all there is to reading. Goodman and Goodman (1977), for example, suggest that readers use three systems: grammatical, semantic, and graphophonic. While the language explanation does assume that children learn something about the reading process itself from being read to, it stresses only the contributions to the grammatical and semantic systems. Because there is evidence that children can also learn letter-sound associations primarily from story reading experiences (Forester 1977), the language explanation is incomplete.

The book knowledge and knowledge of reading explanation, like the language explanation, is different from the others in that it suggests that children learn something about reading from the story reading situation itself. This explanation, however, is rarely extensively developed. Authors only mention it, and then stress the affective effects of story reading through comments such as, "Reading to children is primarily for enjoyment, and anything that detracts from that goal should be bypassed" (Durkin 1970, p. 84). Yet, it is precisely this last, less well-developed explanation that may be particularly interesting and fruitful to explore, because it is consistent with cognitive theory.

A COGNITIVE EXPLANATION FOR THE EFFECTS OF STORY READING

A cognitive explanation focuses on the story reading situation itself as a source of data from which children construct knowledge about rules that govern the reading process. In a cognitive theory of learning, the learner is viewed as active, both in terms of motivation and construction of knowledge. Learning is conceived structurally as schemes or representations of experiences that become reorganized and more highly differentiated as learning progresses (Piaget 1963). Access to complex raw data, or what teachers call "real experiences," is necessary for a learner to develop schemes.

Reinforcement in the cognitive model is thought to be "inherent in the act of information-processing itself" (Hunt 1965). The child engages in activities not for the purpose of gaining external reinforcement (e.g., praise, attention, affection) but because he or she finds the activities interesting.

What data about reading are made available in the story reading situation? What schemes might children construct? How might early schemes become reorganized into more complex schemes?

With respect to the development of knowledge about letter-sound associations, for example, schemes might develop as follows:

Scheme I: Memorized Story Line

In the story reading situation, the reader makes the story line accessible to the child. When the same story is repeated many times (which usually happens), children learn it "by heart." Learning stories "by heart" when they are read can be viewed as a cognitive scheme. The scheme is not the story line of an individual story but the general idea that story lines can be remembered, and general strategies for doing this. Children would then apply this scheme to several, or even many, books that they could learn "by heart."

Scheme II: Locating Print in Books

The story reading situation also helps children locate print in books. Sometimes parents point out words to their children as they read them stories. Even if they do not, children can probably learn which words appear on particular pages through observing when the parent says certain words. In addition, children's "by heart" versions of the story line include not only the words but the phrasing of the story, which they may be able to associate with the turning of pages. These associations would help them "line up" their "by heart" rendition of the story with the words printed in the book. Children probably also associate pictures with certain words that have been read. They know that when the parents say a certain line, a certain picture appears on the page. The picture can then be used to locate the page where a part of the story line that the child knows is printed.

In all of these ways, children probably can determine what the printed words in a book say, and they can then become familiar with how the words look. "Reading" at this point might be "by sight," while earlier it would have been "by heart."

Scheme III: Matching Letters and Sounds

Once the child knows the story "by heart," and also knows the same printed words "by sight," he or she can observe letter-sound correspondence. A third scheme, consisting of the general idea that there is a pattern or some regularity in the correspondence between letters and sounds might possibly develop as a consequence. When a certain degree of learning of this kind has taken place, "reading" using phonics rules can occur.

It should be noted that Scheme III involves a unique interaction between the child and a book, and does not involve a story reader. Scheme III, however, is a product of two earlier schemes that *are* dependent on the story reader.

Each of the above schemes could be expected to take considerable time and experience to develop. The reader need only consider the fact that it takes an infant about two years to develop a complete concept of the object (Piaget 1963) and about six years to develop concepts of conservation, classification, and seriation (Inhelder and Piaget 1964; Piaget 1965) to appreciate how long it might take a child to develop an understanding of letter-sound associations.

IMPLICATIONS OF THE COGNITIVE MODEL FOR CLASSROOM PRACTICE

If knowledge of letter-sound associations can be constructed by children in a fashion similar to that proposed above, then some ways of reading to children should be more effective than others. Suggestions for possible effective techniques follow.

● **Story reading, to be most effective, should take place in a situation that allows the child to see the print in the book.** Reading stories to large groups of children, or even to relatively small groups (six to eight children), may not give the access to print needed to learn words "by sight."

● **Turning the pages of the book may help children learn the phrasing of the story,** which may, in turn, help them match their "by heart" story line with the printed words in the book. This may be one strategy children use to learn words "by sight." Again, individual or very small group story reading situations would be necessary.

● **The same story should be read to children many times** because repetition is required for construction of the story line. The amount of repetition necessary for individual children to construct the story lines of a particular book would be expected to vary. The "match" between the linguistic abilities of a child and the language in the book may determine in part how much repetition is required. The experiences a child brings to the book would surely also influence the child's comprehension of what it says, and this, too, would probably play a part in determining the amount of repetition necessary for a child to construct the story line "by heart."

It would be important, then, to pay particularly close attention to children's pleas to hear a particular story and to read it again. It is impossible to exhibit this kind of responsiveness when reading to a group of children, because children are different; the book one child wants and needs to hear may not be at all suitable for the others. Again, then, reading to individual and small groups of children would seem to be much more effective.

● **Adults should point out, at least**

occasionally, **where in the book words that "say" what they are reading appear.** Adults should probably also pose questions to the child, such as, "Where do you think it says, 'MEEOW!' on this page?" or "Where do you think it says, 'Will you please come to my birthday party, Peter?' on this page?" Obviously, children would need to be very close to the book to become involved in answering such questions.

• **Listening posts** may be used most effectively when children have individual books of the stories they hear to follow along in.

• **Children would need free access to books** that are read to them at times *in addition* to the story reading time itself. Such access would be critical for children to practice matching their "by heart" story lines with printed words, and for integrating their "by heart" and "by sight" versions to abstract rules about letter-sound associations. Mere access to books that have not been read may not be particularly useful, and no access to books that have been read would limit learning terribly.

• **Observation lists** used to keep records of children's progress should include items such as the following:
—Child chooses frequently to look at storybooks during a free-choice activity period.
—Child asks adult to reread stories often.
—Child pretends to read familiar stories to him- or herself, to other children, or to stuffed animals and dolls.
—Child corrects the adult when he or she alters the story line of a familiar story.
—Child turns pages for adult reader on the basis of phrasing clues only.
—Child asks what the words in a favorite storybook say.

• **Teachers should encourage children to compose stories** that the teacher can write down. These experience stories would be easy for children to read "by

heart" because they composed them. Stories of individual children, rather than total-group experience charts, are likely to be more effective in promoting the development of schemes described above.

SUMMARY AND CONCLUSIONS

If the view presented describes with reasonable accuracy what indeed does occur, then it is clear that the *how* of story reading is critically important. Even programs in which story reading occurs on a daily basis may not be very effective if the stories are always read to the entire group or if the same books are not frequently repeated or if children do not have access to books that are read.

The effects of story reading at home may be quite strong, while the effects of even frequent story reading at school may not be. At home, the child is usually on the reader's lap where he or she can see the print and turn the pages of the book; in the classroom children often are seated far from the book in groups of twenty or more, a situation that limits both physical and visual contact with the book. At home, the child usually chooses the books to be read, thus ensuring repeated access to the same books; in the classroom children often do not select the books that are read to them. At home, a child has easy access to his or her storybooks at other times than when the parent is reading; unfortunately, at school there is often only a short time when children have access to books. In far too many classrooms, books are kept high on shelves or on the teacher's desk, out of the children's reach.

The issue of whether or not young children should be taught "reading skills" also emerges out of this discussion. The real issue is not whether children do or do not need to learn reading skills, but rather, *how* children come to know the skills that indeed are necessary if they are to learn how to read. In a learning theory model, the teacher teaches the skills directly, in one way or another. In a cognitive approach, teachers provide experiences that make knowledge about the reading process accessible to children who are thought literally to construct the skills for themselves. While skills are not directly taught, teachers must pay close attention to the kinds of experiences that are provided.

The cognitive model also suggests possible remedial procedures for children who encounter difficulty in the elementary school. A direct skill-teaching situation may be successful with children who have had all the necessary experiential background, such as having been read to at home by their parents, before they are taught to read in the school situation. They probably already know, at least on an intuitive level, the very skills that they are being "taught," and have learned to use others as well. Thus, they master the phonics training quickly. Because these children are often the best readers, teachers believe erroneously that it is the phonics training that is responsible.

Children without this background, however, may become terribly lost, not knowing the source of these rules. For these children, the cognitive model would predict that no amount of phonics drill or training would be effective, not because it is too "hard" or "advanced," but because the information is too simple, i.e., data-starved. It is isolated from the data-rich context of real reading materials.

Children experiencing this difficulty may profit from the procedure found to be effective by Chomsky (1975). She was able to help four third graders who were having great difficulty learning to read, despite hours of phonics drill, by having them memorize storybooks! Although she attributed her success to the confidence gained by the children in their ability to read, it might also have been due to the knowledge of the reading process itself obtained in the story reading situation described above.

Some possible directions for research are also suggested. We need answers to the question: "What does reading look like before we recognize it as 'real' reading?" We know what behaviors are typical of young children on tasks of conservation and classification, for example, and we know how these behaviors change qualitatively over time. But we do not have comparable descriptions of behavior for early reading.

Instead, we have knowledge about children's ability to recognize or manipulate *isolated elements* thought to be related to the reading process (e.g., alphabet recognition, recognition of rhyming words, etc.). This is very different from knowing how they understand the process of reading as a whole. To use mathematics as an example, it is the difference between knowing that a child can recognize the numerals one through nine and knowing the child still confuses space with number (says there are more cubes in a row when they are spread out then when they are close together). These two pieces of information are likely to lead us to different conclusions if we are trying to determine if such a child is "ready" for instruction in operations on number, e.g., addition, subtraction, etc. They become critical in determining *how* we might attempt to help such a child come to understand addition.

The few researchers who have suggested that cognitive skills are involved in learning to read (Dimitrovsky and Almy 1975; Elkind 1974) have assumed that these consist of the logico-mathematical concepts of conservation and classification. What I am suggesting is that structures *unique to reading* might also develop. The schemes outlined above might possibly be examples of children's early understandings of the reading process. Of course, any theoretically-based hypotheses such as those suggested above need rigorous empirical confirmation.

Finally, the discussion presented here provides an interesting basis for speculation about the relationship between affect and cognition. If the story reading experience is to result in the cognitive learnings outlined above, a closeness between the adult reader and the child is required. In other words, a story reading situation that is loaded with positive affect (e.g., individual attention, physical contact, verbal praise, etc.) is the same situation that is loaded with information for the child. Part of the "loading" no doubt results because the adult is in a situation where he or she can be *responsive* to an individual child's behavior. The adult can be directed by the child to back up or to go forward, to repeat, to answer questions, and so on.

It may be that a child's affective tie to an adult is influenced by the adult's responsiveness to the child's cognitive needs. It has been well-documented in relation to infants, for example, that they like best those adults who are most responsive, i.e., who play with them, etc. (Rheingold 1956; Schaffer and Emerson 1964). It has been suggested by others that infants may like these adults best because they know that with them around they can get interesting things to happen (Schickedanz and Goldstein 1977).

Affect and cognition, then, may truly interact with each other. If this conception is at all accurate, ideas such as "we should limit goals of the preschool to emotional development and leave cognitive development to the elementary school" need to be reconsidered.

REFERENCES

Chomsky, C. "After Decoding, What?" *Elementary English* 52, no. 6 (March 1975): 288–296, 314.

Department of Education and Science. *A Language for Life*. London: Her Majesty's Stationery Office, 1975.

Dimitrovsky, L., and Almy, M. "Early Conservation as a Predictor of Later Reading." *Journal of Psychology* 90 (1975): 11–18.

Durkin, D. *Children Who Read Early*. New York: Teachers College Press, 1966.

Durkin, D. *Teaching Them to Read*. Boston: Allyn & Bacon, 1970.

Elkind, D. "Cognitive Development and Reading." *Claremont Reading Conference Yearbook* 38 (1974): 10–20.

Flood, J. "Parental Styles in Reading Episodes with Young Children." *The Reading Teacher* 35 (May 1977): 864–867.

Forester, A. "What Teachers Can Learn from 'Natural Readers.' " *The Reading Teacher* 31 (November 1977): 160–166.

Goodman, K. S., and Goodman, Y. "Learning about Psycholinguistic Processes by Analyzing Oral Reading." *Harvard Educational Review* 47 (August 1977): 317–333.

Goodman, K. S., and Goodman, Y. "The Psycholinguistic Nature of the Reading Process." In *The Psycholinguistic Nature of the Reading Process*, ed. K. S. Goodman. Detroit: Wayne State University Press, 1968.

Gordon, I. "Parenting, Teaching, and Child Development." *Young Children* 31, no. 3 (March 1976): 173–183.

Guinagh, B., and Jester, R. "How Parents Read to Children." *Theory into Practice* 11 (June 1972): 171–177.

Hunt, J. McV. "Intrinsic Motivation and Its Role in Psychological Development." *Nebraska Symposium on Motivation* 13 (1965): 189–282.

Inhelder, B., and Piaget, J. *The Early Growth of Logic in the Child*. New York: Norton, 1964.

Olson, D. "From Utterance to Text: The Bias of Language in Speech and Writing." *Harvard Educational Review* 47 (August 1977): 257–281.

Piaget, J. *The Child's Conception of Number*. New York: Norton, 1965.

Piaget, J. *The Origins of Intelligence in Children*. New York: Norton, 1963.

Rheingold, H. "The Modification of Social Responsiveness in Institutional Babies." *Monographs of the Society for Research in Child Development* 2, no. 63 (1956).

Sakamoto, T. "Beginning Reading in Japan." Paper presented at the International Reading Association annual meeting, May 1977, Miami, Fla.

Schaffer, H. R., and Emerson, P. E. "The Development of Social Attachments in Infancy." *Monographs of the Society for Research in Child Development* 29, no. 94 (1964).

Schickedanz, D., and Goldstein, G. "The Relationship Between Moderate Novelty and Effectance Motivation in Determining Children's Visual Attention and Instrumental Behavior." Paper presented at the Eastern Psychological Association annual meeting, April 1977, Boston, Mass.

Sheldon, W., and Carrillo, L. "Relation of Parents, Home, and Certain Developmental Characteristics to Children's Reading Ability." *Elementary School Journal* 52 (January 1952): 262–270.

Smith, F. "Making Sense of Reading—and of Reading Instruction." *Harvard Educational Review* 47 (August 1977): 386–395.

Sutton, M. "Readiness for Reading at the Kindergarten Level." *The Reading Teacher* 22 (January 1964): 234–239.

When Should We Begin to Teach Reading?

WALTER H. MACGINITIE

If ever there was a question that should be answered with another question, it is "When should we begin to teach reading?" The proper answer is: "What do you mean by 'begin to teach reading'?" The definitions of *beginning* to teach reading could include reading stories aloud to children, or showing them how to print their names when they ask, or casually teaching them the names of a few letters over a period of several months, or teaching them to recognize a few survival words such as "POISON," "DANGER," and "EXIT." The most common definitions of what beginning to teach reading means might be something equivalent to starting to do a lesson a day from the teachers' manual of a reading series. But current practice, as defined by teachers' manuals or syllabi, is not sufficiently uniform for us to say what it means to "begin to teach read-

From *Language Arts,* Vol. 53, No. 8 (November/December, 1976). © 1976 by the National Council of Teachers of English. Reprinted by permission.

ing." Among different reading programs there are considerable differences in the approach to instruction and in the rate at which it proceeds. Compare a few different teachers' manuals for the first grade and just see how different they are in both approach and pace. Furthermore, many children are being taught to read today by individualized or language experience approaches that vary enormously. Among teachers, too, there are differences in the style of presentation, the integration of reading into other tasks, and the pace at which demands on the child accumulate. It cannot be assumed that "begin to teach reading" means about the same thing to everyone.

When we should begin to teach reading also depends, of course, on the circumstances of the individual child. That is, the readiness question is involved. I have argued elsewhere (MacGinitie 1969), however, that the readiness question, too, is meaningless unless the kind of instructional program is specified. That is, we cannot answer "Is the child ready?"

unless we specify "Ready for what?"

From the extensive research on reading readiness, we would expect to learn a lot about when children with different characteristics could profitably begin to learn to read. However, so much of that research has ignored the fact that children are taught in different ways, that it tells us relatively little about what abilities are important for success in any *particular* instructional program. For example, some of that research indicates that it is almost impossible for the average five-year-old child to learn to read. "Nearly every six-year-old is ready to learn *something* about reading (Mac-Ginitie 1969)." Surely the same is true of nearly every *five*-year-old or every *four*-year-old, as long as the "something" that is to be learned is scaled to the child's background and is introduced gently enough. This possibility for appropriate scale and pace of instruction is, in my opinion, the principal argument for introducing the rudiments of reading prior to first grade.

Under our present system, we expect nearly all children to start learning to read during the first-grade year. With some of the children, the teacher will begin reading instruction right away. With others, who are deemed not as ready, the teacher may wait as much as six months or more out of the ten-month school year before beginning formal reading instruction. In the interim, these children will be given "readiness instruction."

It is interesting to observe that we are now talking about teaching reading before first grade when but a few years ago it was taboo in many schools to teach anything directly about reading as part of readiness instruction. I have never been able to understand the sort of reading readiness instruction that involves learning to discriminate a rabbit with one ear from a rabbit with two ears, but does *not* involve discriminating *a* from *b*. If early reading instruction does nothing else, perhaps it will result in more meaningful

reading readiness instruction. To me, meaningful reading readiness instruction means a slow and gentle introduction to reading itself—often gamelike, often hidden in other activities.

When children are started on formal reading instruction in a given classroom, the typical procedure has been to give pretty much the same instruction to all the children, though some will have started half a year later and will proceed a little more slowly. It is easy to show that waiting half a year is *not* much of an adjustment to make for the range of abilities found in the typical first grade. In a typical first grade in the first month of school, some children will be 6¾ years old; others will not reach 6 for another two months. The children's *IQs** are likely to range from 85 or less, to 125 or more. Under these conditions a mental age spread from less than 5 years to about 8½ years should be expected in the typical first grade classroom—a range of more than 3 years. In the face of a range of mental ability of more than three years, delaying the start of reading for some children by half a year is *not* much of a concession to individual differences. We need to provide a great variation in the instruction itself.

We expect children to begin to learn to read in first grade, and those who don't are likely to be in trouble in school forevermore. Evidence clearly shows that children who do not learn to read in first grade tend to be those who are the lowest achievers in most subjects clear up into secondary school (Breen 1965; Thorndike 1973–74). Part of this relationship is natural and to be expected. Some children learn faster than others. They will learn to read faster than others, and they will continue to learn a lot of other things in school faster than others.

But do we have to be so do-or-die about reading in the first grade? Yes, I'm afraid we do. At least at the present time, we do. Parents wouldn't stand for

---

*General IQ may not be the best index of ability to learn to read, but any reasonable index you might pick as relevant to the particular reading program would show about the same range.

anything else; and most educators would side with them. We insist on believing that certain school tasks are divinely assigned to certain grades. We insist, by our demand that reading be learned then and there, on turning the first grade into a "child's garden of reverses" (Mac-Ginitie 1973).

Even little children know that it's often easier for them to learn something as they grow more mature. McConkie and Nixon (1959) and Stewart (1966) conducted interesting studies of what kindergarten and first grade children think reading is and why we learn to read. They also studied the children's ideas about why some children have trouble learning to read and what happens when they do have trouble. Each child was shown a picture of a group of children and was told, "This is a group of boys and girls in the first grade. They are learning to read." Then the child was asked a series of questions, including, "Will it be hard to learn to read?" "Have you ever known anyone in the first grade who didn't learn to read?," and "Why didn't they learn how?"

"Why didn't they learn how?" Some of the answers from kingergarteners are instructive: "Maybe he was too little and couldn't do it right—maybe he was born after the other children." "He wasn't concentracing (sic) on the teacher." "I think she didn't listen or do what the teacher said." "He'll just have to get older and then learn how." "Maybe the class was too fast and he should try to start from the beginning."

"Will it be hard to learn to read?" the investigators asked. "It will if they don't know their words and if it's done fast," replied a kindergartener. These answers stress the need for reading instruction to proceed at a pace that is appropriate for the particular child. Out of the mouths of kindergarteners can come useful commentary on our curriculum.

"What will happen to a boy or a girl who cannot read?" the children were asked. "He'll be in trouble if he's lost in the desert. He'll find a mailbox, but it won't be any good. He can't write. He'll have to turn himself over to the police." A more mundane response that still recognizes the problem was, "He will learn sometime or other, and if he doesn't he will be in a thick problem."

He *will* be in a "thick problem." What can we do for first graders to help them steer clear of that thick problem? Paradoxically, one way out may be to begin teaching reading earlier than we now do.

If reading instruction is already too pressured a situation for some children in first grade, how can it help to extend reading instruction down into the earlier years? It can help simply because we can allow more time for the child to assimilate the elementary processes that are involved. The healthy thing about most early reading programs at the present time is that both teachers and students can be relatively relaxed. Whatever is learned in an early reading program is often regarded as just a start. Teacher and child can be less tense, for it is still in the first grade that we seem to believe the task *must* be accomplished. We appear to believe that first grade is early enough for frustrations and disappointments. Also, if a child does not learn to read in the early reading program, the first-grade teacher is able to start again at the beginning.

Wardhaugh (1971) has pointed out that one of the major differences between initial language learning and learning to read is that the child is required to learn to read in a relatively short time in a formal training situation. An early reading program *can* provide the opportunity for the learning of reading to be more like initial language learning. Note that I am not suggesting that early formal schooling for all children is desirable, only that a chance to learn some of the elements of reading before first grade could be helpful to many children. As a result, some children will actually learn to read rather well before first grade—an appropriate manifestation of individual differences.

We should resist tenaciously, however, any steps toward making early reading achievement a standard that all children are expected to attain.

In talking about these possible advantages of early reading instruction, we should not lose sight of the initial point—that we must define what we mean by "begin to teach reading" before we can sensibly talk about the age or developmental level where it should take place. As a corollary, we need to consider some of the evidence on the mental development of children under the age of six and suit whatever reading instruction *is* given to that development. It is not yet clear what all the characteristics of a good early reading program should be. Clearly it is not appropriate simply to move down a year or two what the first grade teacher is now doing. In particular, reading for younger children should be less oriented toward teaching formal, complex rule systems than are some present first grade programs. In the first place, children seem to have difficulty analyzing language into the units that are manipulated by the rules. In the second place, the cognitive tasks that some phonics lessons represent are quite literally beyond the understanding of many six-year-olds (MacGinitie 1976).

Obviously, most children eventually learn to function according to the rules of grapheme-phoneme correspondence, for they *do* learn to read; but they do not necessarily *understand* what the rules are and what they mean.

In this sense, learning to read should be, for many children, like the initial learning of spoken language. The rules become internalized and functional, but cannot be verbalized. Being told what the rule is has *not* been the basis for learning to follow it. For example, you and I, and most six-year-olds, could say that if something is called *lun,* then two of them are *luns.* We know that if something is called a *bik,* two of them are called *biks;* and that if something else is called a *nizz,* two of them are *nizzes.* We would correctly *use* three different plural allomorphs, /-z/ (in *lun-luns*), /-s/ (in *bik-biks*) and /-iz/ (in *nizz-nizzes*), but most of us, even now, do not know that there is a rule to the effect that English /-iz/ is used to indicate the plural only after affricates and alveolar and alveopalatal fricatives, that /-s/ is used only after voiceless stops and labiodental and dental voiceless fricatives and that /-z/ occurs after all other consonants and all vowels.

This example illustrates the difference between functioning according to a rule (we all do that) and understanding a rule intellectually (few of us know very much about our language in that sense). Most children learn to read by learning to function according to rules, not by gaining an intellectual understanding of the rules. After all, how many adults who are excellent readers could explain that the *s* that signifies plural is pronounced /-s/ only after voiceless stops and labiodental and dental voiceless fricatives? Yet that is the rule we all follow when we read aloud.

Many other phonological rules are involved in learning to read. Many are simpler than this, but all except the most direct are probably better learned by young children by example and practice than as rules stated as guides to pronouncing printed words. The younger the children, the harder it will be for them to use a verbalized rule as a logical proposition for analyzing written language. This fact is clear to most teachers and therefore *early* reading programs are, appropriately, not so likely to be presented as the verbalizing of formal rule systems.

I only hope that as early reading programs become institutionalized they do not become more institution-like—more formal, more uniform, more demanding, less tolerant of deviation. At the present time, early reading programs are likely to present the child with the opportunities for extensive practice and thorough acquaintance with letters and simple correspondences, with a gradual development of objectives, and with frequent, yet brief and often adventitious attention to reading that neither bores nor bewilders. Probably those features account for much of the clear success that many early reading programs have had.

REFERENCES

Breen, J. M. "Differential Prediction of Intermediate Grade Skills Achievement from Primary Grade Aptitude and Achievement Measures." Doctoral dissertation, University of Connecticut, 1965.

MacGinitie, W. H. "Evaluating Readiness for Learning to Read: A Critical Review and Evaluation for Research." *Reading Research Quarterly* 4 (1969): 396–410.

MacGinitie, W. H. "What are We Testing?" In *Assessment Problems in Reading,* edited by Walter H. Mac-Ginitie, pp. 35–43. Newark, Delaware: International Reading Association, 1973.

MacGinitie, W. H. "Difficulty with Logical Operations." *The Reading Teacher* 29 (1976): 371–375.

McConkie, G. W., and Nixon, A. J. "The Perceptions of a Selected Group of Kindergarten Children Concerning Reading." Doctoral dissertation, Teachers College, Columbia University, 1959.

Stewart, D. Jr. "The Perception of Reading of Kindergarten and First Grade Children." Doctoral dissertation, Teachers College, Columbia University, 1966.

Thorndike, R. L. "Reading as Reasoning." *Reading Research Quarterly* 9 (1973–74): 135–147.

Wardhaugh, R. "Theories of Language Acquisition in Relation to Beginning Reading Instruction." *Reading Research Quarterly* 7 (1971): 168–194.

Beginning Reading: When and How

ETHEL M. KING

Throughout the world, there appears to be an increasing interest in the methods by which children are taught to read. The press reflects the concern of the public by reporting frequently on different reading programs.

Many questions are being asked regarding the age at which formal reading instruction should begin, particularly since recent programs for teaching the very young to read have received wide publicity. Then, too, reports from differ-

From *The Reading Teacher,* Vol. 22, No. 6 (March 1969). Reprinted with permission of the International Reading Association and Ethel M. King.

ent countries of the world indicate that children begin to receive formal reading instruction at varying ages. In North America, pupils generally begin to receive reading instruction at age six, although a few children have already begun to read by this age and some are not ready until later. Advocates of earlier reading instruction cite examples such as England, where reading instruction begins at age five or even at age four. On the other hand, reading instruction is delayed until age seven in Russia and Sweden, and until age eight in Denmark. Pressure to provide systematic reading instruction at an earlier age seems to be growing and yet teachers involved in a serious study of reading express many reservations. Educators have known for a long time that it is possible to accelerate the age at which reading instruction begins for most children. This is not the important issue. Of more concern than when *can* reading instruction begin, is when *should* it? This is a difficult question because of a number of factors.

Individual Differences

Children vary greatly in such matters as home environment and experience, ability to perceive minute differences in sounds and printed symbols, motor co-ordination, language ability, vocabulary, and interest in reading. To the amazement of their parents, they may vary widely in their abilities and interests within the same home. The range of differences will be much greater in any given classroom, or community, or nation. Obviously, when children come to school they will differ in their needs for a preparatory program which will subsequently affect the age at which reading instruction should begin.

Before making comparisons from one system of teaching reading to another, or from one language to another, it is necessary to examine very critically the specific skills involved. It is quite possible that the minimum age which would be best for most children for initial instruction in reading would vary from one program to another and a comparable difference may well exist for teaching reading from one language to another. On these questions there is little real knowledge, and yet information from comparative studies of the beginning reading age in different programs and languages might lead to some important linguistic and pedagogical findings.

In any country, there will always be some children who learn to read before coming to school because of certain interests and opportunities. Studies indicate that children who learn to read at an early age before coming to school do so in a manner which is quite different from the way they are taught in school. Also, the materials they read are usually quite different. Because some children receive reading instruction in one language earlier than in another or because some children learn to read on their own at an early age, the question is often raised as to whether or not this should be stimulated on a mass basis by lowering the age at which formal reading instruction begins.

Young children need protection from two extremes in the teaching of reading: an excessive pressure to learn to read which ignores the child's level of development, and a lack of knowledge or sensitivity for the "right" moment to begin so that time is not wasted. The total reading program should not be organized so rigidly as to delay children who have started to read on their own, or to deny the opportunity for learning to read to those who are ready to do so at school entrance. Nor should a pre-reading program ever be unnecessarily prolonged for those children who have only a few specific needs. Nevertheless, for children who are immature, who have certain physical handicaps, who are weak in auditory and visual perception, whose language is inadequate, or whose native tongue is not the language of instruction; special activities should be used to prepare them for the regular reading program. This preparation should be viewed as insurance for a successful beginning and as prevention against certain kinds of reading problems. A pre-reading program will not necessarily solve all the reading problems but it does promote a good beginning so that the initial experiences in learning to read will be rewarded with a desire to use the newly-acquired skills more and more independently.

Developing Readiness

Educators generally agree that reading instruction should not begin before children are ready, but there is not complete agreement as to the best method of fostering readiness. A few believe that readiness for reading is an individual matter which will result from maturation. Many more now believe that the pre-reading period should be planned to teach specific skills. The evidence is accumulating that readiness for reading can be promoted by the implementation of a good pre-reading program. Through research, a beginning has been made in identifying certain skills that will facilitate learning to read, and others which are of little value. These findings suggest that learning is not adding to the program, but rather selecting the kinds of activities which will contribute to the acquisition of reading skills.

Few people remember exactly how they learned to read. They are unaware of how simply children must start to learn to read and how carefully selected must be the initial learning activities that develop reading skill. Much has been written on what skills should be developed in the pre-reading period and how these should be developed. A few examples of the important skills illustrate the kinds of emphases that most children need in a pre-reading program.

Studies show that two of the specific skills needed in acquiring a reading vocabulary can be taught advantageously to children prior to formal reading instruction. These skills are the ability to see letter differences in printed words and the ability to hear separate sounds in spoken words.

The ability of the eyes to adjust for near vision begins developing in infancy. By the time the child is five or six he has made considerable progress in focusing both eyes on fairly close objects and has usually developed some measure of eye and hand coordination. During the pre-reading period even greater demands are made upon the child to make finer discriminations of shape, size, space relationships, and arrangement of visual details. In addition, he must now learn to direct his eye movements in the ap-

propriate direction for the language he is reading. Children vary greatly in the development of these visual skills, because of physical and experiential differences. Those who have had many experiences with manipulative toys and equipment have usually developed the ability to adjust their eyes and focus attention on close work much more readily than those lacking such experience. Many more years of training are required for the reader to acquire the visual skills needed to become a mature, efficient reader.

When children come to school they have also had a number of years of experience with sound; that is, they have been hearing a great deal. Many adults assume that they have also learned to listen but this is not necessarily so. Rarely have children at school entrance age learned to make the very fine discriminations required for efficient progress in learning to read. Initially, pupils need to develop skill in attentive listening at a level not usually demanded in pre-school activities. Next, they need to refine their skill in differentiating the characteristics of sounds: intensity, pitch, quality, duration, and sequence. Finally, they must develop a recognition of sounds in words and sentences.

At the pre-reading level, pictures, stories, and experiences are the main materials used, instead of printed materials, to develop comprehension. The thinking processes required for interpretation are similar to those needed in reading. Pictures, as with words, become meaningful from the child's previous experiences and his ability to verbalize. Important language abilities include the child's ability to express his own ideas in words, and the ability to interpret the language he hears. In this regard, children should listen to many stories and have the opportunity to participate in many kinds of discussion activities. One of the most important steps in preparing for reading or interpreting the printed language, then, is to develop the ability to use and interpret oral language.

Young children need many informal,

functional experiences with reading symbols. These experiences should grow out of current interests and activities in the classroom and the alert teacher seizes on opportunities for exposing children to reading symbols. Some children will start reading words by themselves, others will ask what words are, and others will recognize certain letters in words. Some children will *appear* not to benefit from exposure to reading symbols in the pre-reading period. This is not cause for alarm but rather we should be content with the exposure only in the early stages. Eventually, the children will reach the maturity for beginning reading instruction from the accumulation of benefits from previous experiences. This readiness will occur at different times for different children.

Young children, when questioned on what they are looking forward to most when they go to school, will usually reply, "Learning to read and write." It makes good sense to capitalize on this enthusiastic desire as soon as possible. As children gain competency in pre-reading and related skills, they soon learn to recognize a few printed words.

A pre-reading program should merge inconspicuously with the beginning reading program so that it is difficult to say when formal reading instruction actually begins. A stimulating pre-reading program, which includes literature, language, and specific visual and auditory training, will contribute *directly* to learning to read. Pupils with this kind of initiation into reading instruction usually understand and enjoy reading more than those who are pressured into reading too early. Forced early reading may develop a reader who can name the words but who understands little.

Questioning caution should be the key in evaluating the preliminary evidence on new approaches to teaching reading, and especially on those programs which attempt to teach the very young to read, until we see what the results are, not only on reading achievement but also on the desire to read.

The age at which children are ready to learn to read could well vary from one program or method or language to another. When the language of instruction is English, age six still seems to be an appropriate age for the majority of children to begin formal reading instruction, if we add two important qualifications. First, provision should be made in a school program for the small group of children who can already read by this age or who are ready to learn to read before this and for the group of children who are not ready until later. Second, provision should be made for a pre-reading program which is planned carefully for the particular children in a group. The pre-reading program is important for the development of certain skills, and should merge unobtrusively into the beginning reading program.

Reading in Kindergarten

CHRISTINE LA CONTE

The controversy over the teaching of reading in the kindergarten has been the subject of much philosophical discussion in the educational literature in the nineteen sixties; however, not since the publication of the *Harvard Report: Reading in Elementary Schools* (Austin & Morrison, 1963) has a serious attempt been made at assessing the amount of reading being taught. The purpose of this investigation was to examine opinions and practices of kindergarten teachers in two northeastern states.

Procedures

A questionnaire was devised which sought information on opinions, reading skills taught, and reading materials employed. The opinion items represent some commonly cited views on both sides of the controversy, the skills items represent a possible continuum of prereading and reading skills; and the practices items represent some commonly accepted beginning reading materials. For each skill (and practice) the respondent indicated whether she taught it (employed it), how often, to whom, and her reasons for teaching or not teaching it. Biographical information included length of kindergarten teaching experience, educational preparation level, size of community in which the respondent taught, and ability level of respondents' pupils. The final version of the questionnaire was mailed to 775 teachers—a 20 per cent sample randomly selected from state department of education lists. Follow-up questionnaires were mailed to non-respondents.

To increase validity and to insure maximum depth of response, a 10 per cent subsample of respondents was selected to be observed teaching in their kindergarten classrooms, and a 4 per cent subsample of respondents was selected to be interviewed. The chi square technique was used in the statistical analysis.

Findings

A 73 per cent questionnaire return included 563 kindergarten teachers who showed a wide range of teaching experience and professional preparation. Length of kindergarten teaching experience seemed to be the only biographical variable on which they were fairly evenly divided. Of the respondents, 72.9 per cent had completed the BA and BA + levels of preparation; 62.7 per cent taught in communities having between 10,000 and 99,999 people, and 61.3 per cent judged the majority of their pupils to be "average" in ability.

Opinions

Although closely divided in their overall positive and negative responses (49.4 per cent positive, 50.3 per cent negative), the teachers displayed marked differences in their responses to individual opinion items (Table 1). The biographical variables which showed the greatest differences among respondents were lengths of experience and size of community in which they taught. Teachers with long experience reported a much

From *The Reading Teacher*, Vol. 23, No. 2 (November 1969). Reprinted with permission from the International Reading Association and Christine La Conte.

higher frequency of negative opinions than did relatively inexperienced teachers. Those from large communities (over 100,000) reported a much lower frequency of negative opinions than did those from smaller cities and towns.

Skills

Of the total response reported in Table 2, 50.2 per cent indicated occasional teaching of reading skills, 30.9 per cent regular teaching, and 18.9 per cent never teaching. The overwhelming majority of the responses indicated that these skills were taught to the whole class as opposed to individual pupils or to small groups. Highly experienced teachers reported teaching many more skills than teachers with little experience, and

teachers from large communities reported teaching considerably *fewer* skills than did those from smaller communities.

Asked why they taught the skills they did teach, respondents replied most frequently (43.6 per cent) "I like to teach it." On the other hand, the reason most often reported for *not* teaching these skills (62.6 per cent) was, "It is against school policy."

Practices

Tabulation of frequencies of reading materials used (Table 3) shows that of the total response 39.5 per cent indicated that these materials are used regularly, 33.2 per cent that they are used occasionally, and 27.2 per cent that they are never used.

Table 1 **Agreement or disagreement with controversial opinions found in literature**

Opinion	N	Agree		Disagree	
		N	Per cent	N	Per cent
Kindergarten children not ready to read	522	356	67.2	166	32.8
Teaching children to read in k. will cause dislike for reading	506	127	25.1	379	74.9
Teaching children to read in k. harmful psychologically	512	159	31.5	353	69.5
Children who begin to read in k. will be better students throughout school	495	99	20.0	396	80.0
Television has stimulated children to read earlier	518	344	66.5	174	33.5
The teaching of reading is not a concern of k.	527	225	42.7	302	57.3
Today's children know how to read when they enter k.	526	38	7.2	488	92.8
Parents are "pushing" the very young these days	535	405	75.7	130	24.3
Those children who are ready should be taught to read in k.	509	336	66.0	173	34.0
Teaching children to read in k. will hurt their eyes	479	88	18.4	391	81.6

Table 2 **Teaching of reading skills in kindergartens**

Skill	N of respondents	Regularly N	Per cent	Occasionally N	Per cent	Never N	Per cent
Sensing motion and distance in pictures	539	171	31.7	319	59.2	49	9.1
Naming letters of the alphabet	549	246	39.9	242	44.1	61	11.0
Writing letters of the alphabet	514	149	29.0	230	44.7	135	26.3
Associating sounds and printed letters	557	208	37.4	294	52.8	55	9.8
Noting likeness and difference between words	530	167	31.5	285	53.8	78	14.7
Reading words	517	84	16.2	283	54.8	150	29.0

Table 3 **Frequency of reading materials reported used in Northeast kindergartens**

Material	N	Regularly N	Per cent	Occasionally N	Per cent	Never N	Per cent
Reading readiness test	457	153	33.4	158	34.6	146	32.0
Reading readiness workbook	466	182	39.1	44	9.4	240	49.4
Duplicated materials to develop visual perception	495	193	39.0	200	40.4	102	20.6
Alphabet chart	477	146	30.6	177	37.1	154	32.3
Experience chart	473	141	29.8	288	61.0	44	9.2
Classroom library	498	383	77.0	78	15.6	37	7.4
Preprimer	416	21	5.1	40	9.6	355	85.3
Primer	404	7	1.8	20	5.0	377	93.2

Observations and Interviews

Kindergarten teachers expressed preference for informal reading activities over formal reading activities by a margin of ten to one. Generally, the teachers are agreed that most kindergarten children are not ready to read, and that the few who are ready should be taught to read, but that these few comprise such a small minority that the teachers do not feel justified in changing their present kindergarten program to meet the needs of this minority.

Observation indicated that they did teach reading skills informally three times as often as they did formally. "Naming letters of the alphabet" and "associating sounds and printed letters" were the reading skills most frequently observed taught, while "reading words" was the skill least frequently observed taught.

Comparison of Findings with the Harvard Report

Very briefly, Austin's findings indicated, compared with the present findings, that

1. 26.8 per cent of kindergartens had reading taught in a planned, sequential approach; this study found 39.9 per cent.

2. Half of the kindergartens which taught reading did so for small, selected groups within a class; this study found that small group instruction is very rarely given.

3. One third of the kindergartens which taught reading offered whole class instruction; this study found that nearly all instruction is for the whole class.
4. 15 per cent of the kindergartens which taught reading offered instruction to individual children as they saw themselves ready to take it; this study found that individual instruction is very rarely given.
5. All of the kindergartens which taught reading used experience charts; this study found 99.1 per cent.
6. Homemade worksheets were used more frequently than commercially prepared materials; this study found that the opposite is true.
7. Half of the kindergartens which taught reading used workbooks (approximately 14 per cent of all kindergartens); this study found workbooks used in 47.6 per cent of all kindergartens.
8. One third of the kindergartens which taught reading introduced basal readers; this study found that preprimers and primers are very rarely, if ever, used.

Conclusions

Kindergarten teachers in this survey believe that most kindergarten children are not ready to read, and that parents are "pushing" the very young these days. Further, these teachers believe that in the long run teaching reading in kindergarten will neither harm nor benefit most children. Finally, the teachers believe that those very few children who can read or who are ready to learn should be taught in the kindergarten; however, the teachers are not willing to meet the needs of such a small minority at the present time.

In the classrooms of these teachers there is a better than even chance that reading skills are taught occasionally (from time to time as the need arises), but only one in three that they are taught regularly (in a planned, sequential program). There is only one chance in five that reading skills will not be taught at all.

Reading materials, in general, such as reading readiness tests, workbooks, duplicated materials, alphabet charts, experience charts, classroom libraries, and preprimers and primers are being used in northeastern kindergartens. Specifically, in programs of planned, sequential activity, reading readiness workbooks are used regularly in approximately four in ten northeastern kindergartens, and alphabet and experience charts are used regularly in three in ten classrooms, but preprimers and primers are being used regularly in fewer than one in twenty classrooms. Whole class instruction prevails.

Implications

Although kindergarten children are generally considered by their teachers as not yet ready to read, these same children are being exposed to mass instruction in reading readiness and beginning reading skills. The teachers seem to be unaware that their classroom practices are inconsistent with their attitudes. If attitudes may be inferred from practices, it is possible that kindergarten teachers in the northeast are more amenable than they have ever been before to the notion of reading in the kindergarten.

REFERENCE

Austin, Mary C., and Morrison, C. *The first r: the Harvard report on reading in elementary schools*. New York: Macmillan Company, 1963.

Early Reading

A Developmental Approach

ELIZABETH M. GOETZ

Teachers have known for years that very young children sometimes begin to read on their own or with help from family members. This common knowledge has been verified by research (Durkin 1966). Early readers—whether self-taught or trained—who have the same IQ's as nonreading peers maintain their head start in reading throughout the elementary years, given appropriate curriculum adjustment (Durkin 1966; McKee and Brezinski 1966). This acceleration in reading, in turn, enhances their performance in other school subjects. The University of Kansas Child Development Laboratory therefore concluded that, if feasible, early reading might be a desirable curriculum option for children as young as three or four years old, provided they are ready.

Any program for teaching children to read at these early ages is likely to raise some eyebrows. Two points must be emphasized: Participation in the program is strickly voluntary with each child and is carefully geared to the readiness of the particular child. It is not our objective to promote the teaching of reading in early childhood programs generally or to induce others to accelerate satisfactory existing schedules for reading instruction. Instead, we are simply interested in finding out what, if anything, might be done to assist the young child who manifests a readiness for reading by self-instruction or requested instruction. Since the effectiveness of such programs is still in the exploratory stage (Robison 1977, p.

Reprinted by permission from YOUNG CHILDREN, Vol. 34, No. 5 (July 1979), pp. 4–11. Copyright © 1979, National Association for the Education of Young Children, 1834 Connecticut Avenue N.W., Washington, D.C. 20009.

139), we feel that a laboratory such as ours is making a contribution.

Interest in early reading has been developing rapidly (Allen 1978; Popp 1975) and probably will accelerate with the federal mandate (P.L. 94-142) that individualized education programs (IEP's) be designed for the gifted as well as the handicapped. Preschool teachers have been advised to handle the teaching of reading in a responsible manner ("Reading and Pre-First Grade" 1977). They also have been warned to provide reading instruction befitting each child's developmental stage rather than blindly following commercial reading programs that do not consider the individual child's learning style, deficits, and assets.

Unfortunately, few early childhood specialists have been trained to assess reading readiness or teach beginning reading in a manner suited to the developmental level of very young children. The instruction of these children has concentrated on enhancing the child's total development: social, physical, intellectual, and emotional (Leeper, Dales, Skiller, and Witherspoon 1971; Robison 1977; Stevens and King 1976). Intellectual development is a part of the total child at an early age, not something to be set aside for later years. From the beginning, one ought to teach as much as each child, as an individual, is comfortably, naturally, and rightfully ready for—even reading (Hymes 1973). Care must be taken of course to avoid any threats, punishment, or emotional pressures to induce a child to learn to read (Smethurst 1975).

Children are never totally ready or unready to read. Reading "readiness," after all, is nothing more than reading instruction in its early stages. Consequently, reading "readiness" and beginning reading are taught simultaneously (Durkin 1976). This same activity may be used as a readiness activity for one child and as a reading activity for another. This versatile method of teaching reading is seldom part of formal early childhood teacher training (see Emery 1975, p. 51).

Research on appropriate reading methods has dealt primarily with children of kindergarten age and older (Chall 1967; Goetz 1977; Stauffer 1967). The purpose of this article is to describe recommended procedures for assessing reading readiness and the teaching of beginning reading for three- and four-year-olds that have been used successfully at the University of Kansas Child Development Laboratory. These procedures might provide the basis for future research that may ultimately provide a data-based methodology.

Reading Readiness Assessment

Commercial tests do not adequately assess reading readiness, in part because they do not take into account the developmental level of very young children: (1) their need for informality; (2) their need for praise; (3) their need for active involvement; (4) their limited language skills; (5) their need for individualized instruction; (6) their lack of pencil and paper test-taking skills; and (7) their inability to process complex stimuli on a complex background.

Readiness tests are generally given to children in groups and focus on vocabulary, visual discrimination, and auditory discrimination. These three abilities usually are assessed by having the children mark the correct picture on a page with several rows of pictures, some of which may be foreign to the very young child's experience. The child may be asked to mark the correct picture for a spoken word, for a match of an original picture, or for a picture's label that rhymes with

or has the same beginning sound as the original picture (Durkin 1976, p. 70). Such test results predict future reading achievement only 16 to 34 percent better than chance (Ladd 1978; Olson and Rosen 1971).

Teacher judgment often may be more reliable than such test scores for predicting reading achievement (Sparberg 1973). Emery (1975, Chapter 6) has suggested an informal reading readiness assessment that we have used along with several innovations of our own. His primary indicators of reading readiness are: (1) oral vocabulary; (2) reading curiosity; (3) auditory discrimination as it relates to clear speech and learning letter sounds; and (4) visual discrimination of letters.

Vocabulary may be assessed by observing and listening to the child in the natural early childhood setting for several weeks. While Emery considers a good working vocabulary to consist of 1,540 words, teachers are not expected to count the words but just to get an overall impression. A child who talks freely and has a good oral vocabulary is easily recognized by an experienced teacher. Reading curiosity is judged by observing the child during the school day: Does the child seem interested in books, look at books, and ask questions about letters and words? The environment, of course, should provide opportunities for reading curiosity to occur.

Auditory discrimination is assessed informally, in part, through everyday conversation. If a child's speech is clear, it is an indication that the child is hearing exact sounds and can reproduce them. A short test is conducted on an individual basis to determine if a child can learn the correct sounds for single letters and groups of letters. For visual discrimination, another short test is conducted on an individual basis to determine if the child can determine whether two letters are the same or different. Usually, auditory discrimination tests on sounds and the visual discrimination tests on letters are conducted within a regular activity involving letters (e.g., grocery store with numerous foods labeled, storytime with books, etc.).

To Emery's (1975) primary indicators, our staff added tests for left-to-right and top-to-bottom visual tracking of words printed on a page and for sound blending. For tracking, the child is asked to show with his or her finger in what direction words are read on a printed page. For blending, the child is given two sounds accompanied by matching letters and asked what sound is made when the two sounds are put together.

All these readiness tests are either observations in the natural environment of the program or individual tests that do not require pencil and paper test-taking skills. In the case of individual tests, there is much teacher help and encouragement. When the child does not know, the answer is given and rehearsed, and the assessment then becomes a learning activity. Observation-type tests and individual tests given by friendly, helpful teachers eliminate test anxiety and provide the child with relaxed opportunities to demonstrate knowledge while actively involved in situations that tend to keep motivational level high. Individual tests also allow the teacher to note subtle characteristics that might not be apparent in groups.

Emery (1975) also listed secondary indicators of reading readiness: (1) attention; (2) compliance; (3) memory as it relates to the general idea of a story; (4) concepts such as top/bottom, up/down, open/closed, etc.; (5) writing in terms of copying straight lines, circles, etc.; and (6) page turning. Our staff found it is not necessary to test specifically for these secondary indicators. Instead, with these indicators in mind, we observe the children during typical activities that provide opportunities to demonstrate these skills.

After considering these observations and tests for primary and secondary indicators and conferring with parents who contribute their own observations, our teaching team can intelligently decide what type of reading instruction a child is best-suited for.

Reading Instruction

During the assessment for reading readiness, all children are introduced to our organic reading center, one of the free-play options along with the blocks, art, concepts, science, and house centers. This reading center is a modified version of Ashton-Warner's organic reading program with Maori children in New Zealand which is described in *Teacher* (1963). It is based on the reading of words that grow out of the child's own life experience. Each child selects the key vocabulary to learn to read; thus, the words were *organic* or *natural* for that child.

There have been two doctoral dissertations on the key vocabulary (Barnette 1971; Duquette 1970), and research is currently being conducted with five- to seven-year-olds in Vancouver, British Columbia (Wassermann 1978). Not only do key vocabulary children learn to read and show growth in language skill development, but compared to control subjects they show a more favorable attitude toward reading. The positive results of Ashton-Warner's (1963) experience and subsequent research, along with Durkin's (1976) advice that the same activity could be used either for reading "readiness" or instruction, inspired us to devise an organic reading program that would be appropriate for three- and four-year-old children.

The organic reading center, tucked in a quiet corner of our classroom, consists of an electric primary (large type) typewriter on a child-sized table, two small chairs (one for the child and one for the teacher), a pack of $3'' \times 5''$ cards, crayons, each child's reading envelope, and a data collection notebook in which the teacher records each child's words, sentences, and performance in reviewing them along with anecdotal notes. The teacher works with the child on a one-to-one basis, thereby stimulating a feeling of success and excitement about reading for each child. Children are free to come into the area or not, but only one child may be there at a time. The reading procedure involves the following steps:

1. The child is asked, "What word would you like to learn to read today?"
2. The teacher types the word given by the child on the middle-top of the 3″ × 5″ card.
3. The teacher and child read this word together with the child underlining from left to right.
4. The child is asked, "What can you tell me about this word?" (The teacher may help the child make a sentence using that word.)
5. The teacher types the sentence in the middle of another 3″ × 5″ card with the words four spaces apart.
6. The teacher and child read this sentence together, with the child underlining the words from left to right. The period at the end of the sentence is pointed out to help the child understand its significance as marking a completion of thought.
7. The child is asked to take the card with the word only and slide it under the sentence to find the matching word.
8. When the child finds the matching words, the words are read and then framed with the child's hands.
9. The teacher asks follow-up, open-ended questions related to the sentence to help build inferential and analytical comprehension skills in the child.
10. The child is asked to draw a picture on the front or back of each card to remind the child of the word.
11. Finally, the cards are put in the child's reading envelope to be reviewed before beginning a new word the next time the child comes into the center.
12. When a child has four words, the teacher and child make up a story with them. The story is typed, and they read it together with the child

underlining from left to right. Individual words that have been incorporated into the story are no longer reviewed, but the story may be reviewed if the child chooses.
13. The child takes the reading packet home over the weekend every other week and returns it the following Monday.

As Durkin has advised, this reading procedure is carried out with many variations depending on the child's developmental level determined from skills evaluated informally during the first few weeks in the program. For a child with a sparse vocabulary, this procedure becomes primarily a language activity since emphasis is on oral expression rather than reading typed words. A child who hesitates to provide a word with an accompanying sentence is helped with such questions as, "What is your favorite color? What things are that color?" or perhaps a more thought-provoking question such as, "What did you do over the weekend?" or "Did you hear the thunderstorm last night?" If a child is having difficulty reading the typed words, the teacher reads the words for the child to prevent the situation from becoming embarrassing or painful. But even a child with a poor vocabulary in this oral variation of organic reading is learning something about reading. Words are simply speech written down.

A child with normal language development who readily says words and sentences to be typed and read is allowed to have as many words and sentences as desired—within reason, of course. Unlike the child with weak language, this child often says, "Let me read it myself."

Though organic reading for these three- and four-year-olds is basically sight word recognition, some children are beginning to learn phonic sounds selected from their organic words and the blending of sounds. The teacher tries to direct these children to learn very different consonant phonic sounds first and then short vowels. Long vowels are taught last with the rationale that this is another way of pronouncing those letters that formerly were learned as short vowels. Yet, the basic rules of phonics have not been taught since these children have not seemed ready for such structured activities.

Some children ask to type their own words, sentences, and stories and are allowed to do so. Some ask to write their words, by hand, and this also is allowed with the teacher providing a handwritten model. Some children stop the matching, framing, and underlining of words on their own, without any adverse effect on learning. Some type messages to take home such as "Keep out, this room is private." Some children even use their reading for therapeutic purposes. For example, one said, "My sister isn't nice because she kicks and bites me." These situations are supported by talking about it as well as reading the typed sentence.

Whatever the child's developmental level, an appropriate variation of organic reading can expose each child to concepts of a word, a sentence, a story, and left-to-right and top-to-bottom tracking. All children are encouraged to increase their attention span through an activity that entices them to continue. What is more interesting than talking and reading about topics of one's own choice? Most important, all children are introduced to the reading process as meaningful communication, since organic reading is based on each child's language aptitude, rather than on rote learning of isolated word and phonics sounds. This approach is supported by findings of reading specialists (e.g., Giordano 1978; Goodman 1976; Pflaum-Connor 1978; Smith 1971) that it is especially important for beginning readers to understand the communication aspect of reading.

Although our reading program probably could have been implemented with handwritten words and sentences, we found that use of the electric primary typewriter has significant advantages. Typing words and sentences can be accomplished quickly to avoid having the young child wait around without active involvement. Since the type is more legible than some teacher's handwriting, reading is not hampered by variations in lettering. Children who want to type their words can do so easily (whereas individual handwriting skills might otherwise rule out writing) which is very helpful in learning letter order.

Conclusion

The teaching of reading to young children should be an important concern. The informal reading assessment and organic reading procedure presented here represent a modest proposal for such instruction of three- and four-year-olds. Looking back on our experience, it seems that Emery's (1975) informal readiness assessment combined with our own innovations provide a reliable guide for determining each child's developmental level in reading. And Durkin's (1976) advice was sound—the same type of reading activity may be used in a competent manner for "readiness" or reading instruction by varying it to match each child's stage of development.

For us, the procedure seems to be working extremely well, but research is needed to affirm its validity. To date, such research has been hampered by unavailability of standardized reading tests appropriate for very young children and the difficulty of making certain that each organic word chosen by the child is not already in the child's reading vocabulary; apparent reading progress could be contaminated by known words. But despite the present lack of supporting data, we know our children enjoy coming to the organic reading center and are becoming readers by their own choice. They look forward to taking their reading envelopes home to share with their parents. In fact, we need more reading teachers and typewriters to handle all the children all the time they want to participate. It is hoped that other practitioners will find these procedures useful and will share their techniques for assessing and teaching reading.

REFERENCES

Allen, K. E. "Reading and the Young Child: Ancient and Recent History." Paper presented at the annual meeting of the Midwest Association for the Education of Young Children, Dearborn, Mich., March 1978.

Ashton-Warner, S. *Teacher*. New York: Simon and Schuster, 1963.

Barnette, E. "The Effect of Key Vocabulary upon Attitudes Toward Reading and Self." Doctoral dissertation, Arizona State University, 1971.

Chall, J. *Learning to Read: The Great Debate*. New York: McGraw-Hill, 1967.

Duquette, R. "An Experimental Study Comparing the Effects of a Specific Program of Sight Vocabulary upon Reading and Writing Achievement of Selected First and Second Grade Children." Doctoral dissertation, Arizona State University, 1970.

Durkin, D. *Children Who Read Early*. New York: Teachers College Press, 1966.

Durkin, D. *Teaching Young Children to Read*. Boston: Allyn and Bacon, 1976.

Emery, D. G. *Teach Your Preschooler to Read*. New York: Simon and Schuster, 1975.

Giordano, G. "Convergent Research on Language and Teaching Reading," *Exceptional Children* 44, no. 8 (1978): 604–613.

Goetz, E. M. "The Traditional and Operant Approaches to Reading Research." Unpublished manuscript, University of Kansas, 1977.

Goodman, K. S. "Behind the Eye: What Happens in Reading." In *Theoretical Models and Processes in Reading*, ed. H. Singer and R. B. Ruddell. 2nd ed. Newark, Del.: International Reading Association, 1976.

Hymes, J. L. "Teaching Reading to the Under-Six Age: A Child Development Point of View." In *Perspectives on Elementary Reading*, ed. R. Karlin. New York: Harcourt Brace Jovanovich, 1973.

Ladd, E. M. "Informal and Formal Screening and Assessment." Paper presented at the annual meeting of the International Reading Association, Houston, Tx., May 1978.

Leeper, S. H.; Dales, R. J.; Skipper, D.S.; and Witherspoon, R. L. *Good Schools for Young Children*. New York: Macmillan, 1971.

McKee, P., and Brezinski, J. E. "The Effectiveness of Teaching Reading in Kindergarten." Cooperative Research Project No. 50371. Denver, Colo.: Denver Public Schools, 1966.

Olson, A. V., and Rosen, C. L. "Exploration of the Structure of Selected Reading Readiness Tests." Paper presented at the annual meeting of the American Educational Research. Association, New York, February 1971.

Pflaum-Conner, S. *The Development of Language and Reading in Young Children*. Columbus, Ohio: Merrill, 1978.

Popp, H. M. "Current Practices in the Teaching of Beginning Reading." In *Towards a Literate Society*, ed. J. B. Carroll and J. S. Chall. New York: McGraw-Hill, 1975.

"Reading and Pre-First Grade." A joint statement of concerns about present practices in pre-first grade reading instruction and recommendations for improvement. Newark, Del.: International Reading Association, 1977.

Robison, H. F. *Exploring Teaching in Early Childhood Education*. Boston: Allyn and Bacon, 1977.

Smethurst, W. *Teaching Young Children to Read at Home*. New York: McGraw-Hill, 1975.

Smith, F. *Understanding Reading: A Psycholinguistic Analysis of Reading and Learning*. New York: Holt, Rinehart & Winston, 1971.

Sparberg, N. Z. "A Quick Teacher-Administered Screening Test to Predict Future Academic Failure in Kindergarten Children.'' Paper presented at the annual meeting of American Educational Research Association, New Orleans, February/March 1973.

Stauffer, R. O. *The First Grade Reading Studies Findings of Individual Investigations.* Newark, Del.: International Reading Association, 1967.

Stevens, J. H., and King, E. W. *Administering Early Childhood Education Programs.* Boston: Little Brown, 1976.

Wassermann, S. "Key Vocabulary: Impact on Beginning Reading." *Young Children* 33, no. 4 (1978): 33–38.

Pre-Handwriting Instruction

- A planned, sequential curriculum . . . is necessary prior to formal handwriting instruction.

  Linda L. Lamme

- Developmental information already exists as a tool to chart children's growth and difficulties.

  Donald H. Graves

- The teacher takes advantage of the child's playfulness, wonder, curiosity, and just plain fun in constructing and reconstructing in writing.

  Georgia L. Peterson

- Various synergies and coordinations must be put into operation to perform the graphic movement; they develop during the pre-writing stage.

  J. de Ajuriaguerra and M. Auzias

INTRODUCTION

To many young children, handwriting instruction is greeted enthusiastically because it is a rite of passage. Written products, even in their most rudimentary form, signify that a transition has occurred from "babyhood" to pupil status. Pre-handwriting instruction, therefore, produces the first concrete evidence of this passage.

Lamme outlines the skills that are prerequisite to handwriting, while Graves treats the introductory stage of handwriting in a more general manner. The comments of the latter contributor range from a discussion of the new interest in handwriting to the relationship between handwriting and other subject areas.

Hall and her colleagues describe the conditions under which children begin to write spontaneously and Peterson recommends some unstructured classroom techniques. In the final paper in this section, de Ajuriaguerra and Auzias examine in some depth the development of writing in the child from several perspectives, considering both the task and the characteristics of the learner.

Handwriting In an Early Childhood Curriculum

LINDA LEONARD LAMME

Handwriting is being taught to young children today in more and more kindergartens and early childhood programs. Children have long been taught to write their names (usually in upper case letters) at home by eager parents who find them highly motivated to acquire this skill. But to assume that children who can write their names are ready to write all letters and words may be a fallacy. Some children are being pushed into handwriting before they have acquired adequate pre-handwriting skills. Handwriting is difficult for these children, causing them to become discouraged. They overcompensate for the pre-handwriting skills they lack, thus causing poor writing habits that are very difficult to correct later.

What are the skills prerequisite for handwriting, and how can we help children acquire them? When should formal

Reprinted by permission from YOUNG CHILDREN, Vol. 35, No. 1 (Nov. 1979), pp. 20–27. Copyright © 1979, National Association for the Education of Young Children, 1834 Connecticut Avenue N.W., Washington, D.C. 20009.

writing instruction begin? Until recently development and assessment of children's readiness for handwriting have received little attention in instructional programs or in professional literature. Barbe (1974) states that "the readiness phase of instruction in handwriting is as important as a sound readiness program in reading" (p. 209). There appear to be six prerequisite skill areas for handwriting: small muscle development, eye-hand coordination, holding a writing tool, basic strokes, letter perception, and orientation to printed language.

Small Muscle Development

The first skill children need to develop is small muscle coordination. Those who have difficulty holding a pencil properly often lack a high degree of small muscle control. Although small muscle activities are rarely thought of as prerequisite skills for handwriting in an early childhood curriculum, motor development clearly is needed prior to using a writing tool.

Activities that enhance small muscle development include many manipulative tasks. Jigsaw puzzles can be graded from easy (with a few large pieces) to complex (with many small pieces). Manipulative toys such as Legos, Tinker Toys, and snap beads are excellent for small muscle development. Play with small motor vehicles, miniature gas stations, dollhouses, etc., gives children experience in using small muscles with precision.

Molding opportunities are indispensable. Clay, sand, play dough, real dough (for baking), putty, sawdust, oatmeal, and papier maché offer children a variety of molding experiences.

Children can also participate in activities common in daily experiences to promote small muscle coordination — zipping, buttoning, sewing, screwing caps on small jars, screwing nuts and bolts, typing, tying knots and bows, and playing a piano. The art curriculum can enhance small muscle development with activities such as painting (with easel or larger brushes), coloring, drawing, sketching, tearing paper, folding paper, and for older children, cutting paper with scissors. Scissors are often introduced into the curriculum too early. Children can be seen struggling with scissors when tearing would be a more appropriate activity. A child who can cut easily with small scissors is very likely ready for handwriting instruction.

A word is in order about the left-handed child. Approximately ten percent of the population is left-handed (Foerster 1975). The small muscle activities listed above will help each child develop hand dominance as well as provide opportunities for teachers to observe and respect the child's handedness. As instruction in letter formation is begun, it is recommended that left-handers be grouped together for instruction (Enstrom 1969).

Eye-Hand Coordination

The second series of handwriting skills in a good early childhood curriculum consists of eye-hand coordination skills. These skills are clearly related to the small muscle development skills, for one must have the muscle control to accomplish what the eye and brain wish to be done. Many of the small muscle activities mentioned above also enhance eye-hand coordination.

Any of the manipulative activities requiring utensils develop eye-hand coordination. Constructing with Legos, blocks, or popsicle sticks builds eye-hand coordination. Balancing objects such as blocks requires precise hand motions. Other precision motor activities include playing the piano, playing with a cash register, pushing buttons, typing, working puzzles, stringing beads, weaving, and sewing. Even large muscle activities such as climbing a ladder, playing Simon Says, and jumping rope help build eye-hand coordination.

Numerous paper-oriented tasks can refine eye-hand coordination skills. Coloring, painting, and drawing are commonly part of an early childhood curriculum. Following dots and completing mazes are enjoyable games for most children. Pasting and finger painting can also enhance eye-hand coordination.

Copying is often part of a handwriting program. However, young children frequently have difficulty with far-to-near copying such as from a chalkboard or chart paper. Children's immature eyes have difficulty translating distant images to closeup images. It is better to have young children copy on paper with the same size letters as the model, first copying directly below the model, then copying from a model placed nearby.

Tracing likewise appears in some early childhood curriculums. At least two research studies have shown that copying is more effective than tracing for initial handwriting instruction (Hirsch and Niedermeyer 1973; Askov and Greff 1975). When tracing, children focus more on staying on the line (or dots) than on visually perceiving what the overall letter or word looks like (Foerster 1972). Tracing actually can inhibit the development of strong basic handwriting strokes.

To observe how well developed eye-hand coordination is, look for children who can consistently hammer nails straight into wood; build a tall building out of blocks without knocking it down; copy sophisticated designs in Legos constructions; follow mazes without touching exterior lines. These children would have the prerequisite eye-hand coordination skills to begin handwriting.

Holding Utensils or Tools

There is a hierarchy of difficulty in using tools or utensils for writing. Pencils are one of the most difficult tools to manipulate effectively; therefore pencils should be the last tools given to children. If you doubt that pencils are the most difficult writing tools, try this experiment: Give young children an opportunity to write their names with four writing tools—chalk, a felt-tip marker, a pencil, and a crayon. Then ask the children which tool was the easiest and which was the most difficult utensil to write with. In most early childhood classrooms where this test has been tried, children overwhelmingly chose markers as the easiest tools to use, followed by chalk, crayon, and pencil, in that order. When asked which tool they enjoyed the most, markers again headed the list.

Children enjoy playing with utensils before they are ready to write. Children need to manipulate tools as part of their early childhood curriculum. A water table with sponges, funnels, straws, and squeeze bottles is essential. Likewise, a sand table with sieves, strainers, containers of various sizes and shapes, sticks, shovels, and pails gives children opportunities to use tools. Gardening adds raking, hoeing, watering, digging, and weeding. Kitchen utensils such as beaters, spoons for stirring, spatulas, and pancake turners make cooking a vital part of the curriculum. Prior to writing, children need many experiences drawing and painting with paint brushes, markers, sponges, chalk, crayons, and

pencils. Charcoal is less suitable because it crumbles easily.

Actual handwriting experiences can begin with markers and felt-tip pens. After the child gains confidence in making firm strokes while holding the tools in a relaxed manner (since they require little pressure), crayons and eventually pencils can be introduced. Crayons, often used as beginning writing tools, require more pressure than markers in order to produce the brighter colors to which children have become accustomed. There is no particular advantage to the large child-sized pencils. In fact, some children write better using regular adult-sized pencils from the start. Although no research studies have involved preschoolers, there is evidence that older children write better with felt-tip and ballpoint pens than with pencils (Krzesni 1971).

It is important that children learn how to hold the writing tool properly from the beginning, because incorrect habits are difficult to break later. The pencil should be loosely gripped with the fingers above the shaved tip to about an inch from the tip. Only the index finger should remain on top of the pencil, not two or three fingers. Left-handers should be encouraged not to "hook" (Enstrom 1969). However, do not stress position of the pencil to such a degree that you discourage the young writer. Rather, simply provide a variety of tools for writing. The child naturally will select those that are easier. Children who select pencils are ready for instruction on the correct position for holding that tool.

There are two indicators that determine if children are holding a pencil correctly. Children who are experiencing stress will grip the pencil too tightly and tire easily and thus will not be able to write for long periods of time. You should be able to easily pull the pencil from the writer's hand as he or she is writing. Look at the child's teeth. Are they clenched, or is the child relaxed? A second indicator of correct pencil usage is the depth of impression on the page caused by the amount of pressure used. Children should always be given soft lead pencils. Then, if the strokes are too light or too dark or if the paper has holes in it, the child is using either too little or too much pressure. Pressure should be even, or the child will become a slow writer.

Basic Strokes

A fourth skill needed prior to instruction in handwriting is the ability to form basic strokes smoothly, in the appropriate direction, and with clean intersections. Observe a child's drawings. Circles and straight lines occur natually in children's drawings. Are the circles round and closed? Do the straight lines intersect properly in such cases as body parts attached to bodies, kites to strings, etc.? Until these strokes occur naturally in such drawings as wagons, cars and trucks, houses, people, flowers, etc., the child is not ready for formal handwriting instruction.

Activities in addition to drawing and painting that give children opportunities to use basic strokes include stirring, sand play, water play, and finger painting. It is important that children not be taught how to make basic strokes in their artwork, but rather that these strokes evolve through time and experience, enhancing creativity as well as indicating readiness for handwriting. Basic strokes can then be "taught" as a part of the handwriting curriculum. Wright and Allen (1975) recommend practice in basic strokes before formal writing begins, so correct sequence of strokes within letters and letter formation can be taught from the start. Teachers should supervise initial writing attempts to discourage the development of bad habits (Enstrom 1965).

The transition from drawing to handwriting is a slow one involving basic strokes in both artistic and written form. A number of principles can be used to identify children who are ready for handwriting.

- Recurring principle—the child repeats patterns (or letters or words) over and over.
- Directional principle—the child goes from left to right and then return sweeps to begin again at the left.
- Generating principle—the child realizes that letter elements can recur in variable patterns.
- Inventory principle—the child lists all of the letters (or words or symbols) he or she knows.
- Contrastive principle—the child perceives likenesses and differences among letter elements, concepts, letters, and words. (Clay 1975)

Not only is it important to observe as a child demonstrates each principle, but abundant drawing and writing experiences should be provided to support the child's acquisition of these skills.

Letter Perception

Sometimes handwriting is viewed solely as a physical activity demanding small muscle coordination with little visual perception. In a longitudinal study of children's handwriting development emphasizing the perceptual-motor nature of handwriting, Furner (1969a, 1969b, 1970) demonstrated that attention to perception in a handwriting program develops better writers than a conventional program.

Furner's program suggests that young children need to be able to recognize form, notice likenesses and differences, infer movement necessary to the production of form, and give accurate verbal descriptions of things they see. Children should observe the finished product (letter or word) as well as the formational act (adult writing the letter or word as a model). Left-handers need left-handed models (Foerster 1975). Self-correction of initial attempts at handwriting can also aid in the development of letter perception (Furner 1969a, 1969b).

Knowing the alphabet is not a prerequisite skill to handwriting. However, the ability to recognize alphabet letters (not necessarily in alphabetical order) is necessary for children who wish to write words and need help in spelling. Early childhood literature is replete with suggestions for helping children learn alphabet letters, so we will not elaborate on those ideas here. In the early stages of handwriting instruction, it is helpful if alphabet letters are kept in meaningful units (e.g., words).

Some letters are easier for children to write than others (Lewis and Lewis 1964). In order from easiest to most difficult, Lewis and Lewis (1964) list: l, o, L, O, H, D, i, v, I, X, E, P, F, V, c, x, T, h, w, J, f, C, N, A, W, K, z, t, B, Q, s, n, Z, r, e, b, S, M, u, Y, d, R, G, a, U, k, m, j, y, P, g, and q. Initially, it is helpful to teach words containing the letters that are formed more easily by young children. Teaching young children to write abstract letters, not associated with words they know, is beyond the developmental levels of most beginning writers.

It is best to use a standard form of manuscript printing initially to teach children to write alphabet letters. The importance of adult modeling of proper letter formation cannot be overemphasized. Have children use unlined paper at first. Children are ready for lines when their writing has achieved a consistent height on a paper without lines. Children write no better on special wide-lined paper than they do on regular adult paper with narrow spaces for writing (Halpin and Halpin 1976).

Reversals occur frequently in the initial stages of handwriting. They usually disappear as children mature. Teachers can however, help solve reversal problems by (a) helping the child see the differences in direction and (b) giving the child practice dealing correctly with the symbols that cause him or her difficulty (Reilly 1972). Children need to perceive visually the way letters are formed; so the more children see the teacher write (on paper just as the child will write), the better. Some letters cause reversal problems with nearly all children—b and d, s, and upper case N; these need to be taught carefully with special attention to the correct beginning point, correct direction of motion, and correct sequence of multipart letters (Enstrom and Enstrom 1969).

Orientation to Printed Language

A final pre-handwriting skill involves a set of skills that parallel reading readiness skills:

- How to attend and orient to printed language.
- How to organize one's exploratory investigation of printed forms.
- How to tell left from right.
- How to visually analyze letters and words. (Clay 1975)

Children can have all of the mechanical skills to perform handwriting tasks, but unless they see the "whole"—what printed language stands for and how it is used to communicate—they will not likely have the motivation to develop good handwriting skills. Just as in reading, we must be careful to avoid subdividing handwriting instruction into minute subskills without at the same time providing lots of examples of the complete end product concurrently.

Herein lies the importance of incorporating numerous language experience activities into the early childhood curriculum. Children need to make lots of books, greeting cards, pictures with labels, charts, maps, letters to mail, signs, etc., where adults do the writing for them. Likewise, they need to "read" lots of favorite songs, stories, and rhymes from charts and class books that have been written in their presence. Each child can have a mailbox or cubby to encourage written communication even before learning to write formally. *Handwriting readiness* ought not to occur in isolation but rather *should be an integral part of the oral and written language program.*

Conclusion

It is important that the six skill areas (small muscle development, eye-hand coordination, holding a writing tool, basic strokes, letter perception, and orientation to printed language) be included but not rushed in an early childhood curriculum. A planned, sequential, curriculum such as the one outlined in this article is necessary prior to formal handwriting instruction. Because children enter school with a wide repertoire of skills and abilities, early childhood teachers need to be able to assess individual differences and provide both pre-handwriting activities for children who are not yet ready for formal handwriting instruction and careful beginning instruction for children who are ready.

Because some children learn to write at home and many others receive at least some instruction from parents, the handwriting curriculum should involve parents (Hall, Moretz, and Statom 1976). Teachers can help parents understand why young children should not be pushed into handwriting before they have acquired these pre-handwriting skills. Ideas for helping their children with these skills can be valuable as they understand the importance of providing their children with many free writing and drawing opportunities. Because many parents do teach their children how to write, they will appreciate knowing how and when to get them off to a good start. The parent component of the early childhood handwriting curriculum is at least as important as (and may be more important than) the school curriculum.

REFERENCES

Askov, E. N., and Greff, E. N. "Handwriting: Copying vs. Tracing as the Most Effective Type of Practice." *Journal of Educational Research* 69 (1975): 96–98.

Barbe, W. B., and Lucas, V. H. "Instruction in Handwriting: A New Look." *Childhood Education* 50 (1974): 207–209.

Clay, M. M. *What Did I Write?* Aukland, New Zealand: Heinemann Educational Books, 1975.

Enstrom, E. A. "Handwriting: Let's Begin in Kindergarten." *Catholic Educator* 36 (1965): 40–41.

Enstrom, E. A. "The Left-Handed Child" *Today's Education* 58 (1969): 43–44.

Enstrom, E. A., and Enstrom, D. C. "In Print Handwriting: Preventing and Solving Reversal Problems." *Elementary English* 46 (1969): 759–764.

Foerster, L. M. "Sinistral Power! Help for Left-Handed Children." *Elementary English* 52 (1975): 213–215.

Foerster, L. M. "Teacher—Don't Let Your First Graders Trace!" *Elementary English* 49 (1972): 431–433.

Furner, B. A. "An Analysis of the Effectiveness of a Program of Instruction Emphasizing the Perceptual-Motor Nature of Learning Handwriting." *Elementary English* 47 (1970): 61–69.

Furner, B. A. "The Perceptual-Motor Nature of Learning in Handwriting." *Elementary English* 46 (1969a): 886–894.

Furner, B. A. "Recommended Instructional Procedures in a Method Emphasizing the Perceptual-Motor Nature of Learning in Handwriting." *Elementary English* 46 (1969b): 1021–1030.

Hall, M.; Moretz, S. A.; and Statom, J. "Writing before Grade One—A Study of Early Writers." *Language Arts* 53 (1976): 582–585.

Halpin, G., and Halpin, G. "Special Paper for Beginning Handwriting: An Unjustified Practice?" *Journal of Educational Research* 69 (1976): 267–269.

Hirsch, E., and Niedermeyer, F. C. "The Effects of Tracing Prompts and Discrimination Training on Kindergarten Handwriting Performance," *Journal of Educational Research* 67 (1973): 81–86.

Krzesni, J. S. "Effect of Different Writing Tools and Paper on Performance of the Third Grader." *Elementary English* 48 (1971): 821–824.

Lewis, E. R., and Lewis, H. P. "Which Manuscript Letters Are Hard for First Graders?" *Elementary English* 41 (1964): 855–858.

Reilly, V. "Reversals in Writing: Some Suggestions for Teachers." *Teaching Exceptional Children* 4 (1972): 145–147.

Wright, J. P., and Allen, E. G. "Ready to Write!" *Elementary School Journal* 75 (1975): 430–435.

Handwriting Is For Writing

DONALD H. GRAVES

Handwriting was one of those early school experiences I have tried to repress. Images of ink globules racing across white paper from deadly scratch pens still give me a heavy feeling. Recollections of endless circles, precise spacing, and comments about my untidiness take away my energy. I had no idea that handwriting was for writing. For years, I have suppressed the connection. Handwriting was punishing, mindless, and mechanical whereas composing with ideas was lofty and worthwhile.

I refused to teach handwriting as a classroom teacher, avoided it as a language arts supervisor, and only recently have begun to understand its place in the language arts scheme. New and old research data and my observations of struggling young writers have revised these earlier opinions.

Children want to write. They want to put down ideas, tell stories, record information, make signs, or act out experiences through their writing. They are more interested in their own marks on paper than the marks of others. But, for many, the handwriting struggle is so great that their important, self-centered objectives are lost. Holding a pencil for more than five minutes or sequencing letters across a line in a set space is simply too great a demand. Ask these same children what writing is about and they will respond: "Keeping neat margins, not writing below the line, and having good spaces between words." Children refer to these details because handwriting is the nature of their struggle. They cannot yet refer to the meaning of writing as including more than mechanical acts.

New Interest in Handwriting

A new interest in handwriting accompanies the recent emphasis on composition itself. Mina Shaughnessy's study (1976) of composition for entering freshmen in the New York City university system found that poor handwriting was a significant barrier to good writing. Shaughnessy observed:

Thus it is not unusual to find among freshman essays a handwriting that belies the maturity of the student, reminding the reader instead of the labored cursive style of children. Often, but not always, the content that is carried in such writing is short and bare, reinforcing the impression of the reader that the writer is "slow" or intellectually immature. Yet the same student might be a spirited, cogent talker in class. His problem is that he has no access to his thoughts or personal style through the medium of writing and must appear, whenever he writes, as a child.

From *Language Arts,* Vol. 55, No. 3 (March, 1978). © 1978 by the National Council of Teachers of English. Reprinted by permission.

Shaughnessy deals with the handwriting issue within the context of where it belongs, the study of composition.

Too much of current handwriting instruction has lost its "toolness." It exists as an end in itself. Handwriting has become the main event, composition the side show. There are several reasons for this. Many teachers do not know what to do with the new emphasis on composition and turn to handwriting as at least outward evidence that writing is taught. Parents and administrators, especially with the new emphasis on basics, value handwriting with its easy visibility and diagnosis (legible or illegible) as proof that the fundamentals are properly stressed.

The misuse of handwriting does not diminish its importance. As Shaughnessy has mentioned there are instances where students' writing is affected simply because of their writings' appearance. These same older students possibly had a poor start with handwriting. Research with very young writers shows they lose out on effective composing because of the slowness with which they put words on paper. Worse, they do not wish to write at all. There are many reasons for these problems. They will be reviewed in this report. Finally, I will outline needed research in handwriting, particularly as it is related to composing itself.

The Development of Handwriting Skill

Teachers are confronted more by individuals than groups in the teaching of handwriting. Images of children and papers flow through their minds. Rex is so physically involved that he sits on his knees, lowers his head, and with bull-like impatience impales the paper with his pencil. Mark scrawls through lines as if they did not exist, whereas Michelle delicately places her paper to the right, and with lightened grip, deftly writes her message across the page. As teachers we wonder what to do tomorrow with these children. We wonder why they write as they do.

There is a body of research that can help us. The Lenneberg's two volume set on *Foundations of Language Development* (1976), which includes the chapter "Preconditions for the Development of Writing in the Child," takes a developmental perspective to introducing children to handwriting. The two authors of the chapter, J. de Ajuriaguerra of the Psychiatric Clinic, University of Geneva in Switzerland and M. Auzias of the National Institute of Health and Medical Research in Paris, France, have both conducted research on handwriting for some time. Their work and that of other continental researchers is summarized in this review of preconditions to writing. Though their continental insularity leads to the neglect of such American researchers as Groff, Otto, Andersen, and Myklebust, their developmental perspectives are useful in helping teachers to help children.

This review is no mere motor analysis of handwriting but one that places handwriting in a much broader language framework. The relation of thinking (inner language) to writing, as well as the full range of developmental issues related to the praxic (motor) aspects of writing are included.

The data from this review will be useful to the degree that teachers can recall and apply their observations to particular children with whom they are working. Developmental data are like that; they challenge us to see for ourselves, to analyze and sequence information until it makes sense in our efforts to aid the child.

There is a need to identify some of the major conventions that are required of children when they try to put something down on paper. An understanding of these conventions, and the developmental issues attached to them, will help us observe what barriers children encounter in handwriting, and how they apply to composing itself.

One caution. As we observe children

there is a temptation to overgeneralize child difficulties. How easy it is to project our protectiveness into the child's world! I have seen a child write for thirty-five minutes, laboring over the creation of a mere thirty words. This child demonstrates unusual staying power, simply because of the importance of the message. There may be a struggle with as many as eight barriers but the importance of the message transcends them all. Another child can be unsaddled by the mere frustration of where to start on a page.

Developmental Factors

How children use space when they write is important diagnostic information. New space, as in a blank piece of paper, places great demands on the young writer. As adults it is difficult for us to appreciate these demands until we work in a new space dimension ourselves. For example, a few years ago I attempted to install some new bookcases in my study. More screw heads were torn and misshapen simply because I did not know how to handle the tools or stand correctly in relation to my work. I knew neither the grip, the angle to work, nor how to guide with my left hand. Force would solve all . . . and it did not. Not until my neighbor deftly positioned himself and quickly guided new screws into their proper locations did I realize the simple facts of experience. My neighbor had dealt with both space, tools, and his own body in relation to that space before. Many hours of practice had taught him how to solve these spacial demands.

Young writers must relate the space of their own bodies to the space on the paper. Look around the room when you are next near children who are writing. You will see many postures, distances from the paper, as well as different positions of the paper on the desk. These are all space discovery features.

Piaget and Inhelder (1948) and Lurcat (1968) have studied the mastery of graphic space for the child. "It is the si-multaneous production of units of graphy and their meaning that enable the child to relate himself to the space on the sheet" (de Ajuriaguerra & Auzias 1975, p. 320). Whether the child is drawing or scribbling, activity is first marked by the exploration of the paper by indiscriminate actions with increased purpose, and good use of space thereafter. "The first strokes (continuous, then discontinuous: circular marks, curves, descending lines, then lateral) are directly governed by the maturation of the motor processes and the role played by the body axis, which acts as an axis of symmetry and affects the direction of the strokes" (de Ajuriaguerra & Auzias 1975. p. 320).

Drawing and writing development are much more closely related than is realized. Both are attempts to represent. At first (with children two to three years of age) there is no difference between them. Later, the child differentiates by drawing a picture and by making continuous scribbles across the page to represent writing itself.

de Ajuriaguerra and Auzias make the point that "Through movement space has been defined." Through praxia, children's drawing and writing on paper, children have discovered how to handle that space, have adjusted it to their own bodies. These same terms are used by persons working in movement education. One of the first tasks in a movement workshop with young children is "to discover your own space." They do this by reaching up and down, around, and by jumping, crawling, or creeping in that small sector of floor space.

There is a mild controversy over how children can best discover space on a page. Alice Yardley from England stresses, "Unlined paper will give the child a surface free of restrictions when his attempts to write are immature and unformed" (1973, p. 118). Children in England work for some time (several years) before lined paper is introduced. On the other hand, in most American schools it is felt that children work best when limits are set through lined paper. Though the lines are well-spaced to accommodate large muscle interference, there is less discovery of an entire page and more discovery of a set space. I do not know of any research that deals with the best approach to space discovery.

Teachers, however, do not have to wait for researchers to act. The careful observation of their own children's exploration of space can tell them. A teacher who provides *many opportunities* for space exploration (art work, construction, movement, writing) does contribute to development.

How children change in their use of space is fundamental to the observation of other changes they make as they become more proficient in their writing. The issue in growth is change. This is the teacher's main concern, change. Although the following variables are not new in considering handwriting fundamentals, their review from the perspective of de Ajuriaguerra and Auzias can be helpful to teachers working with writers of any age. A teacher observing writers can be aided by asking the following questions:

Question

1. How do children change in their use of thumb and forefinger together?

2. How does the continuousness of a child's writing change?

3. How do the position of the elbow and the stability of the body axis change?

4. How does the position of the writing surface change in relation to the child's midline?

5. How does the child's distribution of strength change?

Discussion and Meaning for Writing

1. A poor grip reduces control. At first it is difficult for children to use this position unless they have already used it in composing with other materials.

2. At first children must stop and start due to the unfamiliarity of the movements as well as what they are composing. The observer is interested in finding out if motor issues are contributing to erratic movements as opposed to spelling and idea formulation.

3. The reduction of elbow motion increases the efficiency of thumb and forefinger, and speed and ease of writing. At first there is great elbow motion, along with motion of the entire body. Until this other motion can be reduced, children will have difficulty with the small motor demands of writing.

4. At first children face the paper straight on, not knowing how to accommodate to the left or right of the midline. Gradually children understand the space (the paper) they are dealing with in relation to their own body activity.

5. The child has to suppress large muscles in order for small muscles to gain control. Pressure on the point of the writing instrument as well as body position gives this information. Observe the change in light and heavy lines on the child's paper.

6. How does the child's use of writing space change?

6. (This has been discussed but a few more details are offered to aid observation.) On a sheet of unlined paper a child will first chain letters at most any angle. The control of large muscles also makes it difficult to use space with precision. Also, the meaning of language, word concepts, sentence units, etc., lead to different kinds of spaces between words. At first we note that children run words and sentences together. As language meaning increases the spaces begin to appear. Audience sense also contributes to this development.

These questions should be viewed by teachers in relation to their effect on composing. Any of these factors can contribute to slowness in handwriting which in turn affects the quality and content of writing, and often the child's view of writing itself. It is at the point of speed that we have underestimated the contribution of handwriting to composing. "Getting the words down" is the most dominant early task; gradually the concern for legibility arrives and can be a later irritant, as Mina Shaughnessy has observed. Handwriting is for writing.

When there are problems with handwriting, writing itself is often affected. How and in what ways writing is affected by problems in handwriting is not directly known. Research that uncovers some of these issues is needed.

Needed Research in Handwriting

Seven-year-old Alison has difficulty with both handwriting and spelling. Furthermore, she dislikes writing and looks for ways to avoid composing. Alison speaks with ease when explaining personal experiences, yet rebels at the thought of writing. The crafting of messages, the wait-it-out experience of ordering and making symbols is upsetting.

There are many Alisons. We need to know how and in what order behaviors emerge in spelling, handwriting, and composing that we may understand their relationship. For example, Alison may have good knowledge of sound-symbol relationships. Yet, her motor skills are so poorly developed that her writing speed causes letters to be reversed, or even entire words omitted. Or, she may have strong motor skills but be unable to use sound-symbols to personal satisfaction. She keeps resequencing sounds. "Let's see, 'army'—o-r-m-e-y. No, I'll try it this way—a-o-r-u-m-y." Alison might spend as long as four to five minutes on a single word. The slowness of the process led her to reread constantly to get the sense of where she was in the message. She was very much aware of the discrepancy between her oral and written language. She did not want to write.

There are questions we need to answer as we relate handwriting, spelling, and composing. The data can only be gathered by meticulous observation of the same children over a long period of time. The length of time is dependent on the predictability of information. That is, when the researcher notes that data between cases are predictable and next behaviors are forecast with accuracy, then enough data have been gathered.

There are separate bodies of research on handwriting, spelling, and composing. But only in rare instances have data connected the three. The data can be gathered through meticulous observation of the same children over a long period of time. Through the unity of individual cases, data are gathered simultaneously on the emergence of behaviors in all three areas: spelling, handwriting, and composing. The following are some of the questions such procedures might begin to answer:

Question	*Discussion*
1. How does speed in handwriting affect the content of composition?	1. Until some degree of proficiency in handwriting is reached, children probably do not branch out into more elaborative thinking. Handwriting affects information.
2. How does speed in handwriting affect spelling?	2. The length of time a child must maintain sounding in order to write a letter or even a word probably has a bearing on the accuracy with which the word is spelled. Sounding lags behind the child's capacity to put the letter on paper.
3. How does the child's concept of audience relate to changes in handwriting legibility?	3. Early writing is highly self-centered. Although there is always some audience sense present in the young child's actions, it does not reach proportions significant enough to affect legibility until seven or eight.
4. How does a child's concept of handwriting itself change?	4. Child interviews already show their concepts of handwriting, spelling, and composing change. How these concepts are related to performance and the interrelationships between handwriting, spelling, and composing is not known.
5. How is a child's handwriting related to performance in art work?	5. Children's use of space in art work can also be related to their use of space in handwriting. We need to observe the connection.

Handwriting is for writing. It does not exist to make rows of circles, establish habits of cleanliness, copy epigrammatic statements from the chalkboard, or involve the students in independent activity during reading period. It is not an end in itself. It makes strong contributions to both spelling and writing. Developmental information already exists as a tool to chart children's growth and difficulties as they seek to express their ideas on paper. But research on handwriting is in its infancy when viewed within the context of the entire field of the language arts. We already have data on spelling, handwriting, and composing, but practically none that show how each affects the other.

REFERENCES

de Ajuriaguerra, J. and Auzias, M. "Preconditions for the Development of Writing in the Child." In *Founda-*

tions of Language Development Vol. 2, edited by Eric and Elizabeth Lenneberg. New York: Academic Press, 1975.

Piaget, J. and Inhelder, B. *La Representation de l'Espace Chez l'Enfant.* Paris: Presses Universitaires de France. 1948.

Shaughnessy, Mina P. *Errors and Expectations.* New York: Oxford University Press, 1977.

Yardley, Alice. *Exploration and Language.* New York: Citation Press, 1973.

Writing Before Grade One—A Study of Early Writers

MARYANNE HALL
SARA A. MORETZ
JODELLANO STATOM

Learning to read and learning to write are related processes which deal with printed symbols. The general sequence of language learning is thought to be listening, speaking, reading and writing. Early reading has received considerable research attention; early writing has not although there is evidence that some children do write before formal instruction and that they write before learning to read. (Durkin, 1966, 1970; Read, 1971).

Durkin (1970) suggested that "there might be something 'natural' about the home situation in which the young children learned to read." She noted for some early readers that the ability to read was, at least in part, a by-product of ability in writing and spelling. In his investigation of the "spontaneous spelling" of preschool children Read (1971) found that writing began before learning to read and that in some cases writing began as early as three and a half years. Durkin reported that the most common

time for interest in written language to appear was age four.

C. Chomsky (1971) described an instance of preschool writing similar to those noted by Read. She claimed that forming letters (either using sets of letters or writing by hand) is the first step toward reading, and she suggested reversing the usual order of reading first, then writing.

Pryzwansky (1972) investigated the effects of a program of instruction in manuscript writing as one of three treatments in perceptual motor training in relation to gains on reading readiness tests in kindergarten but did not study the nature of early writing without school instruction. He reported significant findings favoring manuscript writing and suggested that "manuscript training could serve to improve a number of skills."

Factors, especially factors in the home background, which contribute to early reading have been investigated but factors which are related to early writing have not been studied. Little attention has been given to the acquisition of writing prior to direct instruction in the mechanics of writing in first grade. The ef-

From *Language Arts,* Vol. 53, No. 5 (May, 1976). © 1976 by the National Council of Teachers of English. Reprinted by permission.

fect of a reading environment in the home and in preschool settings as a valuable corollary of developing a desire to read before grade one has been stressed by reading authorities for many years. Writing is another facet of becoming literate; yet, a writing environment and its effect on reading readiness and reading achievement has been largely ignored.

Purpose

The purpose of this study was to study factors in the home background of children who were early writers and to ascertain the sequence of learning to write in relation to learning to read.

Definition of Early Writers

For this study early writers were defined as those children who learn to write prior to formal instruction in kindergarten and/or grade one. To be classified as an early writer, a child's efforts at writing should contain legible (distinct) letter and/or word forms, and it should be evident that the child is trying to communicate or represent specific letters, words, or ideas through writing. To be classified as an early writer, the child should show continued interest in writing and should engage in self-initiated writing activities on a number of occasions. Early writers may or may not have learned to read before formal instruction in reading is given. The criteria of self-initiated writing activities, legibility, and frequency are significant considerations in identifying early writers.

Subjects

The early writers attended the four nursery-kindergarten classes for three, four, and five year olds in the Center for Young Children, College of Education, University of Maryland. Twenty-two of the total population of 79 children were identified by teachers as early writers. One child was dropped because of his refusal to be tested, and two were omitted because performance on a writing sample indicated that they were not early writers. The study included ten girls and nine boys with an age range from three years, four months, to six years, one month at the time of identification in February, 1973. It was not possible to hold an interview for one child, so the information reported here is for 18 children (nine boys, nine girls).

Procedures

The procedures included identification of early writers, and obtaining information from the parents through interviews. Limited data on reading readiness performance was also collected and is reported elsewhere (Hall, Moretz, Statom, 1973).

The teachers of the preschool classes identified children who were early writers according to the definition, and the teachers also completed a Checklist of Writing Behavior for all students in their classes.

Interviews were conducted with the parents using a questionnaire developed by the researchers. The seven sections of the questionnaire were: general information about the child; general information about the parents; writing behavior; family writing activities and parent comments about the child's writing; writing, art and other materials in the home; family reading activities and parent comments about the child's reading; and comments about the child's personality. The interviews took from 30 to 45 minutes.

Findings on the Home Background

Most of the parents of the early writers were college graduates with the majority of the fathers holding professional positions or pursuing advanced graduate work. Most mothers were qualified to hold professional positions although half were not working while their children were preschoolers. The sample included five children with foreign backgrounds and two children from lower socioeconomic levels.

All parents reported frequent observation of one or both parents and/or siblings engaging in writing activities. All parents reported writing materials were easily accessible to the child, usually without parental permission. Also, in every instance books were available, and only one parent reported not having newspapers and magazines around. All parents reported that the children liked to be read to and that there was frequent observation by the children of family members engaged in reading activities.

Three patterns to the interest in writing (not mutually exclusive categories) were noted. One pattern was the desire to communicate, often through letters to relatives or friends after a move. Another pattern was introduction to letter names and to writing through direct instruction by the parents. Two parents initiated the direct instruction while in four cases parents gave instruction in reponse to interest evidenced by the children. The majority of parents reported help given at the children's request. The nature of help requested most frequently was with letter formation, recording a child's dictation, and oral spelling of words.

Sesame Street was cited in about half of the cases as contributing to knowledge of letter names, and in five cases as the primary factor in creating an interest in reading.

Findings on Sequence of Writing and Reading

Parents reported that interest in writing preceded interest in reading in 17 out of 18 cases. In six cases ability to read a few words preceded ability to write legible words from memory although these children learned to copy letters and

words before learning to read words with one exception. Two of the children who read before writing legible words from memory were the two whose parents had initiated direct reading instruction.

The extent of reading ability reported by the parents ranged from no reading knowledge in one case to the ability to read beginning books reported for seven with ten instances of children able to read a few words. The early writer for whom no interview was conducted was reported by her teacher to be the most advanced in reading.

Teachers reported less reading ability than parents. Only eight writers were reported by teachers to have some reading knowledge. Four writers were classified as readers by the teachers.

Discussion and Recommendations for Future Research

This initial study of early writing did reveal that learning to write in the preschool years does occur for some children in homes which offer exposure to and models of writing in natural settings. The majority of early writers exhibited interest in and ability to write prior to learning to read.

This study was limited to teacher identification, and since the school environment did little with writing exposure, some writers may have been overlooked. A writing sample might have been a better means of identification. This study was limited to the population of a university school, and the proportion of early writers in other preschool populations may differ.

Comparison of early writers and nonearly writers might identify factors which are common for early writers which are not present for nonearly writers and might reveal certain differences which could have instructional implications. Although the difficulty of testing young children might be a serious obstacle in obtaining certain information for the nonearly writers, comparison studies of children's concepts of language might reveal contributions of writing to cognitive clarity about language (Downing, 1969). Personality characteristics of early writers could also be studied.

The relationships of learning to write to reading readiness and reading achievement merit investigation. Investigations of the ability to reproduce written symbols should examine the relationship of this ability to perform the visual discrimination tasks of reading.

Detailed observational descriptions of the acquisition of writing in the preschool years could provide needed information about the sequence of learning to write and learning to read. We attempted to obtain this information in interviews

but parents were hazy about the time of acquisition and sequence of writing behaviors.

The effect of a writing environment in which children are exposed to written language and writing materials in preschool settings should be investigated.

Recommendations that parents provide reading materials, that they read to their children, and that they demonstrate a model of reading behavior are common. Perhaps corresponding recommendations about writing should also be given. Early exposure to and experience with writing as communication may facilitate interest in both writing and reading and may contribute to initial success in school.

REFERENCES

Chomsky, Carol. "Write First, Read Later," *Childhood Education* 47 (March, 1971) 296–299.

Downing, John. "How Children Think About Reading," *The Reading Teacher* 23 (December, 1969) 217–230.

Durkin, Dolores. "A Language Arts Program for Pre-First Grade Children: Two Year Achievement Report," *Reading Research Quarterly* 5 (Summer, 1970) 534–565.

Durkin, Dolores. *Children Who Read Early.* Teachers College Press, 1966.

Hall, MaryAnne; Moretz, Sara A. and

Statom, Jodellano. "An Investigation of Early Writing," College Park, Maryland: Center for Young Children, College of Education, 1973.

Pryzwansky, Walter B. "Effects of Perceptual-Motor Training and Manuscript Writing on Reading Readiness Skills in Kindergarten," *Journal of Educational Psychology* 63 (April, 1973) 110–115.

Read, Charles. "Pre-school Children's Knowledge of English Phonology," *Harvard Educational Review* 41 (February, 1971) 1–34.

An Approach to Writing for Kindergarteners

GEORGIA L. PETERSON

In working with children new to school, I questioned, "Can five year olds learn about writing and develop abilities to write through some structure or form that maintains the desire and delight that they brought with them to school?" The following illustrates one answer I found. My intent is not to make a case for such experiences but to announce its feasibility. My point is not that this is the best time to do it in terms of developmental readiness, but more in terms of interest readiness. Therefore, neatness and traditional expectations do not exist.

In answering the question I knew what had to happen first and continue to happen in the classroom. Previous and ongoing experiences had to include many forms of verbal expression such as dictating, discussing, reporting, and dramatizing. The classroom environment needed to provide many experiences in listening to stories, records, films, and tapes. Painting, musical experiences, and large and small muscle play were essential to their experiences. More specifically, the children needed to have handled and viewed letters in sandpaper and three dimensions, to have used printing sets, typewriters, and tools which are more traditionally related to writing such as crayons, pencils and pens.

The writing aspect of language expression can only begin when children have had such experiences and indicate that they would like to try and write some of their own words.

In the beginning the children sit comfortably where they can see a large chalkboard. Unlined newsprint and writing instruments of various sizes, colors, and kinds are available so they can choose what suits them best. Such instruments are felt pens, crayons, pencils, and pens.

Because timing is so important and motivation must come from within the children, little explanation or discussion is necessary. However, the explanation that writing is a tool that everyone really needs in life and that they are going to try their hand at doing some seems fitting. It is also important at this point to discuss briefly how writing is one of the skills they need and that it will be in their hands, and not in their heads. They need to develop it in their hands.

Vital features of this approach are where the emphases are placed. It is essential that children understand that the same letter can be made many different ways, that each person's writing is different and unique, that machines make letters in many different ways, and that the letters will be presented in order of their likeness of construction rather than A-Z, for example: PDBR, EFHI, SCOQ, AKLT, MNWV, XYZ. Where in the alphabet the class begins is rather unimportant and the order of presentation of letters is unimportant. Generally, something happens in the classroom in terms of an activity or a discussion that can get it going. Also, beginning with letters that are made with the two basic elements in manuscript writing, I and O has validity. Large and small letters are presented together to avoid later confusion.

The teacher might begin by making a (P) on the board, naming it, and making a brief statement about its construction, then go on to say, "This is mine, you make one." The teacher then looks at

From *Elementary English*, Vol. 52, No. 1 (January, 1975). Copyright © 1975 by the National Council of Teachers of English. Reprinted by permission.

everyone's letter, with praise and attention to each being unique and vital.

In the education of any student, but particularly young children, the teacher's main concern should be in valuing the student and his or her work. It is possible and vital in every instance to consider what students do in their first attempts as acceptable and adequate.

The next possible step in the approach would be to make a small (p), emphasizing its likeness and comparison to big (P). Each child then could make some little p's and some big P's. At this point the teacher might say, "I'm coming around to see how things are going and I'm going to circle one super big P and one super little p." Everyone will have a "super" letter in both sizes because "super" is for that child. The clue seems to be to maintain a feeling of experimentation, wonder, and enjoyment. Children make comments such as, "I knew you would do that." "I like this one better." To maintain enthusiasm and delight the children should be encouraged to make it as enjoyable, as experimental, and as curiosity-arousing as possible. They should want to parade and strut their letters.

If children make letters upside down or backwards at first it is advisable to leave it until later because it will most likely straighten itself out soon, or teaching sense will indicate when that particular child can handle being corrected. This is generally developmental and may for a while vary from minute to minute or day to day. At this point that is irrelevant because he or she is getting the *feel*, and is getting writing in his hand.

The teacher should take advantage of any clues of fun, interest, curiosity, or wonder that the children give and make use of that in the teaching. An example might be if some child wants to make letters into objects by adding to or taking from. The children will make comments such as, "My name begins with that," or "That letter is in my brother's name." They will also say, "You can make that F into an E by adding another line."

They are then helping you and this should be encouraged.

Once children can make all of the letters, they will need and want practice in seeing and writing them. It is difficult to determine all of the ongoing activities that will aid in this gaining of power in knowing and using the letters.

One of our most successful adventures after everyone could make the letters was the making of a dictionary. It was begun because we were ready for activities that would help us with beginning letters, sounds, etc. We began with A and went to Z making the dictionary. Children suggested words. I wrote them so all could see, they chose ones they wanted to illustrate as individuals, as a group we defined them, and I constructed all of the work into a book. It did not begin with that intention but that is what it worked its way into being.

At this point the children were comfortable with writing. In the mornings they were asking that their dictation be written down so they could write it themselves. This was my clue that enough were comfortable with writing to request some each afternoon session so they could make use of practice and get it in their hands.

For any particular group it is difficult to determine how to do the requiring and what form it should take. I have found that it is easier for children if what they are writing is their own, if it is in front of them to copy, and try for as long as it is necessary to offer to write a while for each of them and let them continue when their hands have rested. All the children's writing will be quite different and unique. At all times this should be respected and provided for because the way children's writing appears is usually relevant to their being.

In summary, two vital points of this approach are no one can do it wrong, and students don't become automatons in their writing. The teacher takes advantage of the child's playfulness, wonder, curiosity, and just plain fun in constructing and reconstructing in writing.

Later, when the child is more secure, particulars that will make it easier can be taught.

The most amazing and reassuring aspect of this approach is in the child's own sense of accomplishment. This alone is reason enough for *doing* writing. There isn't a need to do structured pre-writing that is dull and drilling—just *do real writing*.

Preconditions for the Development of Writing in the Child

J. DE AJURIAGUERRA
M. AUZIAS

In this chapter the conditions for the acquisition and development of handwriting are discussed in the light of many different aspects: motor organization; psychomotor and praxic organization required for writing; speed; hold of the tool; and tonicity. We shall analyze the "directional conventions" view of the spatial constraints of writing. Also discussed are stages in mastery of the graphic space by the child; the most usual tools; methods of learning and handwriting scales; writing disorders that may develop in some children, their causes, and relevant re-education methods. Finally, teaching suggestions drawn from experimental investigations and practice in re-education are given.

The Nature of Writing

We must first determine the place of writing in the human sciences. When studying writing in the context of communication systems, one notices with J.

Derrida (1967) that more antagonism than cooperation is expressed when the history of writing and language science meet on the same ground. This author demonstrates, on the basis of an in-depth analysis, to what extent such diverse authors as J. J. Rousseau, F. de Saussure, Jakobson, Halle, and Levi-Strauss tend to depreciate writing on the grounds of its being external, arbitrary, instrumental, auxiliary, parasitical. It is also accused of lack of authenticity, of misrepresentation, of being harmful and inconsistent. Again, writing is considered static, tyrannical, deceptive, a mechanization of language and a loss of the living idiom.

On a more lyrical note, Voltaire remarks that writing is the painting of the voice; the more it resembles it, the better it is. It is true that writing lacks melody, intonation, the tempo of speech, and its spontaneity. When writing attempts to substitute accents for accent, it is but a hollow sham, remarked Derrida. In some cases, however, poetry tries to overcome the absence of accent.

We are in agreement with Alarcos Llorach (1968) when he points out that the elements that make up writing are graphic signs with a structure analogous to that of linguistic signs; in other words, there are two constituents, the

Pages 311–321 of "Preconditions for the Development of Writing in the Child." From *Foundations of Language Development*, Vol. 2, Academic Press. © 1975 Unesco Publications. Reprinted with permission of Unesco.

signans and the *signatum*. Both of these communication media, speech and writing, share the same *signatum*—human experience in general. It would be useful to undertake a systematic "graphematic" study of the communication function of graphic elements and the problems of their material expression. It is not our intention to take on all of these problems in this chapter. For this we refer the reader to the article by Alarcos Llorach (1968) and to the works collected by the Centre International de Synthèse (1963) under the heading. *L'Écriture et la Psychologie des Peuples.*

We do not intend to define the value of written language here, but to study the framework in which writing as such is situated and how it comes about.

In writing, whether transposition or not, the hand that speaks gives pleasure to the child, for whom it is a "discovery" and a means of representing something within himself. It is speech and motion. "The tyranny of letters," as de Saussure (1916) said? Not necessarily. It is rather mastery of a tool and a new method of handling language. Although its inert forms may restrict the liberty of language, to the child they represent mastery of a new mode of expression. Writing does not become a constraint until certain school requirements make their appearance. Of all manual skills, writing allows the child the least liberty, while affording him the greatest satisfaction, because it can provide an indelible trace of what language can express. Writing is graphic representation using conventional, systematic, recognizable signs. It is linear. In Cohen's words (1958), it consists of a visual and durable representation of language, which makes it transportable and conservable. The essential requirement of writing is that it should be transmissible. It is vehicular. In our society, writing is to be seen and read (although in braille, touch replaces sight).

All modes of representation or transcription of language i.e., braille, deaf/mute sign language, as well as writing are physical gestures conveying meaning. According to Alarcos Llorach (1968), the normal and primary manifestation of language is phonic, while writing (graphic representation) is its secondary manifestation; from the linguistic point of view, it cannot be studied alone, but only in relation to the former.

In the ontogenesis of the child, writing comes after speech. A conventional codified activity, writing is an acquired accomplishment. It is not a gift. It is within our reach once a certain level of intellectual, motor, and affective development has been attained. It is language and movement, but it is restricted by the context in which it takes place, by its rigorous graphic figuration, and the rules of spelling governing transcription of the language. Serving society in line with certain norms, the modes of graphic expression, despite their variability, remain fairly stable in the overall organization of their planning and as a result of the equivalence of writing instruments. The social framework imposes limits on us to ensure that the signs retain their value as a form of general communication.

Every normal individual, given a certain level of development, has the ability to write. But this potential, which depends on the completeness and maturation of several systems, cannot become effective except by learning. As Leischner (1957) states, the systems in question are not the same for the different levels of writing. In *copying,* sight and perception of the form of the visual symbols are foremost, as are the faculties of motor innervation required for execution. In *dictation,* verbal understanding of the text transmitted orally by another and transcription into graphic symbols are essential. In *spontaneous writing,* it is necessary to set down in symbolic form material formulated by the internal language, and a choice must be made from among the forms of speech and the graphic symbols that society has made available to us. What is required, therefore, is the transcription of verbal for-

177

mulations into meaningful graphic formulations. Furthermore, in the last
two instances, a knowledge of spelling
must continuously inform the graphic
transcription.

Writing is praxia and language. It
only becomes possible when a certain
level of motor control has been attained,
a fine coordination of movements in
space. It is a gnosopraxia, both when
copying and when performing the other
graphic activities—the anticipatory image, preformed action, and optical to-
and-fro motions combine in its execution.

In our society, writing follows a
measurable course, since it is controlled
partly by organofunctional maturation
factors, partly by a graduated process of
learning. Consequently, and despite its
arbitrary nature, writing develops in the
child in accordance with laws that can be
compared with those of overall psycho-
physiological development.

On the other hand, like motor control
in general and any expressive activity,
writing has a personal style intimately
bound up with individual characteristics,
and this opens up differential psycho-
physiological horizons.

Writing is not only a permanent method
of recording our ideas and memories; in
our society it is also a method of ex-
change, a medium of communication between ourselves and others. For this reason the child must, within the bounds of
his personal ability, meet certain requirements imposed by society with regard to
legibility and speed.

Although the aesthetics of writing
may have changed with the times and the
canons varied with the teachers, one element has been constant: the *layout*,
which gives writing its "verbal melody"
and value as an ordered narrative. It is
this, rather than the aesthetic qualities,
that modulate this silent way of
expression.

Legibility is determined by both the
shape of the letters and their ligature,
and by the organization of the sequence
of letters.

Speed is one of the requirements of
the modern world; typists are chosen in
accordance with speed scales, and short-
hand was invented to compensate for the
slowness of handwriting.

These three types of requirements are
to a certain extent contradictory and cannot be reconciled except by suitable
teaching methods. According to the
child's ability, these methods will take
into account the shape of the letters, the
ligatures, the tools. The first steps in
learning are decisive, since each child
comes to writing with his own inherent
organization, his motor ability, his faculties of structuration, orientation, and
verbal representation, writing being an
ordered figuration with a meaning. With
this in mind, and on the level of peda-
gogies in general, learning writing should
be approached as a school subject that is
shaped by the data here described, data
that it confirms at the same time, the
hand being no more than the instrument
of a broader frame of reference.

The Motor, Psychomotor, and Praxic Organization in Writing

Calling for skilled handling of the writing tool, graphic activity cannot take
place without the activation of certain
muscles, which, first, maintain the writing position with some force, and second, allow flexibility in the sequence of
movements on a flat surface. In writing,
as in any effector activity, the muscular
activity is controlled by the organization
of various anatomico-physiological systems. This organization develops with
time; it is to a great extent the result of
maturation, but it can only be completely understood and studied in *functional performance*.

In fact, one is in the presence of ideo-
kinesthetic activity patterns (Paillard,
1960), of which the form and meaning
are dependent on the task performed; in
writing, an activity that engages the
whole individual, these patterns are as
much "gnosopraxic" and psychological
as they are motor.

The strictly physiological point of view will not be tackled here; we have gone into it elsewhere (Ajuriaguerra, Auzias, Coumes, Denner, Lavondes, Perron, & Stambak, 1964, Vol. 1), and a great many experimental works exist that are devoted to a study of the mechanics of the inscriptive movement considered as the model of a deliberate gesture of extreme refinement (e.g., Essing, 1965; Luthe, 1953; Michel, 1971).

To achieve writing on a small scale, the hand must be capable of fine prehension; furthermore, it must adopt a specific position (in half-supination when a pencil is used), which must be maintained with some force for a fairly extended period of time. Various synergies and coordinations must be put into operation to perform the graphic movement; they develop during the prewriting stage (Lurcat, 1968); the child improves them gradually with practice. The movements, general to start with, have to become precise; the movements of the fingers must gain in refinement and be differentiated from the movements of the wrist and arm, be capable of slight braking while the body learns to keep still to facilitate the complex distal movement. These elementary motor conditions are achieved around the age of six, but at a minimum. The exercise and development of these motor and praxic abilities will enable the movements to become *organized* and gradually to become smooth, quick, supple, economical, and automatic (Ajuriaguerra *et al.*, 1964, Vol. 1; Freeman, 1954).

To illustrate certain aspects of graphic motor behavior, we shall consider three problems; the hold on the tool, the speed of writing, the regulation of tonicity.

Prehension of a Writing Instrument

The position of the fingers on the tool varies with the tool used (pencil, brush), convention, and more or less conscious imitation. These different factors contribute to an accepted so-called "standard" hold (for a given tool), while the

manner of proceeding of individual adults more or less conforms to this norm, depending on various individual factors.

In children, the position changes with age. For example, a pencil is first gripped by the whole hand before the age of 1. Prehension thereafter gradually becomes more distal, until the ends of the thumb and the index finger are opposite one another near the instrument's point. After 6 years of age, another change occurs: the flexion of the fingers decreases. Sometimes unusual, defective types of prehension occur. They are related either to tension stemming from widely differing origins (too fine a tool, awkwardness, psychic tension about writing), or to gnosopraxic difficulties: difficulties in awareness, representation, and use of parts of the body, particularly the fingers. Lastly, a particular hold may be the mark of an ostentatious attitude intended to attract attention. From this simple example, it is clear that the graphomotor organization is also psychomotor and praxic.

Speed of Writing

Handwriting scales have been designed to measure children's writing speed (Ajuriaguerra *et al.*, 1964, Vol. 1; Bang, 1959; Cormeau-Velghe, Destrait, Toussaint & Bidaine, 1970; Harris, 1960, pp. 622–624), as well as speed of execution of other activities. They show that speed of movement increases with age and depends on maturation factors, especially in the young child. But other factors influence speed of writing. Daily learning and practice contribute to the *organization of graphic movements*. We have studied the organization of writing gestures when performing a "horizontal" sequence. Between 5 and 6 years of age, the action is *discontinuous*, the hand being almost parallel with the line and the paper held straight. Inscriptive movements alternate with the progression of the hand along the line. During the stages that we were able to describe precisely, this infantile progression is replaced by a well-coordinated, *continuous,* and economic progression. The elbow tends to remain in one place (between ages 12 and 14), serving as a pivot for the forearm (Callewaert, 1954), while the hand rests below the line and the sheet of paper is tilted, thus liberating the graphic field. Various improvements in graphic action occur simultaneously with this new organization, particularly an increase in speed.

Still other factors influence writing speed. It can be impeded (1) by synkinetic (Ajuriaguerra & Stambak, 1955) and tonic elements, (2) by spelling difficulties, and (3) by specific emotional attitudes toward writing (as at the outset of infantile cramp, to which we shall refer later).

Tonic Regulation

The writing activity is not related only to brachial and manual mobility. The maintenance of immobility of the central pillar formed by the body axis is all the more necessary as the movements become more delicate and distal. For the forearm to slide easily and smoothly over the table, the body axis must remain motionless, but as Wallon (1928) remarked, in a "very active state of immobility" with imperceptible compensatory reactions. This function of postural regulation, which develops with acquisition of the walking ability, improves with writing. Between five and seven years of age, the child's torso tends to lean sideways, drawn by the distal movement of the arm and hand advancing along the line. Toward the age of 9, the distal movements are better compensated and are more independent of the trunk, which remains still.

With individual variations that may be considerable, tonicity brings about changes in posture (upright position of the torso between ages 5 and 14), changes in support (gradual elimination of trunk leaning on the table and light-ening of the hand), stability of the hand (the constant position in half-supination is acquired between seven and eight years), and elasticity of the shoulder, wrist, and fingers.

Force and pressure are important tonic factors that affect graphic motor control (Essing, 1965; Harris & Rarick, 1959; Luthe, 1953). It is essential for the child to learn, with practice, to use and distribute his own strength (in accordance with his age and tonic typology) in such a way as to limit his energy output. Sometimes it is necessary to help him do this. Experience gained in re-education has demonstrated that the child can improve his writing skill by learning to make a better use of his strength and by correcting unsuitable tonic reactions (Ajuriaguerra *et al.,* 1964, Vol. 2).

Tonic regulation in its various aspects governs the entire writing activity and therefore plays an essential role in handwriting. Serious or even slight defects in tonicity and a lack of strength impede motor control, the support function, and prehension of the implement. On the one hand, good tonicity facilitates writing, and, on the other, is evidence of a positive adaptive response to the situation. Any emotional reaction of displeasure can at the physical level produce *paratonic* reactions (exaggerated tonic reactions that impede movements) because of the close relation between tonicity and affectivity—relations that are established in early childhood (Ajuriaguerra, 1970; Wallon, 1949).

Spatial Constraints on Writing

The writing act is a meaningful graphic movement inscribed on a flat, two-dimensional space. Control over this space, which is always sharply defined, demands of the writer a continuous effort of anticipation. Furthermore, whether writing on a blackboard or on a sheet of paper, one always writes in a *space of representation* that is in relation to the points of reference of the writer's body.

The support facing the writer has a top and a bottom, as well as a right and a left side separated by an imaginary median, the vertical projection of the body's axis. For the writer these spatial references to some extent ultimately become qualities inherent in the support, regardless of its position on the table.

Writing takes place in this particular space in accordance with various conventions relating to the shape of the letters and directions to be used, conventions that vary from place to place in the world. Here we shall consider the *directional* conventions, since they are a factor common to many forms of writing and make it possible to take a detached view of the infinite variety of characters used in the world. For a study of these characters we refer the reader to various works (Centre International de Synthèse, 1963; Cohen, 1958; Diringer, 1948; International Conference on Public Education, 1948). It would be advisable to supplement these studies with a survey updating the list of written languages used at present, since in our own day, as in the course of history, some die, others are born (Houis, 1971), and those that live, evolve. There are countless reasons for the birth of written languages and their evolution (Centre International de Synthèse, 1963). One is the need to bring writing within reach of children and also of illiterate adults (a need felt by many countries).

The directional conventions of writing are related to the following considerations:

1. *The direction of the development of the line:* the first large unit on a written page is broken down into smaller units consisting of graphic signs (words in phonographic scripts using consonantal or alphabetical representation; ideographs or groups of ideographs in ideographic forms of writing).

2. *The sequential production of minimum units of words:* letters in an alphabetical system, groups of strokes in the elements of an ideogram in an ideographic system (letters and strokes do not serve the same purpose) (Alarcos Llorach, 1968; Alleton, 1970).

Regardless of which method of graphic representation of language is adopted, the hand has to delineate the minimum units in accordance with certain codified directions and in a given order; these units, juxtaposed or connected, are grouped in words, which are aligned according to certain directions that are also codified.

Most types of writing follow a horizontal development of the line (or a horizontal progression of the line), the first line being parallel to the upper edge of the paper, each of the following lines being situated below the preceding line (progression on the page thus being vertical, from top to bottom). Horizontal development is characterized by the fact that the characters are placed side by side, as for example, the personages in the well-known pictograms of the Cuna Indians of Panama (Cohen, 1958). Horizontal development can be done systematically from left to right, as in Roman script (Western Europe, North and South America, etc.), in modern Greek writing, Cyrillic script, Indian writing, and so forth; or from right to left, as in Hebrew and Arabic script. There are also boustrophedon inscriptions, as in ancient Greek writing, in which the lines run alternately from right to left and from left to right, and there is the particular arrangement of signs varying from line to line in ancient writing discovered on the Easter Island tablets (Centre International de Synthèse, 1963; Cohen, 1958). In Arabic, as in Hebrew script, written from right to left, numbers (Arabic numerals) are written from left to right, in the opposite direction to the writing. Children must therefore learn to allow the necessary space to write down a number in mid-sentence. After the number is set down, the writing continues from right to left. In Hebrew script, two systems of numerical notation exist simultaneously and are learned by children: Arabic numerals and the ancient

181

Hebrew system using certain letters of the alphabet (direction R–L), of which the principle is analogous to that used in upper case Roman numerals.

In the types of writing used in China, Japan, and Korea, the development of the line (or rather column) was until recently vertical, from top to bottom. Progression on the page was from right to left, each column being placed to the left of the preceding one. In vertical Chinese writing, the characters are placed one below the other (like figures standing one below the other), an arrangement followed in ancient Egypt for monumental hieroglyphics (Centre International de Synthèse, 1963).

At the present time in China, as in Japan, horizontal development, starting in the top left-hand corner of the page, is tending to become institutionalized (Alleton, 1970), which does not change the orientation of the characters; they are placed side by side instead of one under the other. This new arrangement is used in printed publications and is taught at school, while the traditional (vertical) system continues to be used, for example for any type of monumental writing (posters) or for some personal uses (wishes, dedications). Vertical writing, and use of the brush and Indian ink, lend the text a certain emphasis derived from the cultural and sentimental value attached to them.

The *ductus* or direction of the stroke of the small units (letters, strokes) is also codified. This codification is far from arbitrary. It derives from usage that has fashioned writing through the centuries. The ductus of each letter is designed to facilitate the cursive development of a word and, where connected script is concerned, to facilitate the ligatures (connections between letters), which tend to follow the direction of the development of the line established by convention. Where a technical problem of ligature arises (e.g., connections with *a, d, g, q, o, c* in Roman script), codification seeks to solve the problem, codification that can vary from one method to another

(the American Palmer-type ligatures, or the continental-type lift of the pen). Sometimes the organization of motor control and the laterality of the child lead him to produce types of ductus contrary to normal usage. Generally speaking, since the microspace of a letter at the beginning of the learning process renders perception of its form and development a little difficult, large writing on the blackboard is frequently used to facilitate learning. The same principle is applied to adults in literacy courses (*Guides practiques pour l'éducation extra-scolaire,* 1960–1966).

The study of the genesis of writing (Gobineau & Perron, 1954) shows that the child first writes discontinuously; gradually he learns to connect several letters; later he transforms the calligraphy learned into a personal style of writing with new ligatures adapted to it. Some forms of writing are separate by tradition (Arabic and particularly Hebrew), but adult writers also introduce personal ligatures here and there.

Similarly, in cursive Chinese writing, some strokes are connected (Alleton, 1970). It should be remembered that in this writing the various strokes in one ideograph must not only follow certain directions; they must also follow a strict order of succession (they are numbered in the school children's exercise books). Learning the order of succession is facilitated by certain general rules. This order and the ductus of strokes must therefore be carried out by the children for each character they learn (some of which have been simplified since 1958)—in other words, 1000–2000 of the most common characters. This way of writing may seem extraordinarily difficult to users of alphabetic scripts, which all in all have about 30 forms of letters to learn (60 including capital letters). But, in fact, although it takes longer to learn Chinese writing than alphabetic script (Gray, 1958), there is no doubt that the children do finally master this system of writing, and even the still more complicated Japanese system.

But are alphabetic scripts really easier to write? Actually, the intellectual and perceptomotor activity of the alphabetic writer is, if we think about it, just as complex. Any form of writing calls for *anticipation* of the spatiotemporal development of small units in accordance with the development of the narrative and the method of representing language. A sequence of graphemes must correspond to a sequence of phonemes, which is achieved through a graphomotor rhythm and internal formulation of narrative proper to writing, a medium of expression that ultimately acquires a certain autonomy in relation to the spoken language (Alarcos Llorach, 1968).

Matters are still relatively simple—in phonographic systems—when the laws of correspondence between graphemes and phonemes are themselves fairly simple. But the difficulty of certain written languages can be considerably increased by the polyvalence of graphemes and the polygraphy of phonemes, as in French and even more so in English, where the writing system is quasi-semiographic (Alarcos Llorach, 1968, p. 562). One could even go so far as to say that these scripts are at least as complex as ideographic or semiographic writing, because they continue to be taught as phonographic writings—which they basically are, according to the system of representation of language adopted—and because continuous reference to the *signatum* is as necessary as it is in Chinese writing to transcribe the correct sign and correct spelling.

Difficulties inherent in various scripts do not therefore stem exclusively from their particular spatial constraints. However, the child must pass certain stages, on the level of representation of space, to arrange the layout and development on the page of the writing he has to learn.

Stages in the mastery of graphic space by the child have been thoroughly studied by many writers (Lurçat, 1968; Piaget & Inhelder, 1948; Vereecken, 1961). This skill develops through the first spontaneous strokes which gradually take the form of symbolic representations. It is the simultaneous production of units of graphy and their meaning that enable the child to relate himself to the space on the sheet.

The writing movement develops before the definite representation of landmarks in space (top, bottom, right, left). If the child sees others about him drawing and is given the necessary tools, he will start to scribble between the ages of two and three. The origin of such scribbling is primarily a straightforward motor impulse stimulated by the need to imitate. The first strokes (continuous, then discontinuous: circular marks, curves, descending lines, then lateral) are directly governed by the maturation of the motor processes and the role played by the body axis, which acts as an axis of symmetry and affects the direction of the strokes.

The child acts, then considers the result of his efforts. If the adult is encouraging, he takes pleasure in some repetition. Between the ages of three and four, he tries to make the strokes more precise and to vary them (a closed circular stroke, lines in various directions, isolated loops, then the execution of the square) while coordination improves between the movement of the hand and the eyes, which began to develop with the first sensory motor activities. At the same time, a new and very important synthesis occurs: the child interprets the drawing after it is completed. He gives a meaning to as yet indefinite lines: "It's a bird." Some coincidence of form is possible between the graphic marks and the ideographic interpretation, but one is not determined by the other (Wallon, cited in Lurçat, 1970–1971). A new step forward is made when the child anticipates what he is going to draw ("I will draw a tree"). There is a transition from spontaneous (or semideliberate) movements to movements controlled by the intention to depict (Wallon, cited in Lurçat, 1970–1971).

Between the ages of 4 and 6, the

drawing becomes richer and more precise. A pleasurable activity for the child, who enjoys handling color, and a basic educational activity, as has frequently been stressed, drawing plays an important role in the development of the symbolic functions and the affective life of the child. At the same time, drawing enables the child gradually to relate to the space on the sheet of paper. In exploring this space with the point of his tool and placing on it his houses and little men, he builds up landmarks as a result of the confrontation of his movements, the limits of the sheet, and his drawings on it. The top and the bottom acquire a meaning.

During this period, the child also assimilates certain topological relations (Piaget & Inhelder, 1948) from experience: internal–external relationships, intersection, and order. He learns to recognize in himself and on the sheet of paper the right- and the left-hand side, which will be related to the top and the bottom. The acquisition of all these relations necessary to writing and reading will, toward the age of 6, enable him to learn the written language. But well before the age of 6, before he can copy a sentence, the child shows an interest in writing provided he sees it going on around him. Next to the figurative drawings, little signs appear (miniature sketchy curves, or small enclosed figures, or lines placed next to the drawings, or wavy lines like lines of writing); the child will then say that he is writing. In fact, it is no more than an imitation of writing (Wallon, 1952). But this imitation already reveals an intuition of abstract symbolic configuration; when the time comes to learn to write, this will be an advantage.

In the representative drawings and later in the early stages of writing, the moving hand and the eyes that anticipate and guide it together define an external space and identify a before and after, a top and bottom, and so on, on the sheet of paper. Through movement, space has been defined. Then the child can juggle within the system of coordinates that he has organized, go in one direction or another if necessary, depending on the conventions of the writing that he learns. On the other hand, he will be unable to draw characters or learn their order of succession according to a continuous direction if maturation at the level of practice and knowledge is not sufficiently advanced; in other words, before the system of spatial reference is constituted or if it is still uncertain.

REFERENCES

Ajuriaguerra, J. de. *Manuel de psychiatrie de l'enfant.* Paris: Masson, 1970.

Ajuriaguerra, J. de, & Auzias, M. Méthodes et techniques d'apprentissage de l'écriture. *Psychiatrie de l'Enfant,* 1960, *3,* 609–718.

Ajuriaguerra, J. de, Auzias, M., Coumes, F., Denner, A., Lavondes, M., Perron, R., & Stambak, M. *L'écriture de l'enfant* (2 volumes; Vol. 1, *L'évolution de l'écriture et ses difficultés,* and Vol. 2, *La rééducation de l'écriture*). Neuchâtel & Paris: Delachaux & Niestlé, 1964.

Ajuriaguerra, J. de, & Gobineau, H. de L'écriture en miroir. *Semaine des Hopitaux,* 1956, *32,* 80–86.

Ajuriaguerra, J. de & Stambak, M. L'évolution des syncinés ies chez l'enfant. *La Presse Médicale,* 1955, *39,* 817–819.

Alarcos Llorach, E. Les représentations graphiques du langage. In *Le langage.* Paris: Éditions Gallimard, 1968.

Alleton, V. *L'écriture chinoise.* Paris: Presses Universitaires de France, 1970.

Auzias, M. *Les troubles de l'écriture chez l'enfant.* Neuchâtel: Delachaux & Niestlé, 1970.

Auzias, M. La vitesse d'écriture chez les enfants qui écrivent de la main gauche. Revue de neuropsychiatrie infantile, 1973, *21,* 10–11, 667–686.

Bang, V. *Evolution de l'écriture de l'enfant à l'adulte; Étude expéri-*

méntale. Neuchâtel: Delachaux & Niestlé, 1959.

Brachold, H. *Einschulung Schwergeschädigter Armloser, Armbehinderter Kinder.* Stuttgart: Ernst Klett, 1966. (a)

Brachold, H. Synthetischer oder ganzheitlicher Schreibunterricht? *Praxis der Kinderpsychologie und Kinderpsychiatrie,* 1966, *15,* 308–315. (b)

Callewaert, H. 1954. *Graphologie et physiologie de l'écriture.* Louvain: Nauwelaerts, 1954.

Centre International de Synthèse. *L'écriture et la psychologie des peuples.* Paris: Armand Colin, 1963.

Clark, M. *Left-handedness.* London: Univ. of London Press, 1957.

Cohen, M. *La grande invention de l'écriture et son évolution.* Paris: Imprimerie Nationale, 1958.

Cole, L. Instruction in penmanship for left-handed children. *Elementary School Journal,* Feb. 1939, 436–448.

Cormeau-Velghe, M., Destrait, V., Toussaint, J. & Bidaine E. Normes de vitesse d'écriture: étude statistique de 1844 écoliers belges de 6 à 13 ans. *Psychologica Belgica,* 1970, *X-2,* 247–263.

Critchley, M. *Mirror writing.* London: Kegan Paul, 1927.

Derrida, J. *De la grammatologie.* Paris: Editions de Minuit, 1967.

Diringer, D. *The alphabet: A key to the history of mankind.* New York: Philosophical Library, 1948.

Dottrens, R. *Au seuil de la culture; Méthode globale et écriture script.* Paris: Editions Scarabee, 1966.

Essing, V. W. Untersuchungen über Veränderungen der Schreibmotorik im Grundschulalter. *Human Development,* 1965, *8,* 194–221.

Fernandez-Huerta, J. *Escritura didactica y escala grafica.* Madrid: Consejo Superior de Investigaciones Cientificas, Inst. San José de Calasanz de Pédagogia, 1950.

Freeman, F. N. *Teaching handwriting.* Washington, D.C.: Amer. Educ. Res. Ass., 1954.

Freinet, C. *les méthodes naturelles dans la pédagogie moderne.* Paris: Bourrelier, 1955.

Gobineau, H. de, & Perron, R. *Génétique de l'écriture et étude de la personnalité,* Neuchâtel & Paris: Delachaux & Niestlé, 1954.

Gray, W. S. *The teaching of reading and writing; An international survey.* Paris: Unesco, 1958. (2nd ed., 1969.)

Guides pratiques pour l'éducation extrascolaire. Paris: Unesco, 1960–1966.

Harris, T. L. Handwriting. In C. W. Harris (Ed.), *Encyclopedia of education research.* New York: MacMillan, 1960.

Harris, T. L., & Rarick, G. L. The relationship between handwriting pressure and legibility of handwriting in children and adolescents. *Journal of Experimental Education,* 1959, *28,* 65–84.

Hildreth, G. *Learning the three R's.* Minneapolis: Educ. Publ., 1947.

Houis, M. *Anthropologie linguistique de l'Afrique noire.* Paris: Presses Universitaires de France, 1971.

International Conference on Public Education, XIth, Geneva. *The teaching of handwriting.* Publ. No. 103. Geneva & Paris: International Bureau of Education/Unesco, 1948.

Leischner, A. *Di Störungen der Schriftsprache.* Stuttgart: Thieme, 1957.

Lurçat, L. *Etude de l'acte graphique.* Paris et La Haye: Monton, 1974.

Lurçat, L. Genèse de l'idéogramme; graphisme et langage. *Bulletin de Psychologie,* (Paris) 1970–1971, 16/18, 932–947.

Luthe, W. Der Elektroscriptograph. *Psychologische Forschung,* 1953, *24,* 194–214.

Michel, F. Étude expérimentale de la vitesse du geste graphique. *Neuropsychologia,* 1971, *9,* 1–13.

Olivaux, R. *Désordres et rééducation de l'écriture.* Paris: Editions ESF, 1971.

Paillard, J. The patterning of skilled movements. In Hw. Magoun (Ed.), *Handbook of physiology,* Section I: Neurophysiology, Vol. 3. Washing-

185

ton, D.C.: Amer. Physiol. Soc., 1960.

Piaget, J., & Inhelder, B. *La représentation de l'espace chez l'enfant*. Paris: Presses Universitaires de France, 1948.

Rudolf, H. *Schreiberziehung und Schriftpsychologie*. Bielefeld: Pfeffer, 1973 (preface by O. Lockowandt).

Saussure, F. de. *Cours de linguistique générale*. Lausanne: Payot, 1916 (17th ed., Paris, Payot, 1972. *Statistical yearbook*. Paris: Unesco, 1970.

Tardieu, G. Education thérapeutique de l'habileté. *Les feuillets de l'infirmité motrice cérébrale*. Paris (33 rue Blanche): Ass. Nat. Infirm. Motrice Cérébraux, 1972.

Vereechen, P. *Spatial development; Constructive praxia from birth to the age of seven*. Groningen: Wolters, 1961.

Wallon, H. La maladresse. *Journal de Psychologie Normale et Pathologique*, 1928, *25*, 61–78. Also in *Enfance*, 1959, *3/4*, 264–276.

Wallon, H. *Les origines du caractère*. Paris: Presses Universitaires de France, 1949.

Pre-Arithmetic Instruction

- ... children come to kindergarten with considerable knowledge upon which the school can build an interesting, challenging, and sequential curriculum.

  Anthony N. Schwartz

- ... in certain number concepts kindergarten children are relatively mature, while in other number concepts they are poorly developed.

  Emma E. Holmes

- ... appropriate mathematical instruction based upon the child's experience would be beneficial and profitable to the kindergarten pupil ...

  Alfred H. Williams

- If standards are not set and if goals are not stated, it becomes difficult to determine what the program is.

  V. Ray Kurtz

INTRODUCTION

As the contributions in this section attest, there is considerable agreement as to what skills kindergarteners possess or are capable of learning. Holmes studies the responses of young children pre-nursery through kindergarten to arrive at the sequence of skills that emerges during this portion of childhood. Williams and Schwartz concentrated on kindergarten age children to find what concepts, skills, and abilities related to mathematics were either present at entry into kindergarten or were acquired soon thereafter. Kindergarten children were found to be ready and able to learn most concepts and skills that precede formal operations. As Williams reports, however, formal operations (addition, subtraction, and so on) are best reserved for instruction in the first grade.

Whereas the first four selections concentrate on children's abilities, the fifth reports the results of a survey of teachers' perceptions of kindergarten abilities. It is encouraging to note that there is a high degree of correspondence between teachers' perceptions and the measured performance of kindergarten children.

What Do Pre-First-Grade Children Know about Number?

EMMA E. HOLMES

Instruction for understanding is a major objective in teaching arithmetic today. *Understanding* has often been defined as an intellectual grasp of relationships. Because there are innumerable mathematical relationships, teachers have had to single out certain relationships for attention in the classroom.

Teaching has stressed the fact that our number system uses the base "ten" and that the value of a written symbol is determined by its place in the numeral. Manipulative devices such as pocket charts and abaci have been used extensively to teach the place-value principle. Teachers have also emphasized the relations between the fundamental operations. Addition and subtraction as well as multiplication and division have often been taught as inverse processes. When so taught, it has been pointed out that either operation in the pair will undo the

Reprinted from *The Elementary School Journal*, Vol. 63, (1963). By permission of The University of Chicago Press. © 1963. Copyright is held by The University of Chicago.

other. Still other relationships are expressed in the laws that state general mathematical principles. New materials such as those prepared by the School Mathematics Study Group have made use of such laws as the commutative or associative principles.

Concepts of equality, cardinal number, and ordinal number are necessary to an understanding of mathematical relationships. Before the child enters school, what does he understand about number? Have empirical studies contributed to our knowledge of children's concepts of equality, cardinal number, and ordinal number?

A survey of the literature reveals that studies of young children's number concepts have been concerned primarily with children's ability to count and to compute. The investigations of McLaughlin (1), Buckingham and MacLatchy (2), Woody (3), and Brownell (4) led to the conclusion that counting abilities are well developed by the time formal instruction begins in first grade. Recent studies conducted by Bjonerud (5) and Priore (6) corroborated earlier findings.

Few studies have been concerned with children's concepts of equality. Russell, who investigated the subject in the early forties, concluded that children under seven years of age do not fully grasp the notion of *equal* (7).

Piaget has also studied children's concepts of equality. In *The Child's Conception of Number*, he discusses notions of equality in the context of the development of cardinal number (8). This work also treats the development of ordinal concepts. Piaget concludes that there are three stages in the development of the cardinal and the ordinal phases of number. These stages are generally referred to as the pre-operational stage, the stage of concrete operations, and the stage of formal operations. At the first stage the child responds to his immediate environment without taking thought; at the second stage he behaves rationally with respect to the perceived environment; at the third stage he manipulates symbols and considers possibilities removed from the world at hand. Furthermore, Piaget reports that cardinal concepts develop along with ordinal concepts. The fusion of these concepts gives rise to ideas of number. In his writings, Piaget describes unique tests to measure children's number concepts.

The pioneer work of Piaget suggests further studies of children's number concepts. I conducted one such investigation (9). The tests I used to measure concepts of cardinal and ordinal number were adapted from those described by Piaget.

The purpose of my research was to investigate the nature of young children's concepts of cardinal and ordinal number. Three areas of study were delineated: the developmental level of cardinal- and ordinal-number concepts of pre-first-grade children; the change in the developmental level of number concepts as the child grows older; the association between cardinal-number concepts and ordinal-number concepts of young children.

The study was conceived as a genetic survey, and a cross-section approach was deemed appropriate. A test on number concepts was designed and administered individually to 144 pre-first-grade children during the period from March, 1960, to August, 1960. The sample was drawn from children from three to six years of age who were to attend schools in the middle-class districts. The children were members of middle-class and upper-middle class families. Their mean intelligence quotient was above average.

The 144 subjects were divided into four categories on the basis of the year of school entrance. Table 1 summarizes the information on year of entrance and chronological age.

One hundred and forty of the children attended public or private schools in two Iowa towns. Four children attended no school.

Intelligence-test scores were available for fifty-eight children. For thirty-eight kindergartners the mean intelligence quotient on the California Test of Mental Maturity, Primary Level, 1957 Edition, was 120. The Revised Stanford-Binet Scale had been administered to twenty

TABLE 1. *Description of Subjects*

School Level	Number of Children	Year of Entrance to Kindergarten	Chronological Age (Years and Months)
Kindergarten	85	1959	5–4 to 6–4
Preschool	37	1960	4–8 to 5–7
Nursery School	18	1961	3–8 to 4–7
Pre-nursery school	4	1962	3–0 to 3–7

pre-kindergarten children. The mean intelligence quotient was 127.

The test constructed for this investigation consisted of items designed to measure cardinal-number concepts and ordinal-number concepts. *Cardinal number* is generally considered as embracing the quantitative aspect of number. *Ordinal number* has been defined as referring to the serial order of number names, the positional phase of number, or the relational phase of number. For purposes of this investigation, cardinal- and ordinal-number concepts were defined operationally. These operational definitions will be presented. Then the test items will be discussed.

Several dimensions of cardinal number were studied. The child's idea of cardinal number was considered adequate in one respect when he recognized that a certain collection of elements was designated by a given number name. Notions of equality were considered adequate when the child was successful in tests that required judgments regarding identical sets. Tests of cardinal correspondence further defined concepts of cardinal number.

The positional phase of ordinal number was considered adequate when a subject correctly located a designated object in a set. For example, the child was shown a set of ten paper dolls. These dolls, which were identical except for size, were arranged in order by size. The child was told to touch Doll Six. A successful response to such a test depended on the use of the number series. The relational phase of the ordinal aspect of number embodies notions of the connection between elements in a set, when the elements are perceived as unequal. In the set of counting numbers, the series proceeds by adding one to any given number. Hence, the elements may be considered unequal, for adjacent counting numbers differ by plus one (or minus one). Rudimentary notions of ordinal concept of relation were said to be adequate when a subject responded correctly to items of ordinal correspondence.

I believe that a complete concept of number embraces concepts of cardinal as well as ordinal number. The test called "cardinal and ordinal number co-ordinated" was designed to measure the fusion of cardinal and ordinal aspects of number. In these tests, a successful response depended on an understanding of the relation between cardinal and ordinal number.

The fifteen items designed to measure concepts of cardinal number were presented in three subtests. The first subtest was made up of four items of rational counting, which included both reproduction and enumeration. The second subtest was made up of five items related to the equality of two sets of ten beads each. The two groups of ten beads were shown to the subject in plastic boxes or glass bottles. The arrangements of the beads were not predetermined. After each presentation, the child was questioned concerning the equality of the two groups of beads. The third subtest was made up of six tests of cardinal correspondence. The child was shown a group of objects. He was told that another group of objects could be found so that each object in the first group would be matched with an object in the second group. He was asked how many objects would be required to effect this matching. For example, he was shown six pennies. He was told that each penny would buy one piece of candy. He was then asked how many candies could be bought for the pennies.

The twenty-eight items designed to measure ordinal-number concepts were presented in three subtests. The materials for each of the twenty-eight items were either a group of ten paper dolls or ten white cards. The dolls (or cards) were identical but differed in size. The amount by which the dolls (or cards) differed from one another was constant. The first subtest was made up of eight items on locating ordinal number. The child arranged the dolls in order by size. Then he was requested to locate certain dolls by means of ordinal-number names.

The second subtest was made up of four items on seriation and correspondence. The test of seriation and correspondence required the subject, first, to order correctly, by size, the ten paper dolls or the ten cards. Secondly, the subject was required to order a second set, such as doll hats, so that the two sets were in correspondence, that is, each doll would have her own hat. The third subtest was made up of sixteen items on ordinal correspondence. These tests of ordinal correspondence required the subject to match a designated element in one seriated set with its corresponding element in a second seriated set, when the second set was not in direct visual correspondence with the first. The elements in the second set were reversed, displaced (that is, moved to the right or the left), and disarranged or scattered.

There were also eleven items of the subtest "cardinal and ordinal number co-ordinated." This subtest was designed to measure the fusion of cardinal and ordinal concepts. Ten cards, say A to J, were used in these items. Card A was one inch high. The cards differed in height by a constant relationship: $B = 2A$, $C = 3A$ . . . $J = 10A$. After the cards had been seriated, or ordered by size, the test required that the subject grasp the plus-one relationship inherent in the series and then determine the number of cards of the A size that would be contained in a designated card. The ordinal number of the card, of course, gives the cardinal number, or the number of the A elements. Thus, the third, or C, card has three A elements.

The score selected to measure the level of development in each of the seven subtests was the per cent of correct responses to that subtest. For a child's response to a subtest to be considered correct all items in that subtest had to be passed successfully.

At the nursery and the pre-nursery levels children show little understanding of number as measured by this test. This is evident from an examination of Table 2. Furthermore, the per cent of preschool children who performed successfully on the subtests was small.

One other conclusion seems warranted. At the kindergarten and the preschool levels the development of the several aspects of number is character-

TABLE 2. *Per Cents of Correct Responses to Subtests of Number-Concepts Test*

Subtest	Kindergarten	Preschool	Nursery	Pre-Nursery
Rational Counting (to 10)	84.71	29.73	5.55	0.00
Equality	61.18	21.62	11.11	0.00
Cardinal Correspondence	40.00	8.11	0.00	0.00
Locating Ordinal Number	65.88	16.22	0.00	0.00
Seriation and Correspondence	29.41	13.51	0.00	0.00
Ordinal Correspondence	1.18	0.00	0.00	0.00
Cardinal and Ordinal Number Co-ordinated	11.76	0.00	0.00	0.00

ized by unevenness. This observation was substantiated, in part, by statistical analysis. It was reasoned that, if for children in the same category the difference between the per cents of correct responses in two subtests was not statistically significant, the children could be considered as having reached comparable levels of maturity in the concepts measured by those subtests. If, however, for the same individuals the difference between the per cents of correct responses was statistically significant, the children could be considered as having reached different levels of maturity in the concepts measured by those subtests.

The reasoning is based on the assumption that the tests are of comparable difficulty and measure the concepts to an equal extent. The comparability of the tests was established on logical grounds. The tests of rational counting and locating ordinal number were conceived as measuring comparable levels of skill in the cardinal and ordinal aspects of number. The tests of cardinal correspondence were likewise assumed to be of comparable difficulty.

The significance of the difference between proportions of correct responses for kindergarten subjects on two subtests was tested by using McNemar's formula for non-independent proportions (10). At the kindergarten level the difference between the proportions of correct responses to the subtest of rational counting and the subtest of locating ordinal number was significant at the .05 level. The difference between the proportions of correct responses to the subtest of cardinal correspondence and ordinal correspondence at the kindergarten level was also significant at the .05 level. A level of significance equal to .05 was used throughout this investigation. It was felt that this level of significance would provide reasonable control over a Type I error. For samples of the size studied, a smaller significance level might have made the test too insensitive to the possible falsity of the statistical hypothesis.

On the basis of the statistical tests it can be said that for a kindergarten population such as described in this investigation, rational counting abilities are superior to abilities in locating ordinal number. Furthermore, concepts of cardinal correspondence, as measured by the number-concepts test, are more adequate than concepts of ordinal correspondence. Thus, it can be concluded that in certain number concepts kindergarten children are relatively mature, while in other number concepts they are poorly developed.

Of further interest was the development of number concepts over time. The cross-section approach may be used in the investigation of mental growth, if the subjects at the various age levels are selected from comparable segments of the general population. Such was the case in this research. It was thought that, in the general population, older children would demonstrate a more adequate understanding of the cardinal and ordinal aspects of number than younger children. The statistical statement of this hypothesis was in terms of the null hypothesis.

The per cents of correct responses for the nursery-school and the pre-nursery-school subjects were not in a range where the z-test statistic was applicable. However, the differences of the per cents between kindergarten and preschool subjects could be tested for the following subtests: rational counting, equality, locating ordinal number, and seriation and correspondence. All the differences were significant at the 5 per cent level. On the basis of the statistical tests it may be said that the kindergartners evidenced greater understanding of number, as measured by several subtests of the number-concepts test, than the preschool children. Furthermore, as Table 2 shows, it appears that the preschool children lack an operational concept of number.

The third area of study was the investigation of the relationship between any two subtests of the number-concepts test. It was hypothesized that any two subtests were independent; the statistical statement of the hypothesis was in terms of the null hypothesis. The test statistic selected was x^2. The null hypothesis was tested for the twenty-one possible pairs of subtests. The hypothesis was rejected for the five pairs listed in Table 3.

As Table 3 shows, the non-independent subtests formed two clusters, each comprising three associated subtests. The first cluster contains the subtests on cardinal correspondence, on locating ordinal number, and on seriation and correspondence; the second, ordinal number, cardinal and ordinal number coordinated, and seriation and correspondence. The three subtests in each cluster appear interrelated. However, no degree of relationship was determined. It may be hypothesized that the subtests in each cluster measure number abilities that are associated in mental development. Further research is needed to give additional knowledge and understanding regarding the association of various aspects of number.

Additional studies investigating children's understanding of cardinal and ordinal number need to be conducted. Such research could give insight significant to the improvement of mathematical instruction in the elementary school.

TABLE 3. *Five Pairs of Subtests for Which Hypothesis of Independence Was Rejected*

Pairs of Subtests	x^2
Cardinal Correspondence—Locating Ordinal Number	8.11
Cardinal Correspondence—Seriation and Correspondence	4.68
Locating Ordinal Number—Seriation and Correspondence	7.52
Locating Ordinal Number—Cardinal and Ordinal Number Co-ordinated	4.27
Seriation and Correspondence—Cardinal and Ordinal Number Co-ordinated	10.95

REFERENCES

1. Katherine Louise McLaughlin. *A Study of Number Ability in Children of Ages Three to Six*. Chicago: University of Chicago Libraries, 1935.
2. B. R. Buckingham and Josephine MacLatchy. "The Number Abilities of Children When They Enter Grade One," *Research in Arithmetic*. Twenty-ninth Yearbook of the National Society for the Study of Education, Part II. Bloomington, Illinois: Public School Publishing Company, 1930.
3. Clifford Woody. "The Arithmetic Background of Young Children," *Journal of Educational Research*, XXV (October, 1931), 188–201.
4. William A. Brownell. *Arithmetic in Grades I and II: A Critical Summary of New and Previously Reported Research*. Durham, North Carolina: Duke University Press, 1941.
5. Corwin E. Bjonerud. "Arithmetic Concepts Possessed by the Preschool Child," *Arithmetic Teacher*, VII (November, 1960), 347–50.
6. Angela Priore. "Achievement by Pupils Entering the First Grade," *Arithmetic Teacher*, IV (March, 1957), 55–60.
7. Ned Russell. "Arithmetic Concepts of Children," *Journal of Educational Research*, XXIX (March, 1943), 149–62.
8. Jean Piaget. *The Child's Conception of Number*. Translated by C. Gattegno and T. M. Hodgson. New York: Humanities Press, 1952.
9. Emma E. Holmes. "An Investigation of Cardinal and Ordinal Number Concepts of Children Three to Six Years of Age." Unpublished doctoral dissertation, State University of Iowa, 1961.
10. Quinn McNemar. *Psychological Statistics*, pp. 55–60, 229–30. New York: John Wiley and Sons, Inc., 1955 (second edition).

Mathematical Concepts, Skills, and Abilities of Kindergarten Entrants

ALFRED H. WILLIAMS

The needs of society have brought about a revolution in the field of mathematics. Price declares:

The changes in mathematics in progress at the present time are so extensive, so far-reaching in their implications, and so profound that they can be described only as a revolution.[1]

The effects of this upheaval are being felt at all levels of education. "Teach them more and teach them sooner!" is a common demand of today's public. So pervasive is this viewpoint that many persons—lay as well as professional—would attempt to extend the development and improvement of mathematics instruction into the kindergarten program.

If it is assumed that mathematics concepts can and should be introduced at the kindergarten level, some important groundwork must be laid. Before an effective mathematics program can be introduced to know about the children's level of mathematical readiness at the time they enter school.

Research writers have consistently pointed out the desirability of (1) structuring the learning situation so that most of the pupils can experience success, (2) offering a program that will challenge the pupil's abilities, (3) providing proper experience for the development of readiness, interest, and positive attitudes, and (4) helping to establish intrinsic motivation to further new learning.

Information regarding the mathematical achievement of kindergarten entrants is needed by all who are concerned with the selection of content and the determination of scope and sequence for the course of study.

The Problem

The purposes of the study were (1) to ascertain the nature and extent of achievement of pupils who are entering kindergarten with respect to selected mathematical concepts, skills, and abilities as described by test items requiring mathematical insights and/or skills and abilities; (2) to discover the levels of achievement of various groups when categorized by selected psychological and sociological factors; (3) to ascertain by the correlation method the extent of relationship that exists between the test of mathematical achievement and various psychological and sociological factors, and (4) to discover some of the circumstances and conditions existing in the home which apparently influence some kindergarten entrants to attain a high level of mathematical achievement while others of equal mental ability fail to realize proportionate accomplishment.

Procedures and Source of Data

The sample of 595 kindergarten entrants was drawn from six elementary school districts in southern California. These districts were located in the greater met-

---

[1] G. Bailey Price, *The Revolution in School Mathematics,* A Report of Regional Orientation Conferences in Mathematics (Washington, D.C.: The National Council of Teachers of Mathematics, 1961).

Reprinted from *Arithmetic Teacher,* April 1965 (Vol. 12, pp. 261–268), copyright 1965 by the National Council of Teachers of Mathematics. Used by permission.

ropolitan area of the city of Los Angeles.

The various tests used in this study were administered to all the children present in sixteen classrooms, to every third child present in nine classrooms, and on a random basis to children in seven kindergarten classes. Scores for each pupil were recorded on data processing cards. Scores pertained to mental maturity, mathematical achievement, and influence of the home. All data were secured prior to the end of the first four weeks of school in the fall of 1963.

The instrument used to describe achievement in selected mathematical concepts, skills, and abilities of the pupil who is entering kindergarten was developed specifically for this study. The concepts, skills, and abilities to be tested were categorized according to the Strands Report of the Advisory Committee on Mathematics for the State of California.[2] These strands were identified as (1) numbers and operations, (2) geometry, (3) measurement, (4) functions and graphs, (5) mathematical sentences, (6) logic, (7) sets, and (8) applications and problem solving.

The test items were selected on the basis of (1) content validity as determined by textbook analysis and opinions of one jury of experts, (2) item difficulty as determined by the number of examinees in the pilot study who answered the item correctly, and (3) validity index of the item as ascertained by the extent to which the item discriminated among the examinees who differed sharply in the functions measured by the test as a whole.

The reliability of the Preschool-Kindergarten Modern Mathematics Test was determined by means of the Kuder-Richardson Formula 21. The reliability coefficient for this investigation involving 595 kindergarten entrants was .90.

The correlation between the test devised for use in this study and the Quan-

titative section of the *SRA—Primary Mental Abilities—for Ages 5 to 7, 1954,* published by Science Research Associates[3] was .49. The mean IQ for the 301 boys was 101.45, for 294 girls 106.02, and for the total group of 595 pupils 103.71.

Influence of the home was surveyed by means of a parental questionnaire devised to collect information on selected preschool environmental factors. The purpose of the questionnaire was to ascertain whether certain groupings of these factors would reveal any relationship to superior or inferior mathematical achievement.

Computations of the significance of percentages and means, significance of the difference between means, coefficients of correlation, nominal numbers in a geometric progression, and coefficients of contingency were used as statistical tools in this study.

Selected Findings

The results on the Preschool-Kindergarten Modern Mathematics Test devised for this study are presented in Tables 1-8.

The tables present a summary of the findings which pertain to the analysis of the extent and nature of mathematical achievement of kindergarten entrants in the mathematics strands selected for inclusion in the test instrument.

The difficulty level of items was measured in terms of the percentage of correct responses. For subjects in this sample the difficulty level was found to be 75 percent and higher for the items which required (1) identification of three dots, (2) marking of three dots in a larger group of dots and (3) identification of the thermometer with the highest temperature and identification of the longest pencil. This reveals that these items are relatively easy, since more than three-fourths of the sample was able to respond correctly to them.

[2]Advisory Committee on Mathematics to the State Curriculum Commission, *Strands of Mathematical Concepts.* Reprinted from the *California Mathematics Council Bulletin,* XX, 2 (Fall, 1962), 1–11.

[3]Thelma Gwinn Thurston and L. L. Thurston, *SRA—Primary Mental Abilities* (Chicago: Science Research Associates, Inc., 1953).

Table 1

Item analysis of responses to the mathematic subtest: number and operations (N = 593)

Test item	Description of concept, skill, or ability		Number correct	Number wrong	Number omit	Percent correct	SE of percentage	P = .99	.01 confidence interval
Number identification									
2a	Mark box with 3 dots		482	87	24	81.3	1.60	4.13	77.2–85.4
2b	Mark box with 5 dots		305	239	49	51.4	2.05	5.29	46.1–56.7
2c	Mark box with 9 dots		314	193	85	53.0	2.05	5.29	47.7–58.3
2h	Mark single pair of socks		319	212	62	53.8	2.04	5.26	48.5–59.1
Reproduction									
2d	Mark 3 dots		446	110	37	75.2	1.77	4.57	70.6–79.8
2e	Mark 7 dots		288	278	27	48.6	2.05	5.29	43.3–53.9
2f	Mark 9 dots		240	320	33	40.5	2.01	5.19	35.3–45.7
2g	Mark 14 dots		158	378	57	26.6	1.81	4.67	21.9–31.3
Reading numerals									
3a	Mark the numeral 4		336	183	74	56.7	2.03	5.24	51.5–61.9
3b	Mark the numeral 6		259	220	114	43.7	2.03	5.24	38.5–48.9
3c	Mark the numeral 9		222	240	131	37.4	1.98	5.11	32.3–42.5
3d	Mark the numeral 0		228	264	101	38.4	1.99	5.13	33.3–43.5
3e	Mark the numeral 23		102	372	119	17.1	1.55	4.00	13.2–21.2
Writing numerals									
4a	Write the numeral 4		115	318	160	19.4	1.62	4.18	15.2–23.6
4b	Write the numeral 8		107	277	209	18.0	1.57	4.05	13.9–22.0
Illustration									
4c	Make 3 marks		384	157	51	64.9	1.95	5.03	59.9–69.9
4d	Make 10 marks		238	323	32	40.1	2.01	5.19	34.9–45.3
Cardinality									
4e	Two (recognition)		221	287	85	37.3	1.98	5.11	32.2–42.4
4f	Five (recognition)		208	261	124	35.1	1.95	5.03	30.1–40.1
4g	Two (illustration)		210	271	112	35.4	1.96	5.06	30.3–40.5
4h	Five (illustration)		178	262	153	30.0	1.88	4.85	25.2–34.9
Ordinality									
5a	Second		220	329	44	37.1	1.98	5.11	32.0–42.2
5b	First		408	133	52	68.8	1.90	4.90	63.9–73.1
5c	Fifth		92	415	86	15.5	1.48	3.82	11.7–19.3
5d	Between		289	273	31	48.7	2.05	5.29	43.4–54.0
5f	One more		64	428	101	10.8	1.27	4.62	7.5–14.1
5g	One less		41	434	118	6.9	1.03	2.66	4.2– 9.6
Fractions									
5e	Half of a whole		153	406	34	25.8	1.79	4.62	21.2–30.4
5h	Half of a group		170	325	98	28.7	1.85	4.77	23.9–33.5
Operations									
3f	Addition	$2+3=n$	95	343	155	16.0	1.50	3.87	12.1–19.9
3g	Subtraction	$5-2=n$	119	295	179	20.1	1.64	4.23	15.9–24.3
3h	Addition	$2+1=n$	131	294	167	22.1	1.70	4.39	17.7–26.5

Explanation: The "test item" column refers to the test item in the Preschool-Kindergarten Modern Mathematics Test. The column labeled "description of concept, skill, or ability" explains briefly the directions to the subject. The columns "number correct," "number wrong," and "number omit" refer to the status of responses for the total group. The "percent correct" column presents the percentage of correct responses to the item. "SE of percentage" column indicates the degree to which the percent correct is affected by errors of measurement and errors of sampling. The column "P = .99" shows that the percent correct for any example will not differ from the population percent correct by more than plus or minus the indicated amount. The ".01 confidence interval" column indicates that the fiducial probability is .99 that the percent correct for the population lies within the indicated interval and .01 that it falls outside of these limits.

Table 2

Item analysis of responses to the mathematics subtest: measurement (N = 593)

Test item	Description of concept, skill, or ability	Number correct	Number wrong	Number omit	Percent correct	SE of percentage	P = .99	.01 confidence interval
Measurement								
6a	Fewest	169	297	127	28.5	1.85	4.77	23.7–33.3
6b	8 o'clock (recognition)	223	263	107	37.6	1.99	5.13	32.5–42.7
6c	Number of pennies in nickel	64	438	91	10.8	1.27	3.28	7.5–14.1
6d	Number of nickels in dime	90	397	106	15.2	1.47	3.79	11.1–19.0
6e	Thermometer (highest temp.)	445	102	46	75.0	1.77	4.57	70.4–79.6
6f	Longest	500	74	19	84.3	1.49	3.84	80.5–88.1
6g	Shortest	432	114	47	72.8	1.82	4.70	68.1–77.5

Table 3

Item analysis of responses to the mathematics subtest: geometry (N = 593)

Test item	Description of concept, skill, or ability	Number correct	Number wrong	Number omit	Percent correct	SE of percentage	P = .99	.01 confidence interval
Recognition								
7a	Square	368	177	48	62.1	1.91	5.13	57.0–67.2
7b	Circle	387	158	48	65.3	1.95	5.03	60.1–70.3
7c	Rectangle	154	289	150	26.0	1.80	4.64	21.4–30.6
7d	Triangle	312	181	100	52.6	2.05	5.29	47.3–57.9
Properties of shape								
7e	Triangle (number of sides)	154	314	125	26.0	1.80	4.64	21.4–30.6
7f	Square (number of sides)	170	296	127	28.7	1.85	4.78	23.9–33.5
7g	Square (number of corners)	141	288	164	23.8	1.75	4.52	19.3–28.3
7h	Triangle (number of corners)	98	320	175	16.5	1.52	3.92	12.6–20.4
7i	Perception	139	406	48	23.4	1.73	4.46	18.9–27.9

Table 4

Item analysis of responses to the mathematics subtest: functions and graphs (N = 593)

Test item	Description of concept, skill, or ability	Number correct	Number wrong	Number omit	Percent correct	SE of percentage	P = .99	.01 confidence interval
8a	Number line	126	386	81	21.2	1.68	4.33	16.9–25.5
8b	Number line	97	329	167	16.4	1.82	4.70	11.7–21.1
8c	Pictograph	85	423	85	14.3	1.44	3.72	10.6–18.0

Table 5

Item analysis of responses to the mathematics subtest: set (N = 593)

Test item	Description of concept, skill, or ability	Number correct	Number wrong	Number omit	Percent correct	SE of percentage	P = .99	.01 confidence interval
8d	Matching elements of equivalent sets	200	176	217	33.7	1.94	5.01	29.6–38.7
8e	Matching elements of subsets	127	240	226	21.4	1.69	4.36	17.0–25.8
8f	Matching elements of sets not equivalent	49	324	220	8.3	1.13	2.92	5.4–11.2
8g	Adding to a set to make it equivalent to another set	85	328	180	14.3	1.43	3.69	10.6–18.0

Table 6

Item analysis of responses to the mathematics subtest: applications and mathematical sentence (N = 593)

Test item	Description of concept, skill, or ability	Number correct	Number wrong	Number omit	Percent correct	SE of percentage	P = .99	.01 confidence interval
Applications								
9a	Number story $2+1=n$	251	224	117	42.4	2.02	5.21	37.2–47.6
9b	Number story $3+n=5$	47	401	144	7.9	1.10	2.84	5.1–10.7
9c	Number story $5-3=n$	113	326	154	19.1	1.61	4.15	15.0–23.3
Mathematical sentence								
9d	$2+1=n$	243	254	96	41.0	2.01	5.19	35.8–46.2
9e	$n+2=4$	102	326	165	17.2	1.55	4.00	13.2–21.2

Table 7

Item analysis of responses to the mathematics subtest: logic (N = 593)

Test item	Description of concept, skill, or ability	Number correct	Number wrong	Number omit	Percent correct	SE of percentage	P = .99	.01 confidence interval
9f	If. . . , then . . .	196	328	69	33.1	1.93	4.98	28.1–38.1
9g	If. . . , then . . .	283	199	111	47.7	2.05	5.29	42.4–53.0
9h	Geometric construction	104	409	80	17.5	1.56	4.02	13.5–21.5

Table 8

Analysis of responses to all ten subtests of the mathematics achievement test (N = 593)

Subtests	Number of items	Percent correct	Percent wrong	Percent omit
Number	29	40.4	45.9	13.7
Operations	3	19.4	52.4	28.2
Number and operations	32*	33.4*	48.1*	18.6*
Measurement	7	46.3	40.6	13.1
Geometry	9	36.0	45.5	18.5
Functions and graphs	3	17.3	64.0	18.7
Set	4	19.5	45.0	35.5
Applications	3	23.1	53.5	23.4
Mathematical sentence	2	29.1	48.9	22.0
Logic	3	32.7	52.6	14.7
Total	63			
Average		29.3	49.8	20.9

Indicates the combined data for the subtests Number and Operations. These figures are not included in the total or averages.

More than 50 percent of the total group was able to identify five and nine dots and a single pair of socks; read the numeral 4, make three marks, and locate the first object in a series; pick out the shortest object among several, and recognize a square, a circle, and a triangle.

A level of difficulty between 25 and 50 percent indicates that these items were missed by 50 to 75 percent of the sample. Items in this range were considered to be of formidable difficulty. The items that fell within this classification included reproducing 7, 9, and 14 by marking the corresponding number of dots; reading the numerals 6, 9, and 0; making ten marks upon request; demonstrating an understanding of the cardinal meaning of 2 and 5; locating objects in a series that are "second" and "between"; recognizing half of a whole and half of a group of four dots; distinguishing the group with the fewest objects; identifying time on a clock showing 8 o'clock; recognizing the shape of a rectangle and knowing the number of sides of a triangle and a square; using 1:1 correspondence to match elements of equivalent sets; solving a number story involving a $2 + 1$ situation; perceiving the solution to a simple mathematical sentence, and deducing the quantity indicated from an "If . . . , then . . ." situation.

The most difficult items, that is, those to which fewer than 25 percent of the subjects responded successfully, included reading the numeral 23; writing the numerals 4 and 8; locating the fifth element in a series; finding one more or one less of the objects in a series; knowing the sum of the numbers 2 and 3, and 2 and 1, and the remainder for 5 and 2; realizing the number of pennies in a nickel and number of nickels in a dime; showing the number of corners in a square and triangle; perceiving the likenesses and differences among similar objects; deducing the number relationships between line segments and dots, and functions of numbers shown in pictograph form; matching elements of subsets, and making sets not equivalent, or equal in number; solving number stories involving a missing addend or remainder, and deducing the missing elements needed to make two geometric constructions equivalent.

The data revealed that there was a significant difference in mathematical test score means when kindergarten entrants were grouped according to mental age in ranges of six months. These differences were significant beyond the .01 level of confidence. The same significant differences were found between successive levels of IQ, categorized as follows: 89 and below, 90–109, 110–129, and 130 and over.

The data showed that as the chronological age increases, the mathematical achievement of the subjects increases.

The findings indicated that children whose parents' occupations placed them in the higher socioeconomic classes made significantly higher scores on the mathematics test than did those whose parents' occupations were categorized as lower socioeconomic class.

The analysis of the differences in mathematical test scores between children who scored below and above the mathematics test mean and between successive quartile divisions in mathematical achievement revealed significant differences beyond the .01 level of confidence with respect to each of the achievement groups.

An analysis of the relationships between the mathematical achievement of kindergarten entrants and (1) chronological age, (2) mental maturity factors, (3) rote counting ability, (4) socioeconomic status, (5) selected home influences, and (6) patterns of circumstances produced the following results.

Chronological age

The low coefficients of correlation indicated an almost negligible relationship between the two variables.

Mental maturity factors

The correlation coefficient of .70 showed that the relationship between mental age and mathematical achievement was marked. A marked relationship also was found to exist between mathematical achievement and IQ. The coefficient of correlation between these two variables was .75. This same marked relationship was found between mathematical achievement and the mental maturity factors of verbal meaning, perception, quantitative ability, and the factor of space as measured by the *SRA Primary Mental Abilities* test.

Rote counting ability

A substantial relationship was found between rote counting ability and mathematical achievement. The coefficient of correlation was .51.

Socioeconomic status

The .28 coefficient of contingency indicated a definite but small relationship between socioeconomic status and mathematical achievement. The chi-square was significant at the .001 level, which showed that the relationship could not have occurred by chance.

Selected home influences

Of the seventeen home circumstances used to investigate the relationship between home influences and mathematical achievement, nine showed a small but definite relationship, two indicated slight correlation, and six showed no apparent relationship.

The closest relationships were indicated by the contingency coefficients of .38 between knowledge of television channel numbers and mathematical achievement, and .36 between frequency of playing counting games with cards and mathematical achievement. In both comparisons chi-square was significant to the .001 level.

The coefficients of contingency between mathematical achievement and knowledge of house number, knowledge of telephone number, knowledge of telephone dialing, and frequency of playing counting games using spinners and dice were .29, .27, .27, .27, and .23, respectively. Chi-square was significant in all instances at the .001 level.

The relationships between mathematical achievement, interest in counting, and knowledge of songs involving numbers were .24 and .20, respectively. Coefficients of contingency were .17 and .14, respectively, for frequency of counting games played and playmate status.

Patterns of circumstances

Some circumstances and conditions existing in the preschool environment apparently influence some kindergarten entrants to attain a high level of mathematical achievement while others of equal mental ability fail to realize proportionate accomplishments. The higher mathematical achievers among children in the 90–109 IQ group had older siblings and playmates and could count to 20 or more. In the 110–129 IQ group the better mathematics achievers had older siblings and playmates, could count to 20 or more, and knew their age, house number, and telephone number. This

same pattern held true for the higher achievers in the 130-and-above IQ group. No unique pattern of circumstances among the higher achievers in the 89-and-below IQ group was found.

Conclusions

The findings of the study indicate that the extent and nature of mathematical achievement of kindergarten entrants are far-ranging and are associated with a number of factors. These findings appear to support the following conclusions:

1 The substantial number of mathematical concepts, skills, and abilities possessed by kindergarten entrants indicate that mathematics is a part of the preschool child's experience.

2 It would appear that appropriate mathematical instruction based upon the child's experience would be beneficial and profitable to the kindergarten pupil in terms of satisfying his immediate and future needs.

3 When so many kindergarten entrants can respond successfully to questions concerning the mathematical strands of measurement, number, geometry, and logic, it would seem that these topics should be used in the beginning as a basis for extending the mathematical concepts, skills, and abilities of children.

4 Because mental maturity is closely related to successful mathematical achievement, and because pupils differ greatly in general intelligence, important differences in mathematical achievement are to be expected. Therefore, establishment of a differentiated course of study for kindergarten pupils would provide for the wide range of needs.

5 Grouping of pupils according to age level would make it possible to differentiate courses of mathematics study for the different groups.

6 Different instructional programs for

boys and girls would not be particularly beneficial.

7 Differentiated programs for groupings based on socioeconomic status are desirable for the optimum development of kindergarten pupils' mathematics achievement.

8 Since such mental factors as verbal meaning, perceptual ability, and spatial ability are substantially related to mathematical achievement, activities designed to develop these abilities could be incorporated advantageously into the kindergarten course of study.

9 Because rote counting ability is substantially related to successful mathematical achievement, and because pupils differ greatly in rote counting ability, activities designed to develop this ability should be made a part of the kindergarten program. Instruction should fit the needs of the pupil.

10 Since the following factors are related to above-average mathematical achievement, the kindergarten program could well include activities designed to help children develop adequate concepts, skills, and abilities concerning (a) age, (b) house number, (c) telephone number, (d) telephone dialing, (e) television channel numbers, (f) songs involving numbers, and (g) counting games involving spinners, dice, and cards.

11 It would be helpful for underachievers of average IQ to play with older children and to learn to count to 20.

12 It would be helpful for underachievers of above-average or superior intelligence to play with older children, to learn to count to 20 or more, and to learn their age, house number, and telephone number.

The findings of the present study indicate that certain factors are significantly associated with the kindergarten entrant's mathematical achievement described by test items involving mathematical concepts, skills, or abilities.

In view of these findings and other considerations certain educational implications seem to be evident.

1 An assessment of the kindergarten entrants' mathematical concepts, skills, or abilities should be made early in the school year.

2 A planned sequential mathematics program should be developed that encompasses all the mathematical strands described by the Advisory Committee on Mathematics.

3 Time devoted to activities that develop mathematical readiness would also contribute to the development of reading readiness, and vice versa.

4 The wide range of differences in mathematical achievement indicate that intraclass grouping of pupils according to level of mathematical achievement is desirable.

5 The program of instruction should include a wide variety of activities that involve the use of number.

6 Constant evaluation of the pupil's progress is needed to insure proper developmental activities.

7 Schools in different socioeconomic areas should adjust beginning mathematics programs to fit the needs of the pupils.

Assessment of Mathematical Concepts of Five-Year-Old Children

ANTHONY N. SCHWARTZ

ABSTRACT

An instrument, the Schwartz Early Mathematics Inventory (SEMI), was devised to assess, by means of group administration, the mathematical achievement of children ages 3 through 5. The data presented concern only the first stages of the process and deal only with 215 kindergarteners. A reliability of .94 was obtained on the eighty-one items administered on 64 pages. The mean for items correct 43.2. The proportion of correct responses for various items ranged from .85 to .12. The children had satisfactorily acquired the physical and emotional attributes necessary for completing the inventory, namely, holding a pencil or crayon, turning pages, recording responses in designated areas, and maintaining satisfactory attention for the 12 to 28 minutes required for administering each of the three portions of the SEMI.

The development of procedures for the assessment of the capabilities and the measurement of accomplishments of five-year-olds is a major challenge to the educational world. The Research and Development Center in Educational Stimulation, University of Georgia, has unified its total program of activities around early and continuous intellectual stimulation of children, ages 3 through 12. To carry on such a program requires a sound

From *The Journal of Experimental Education*, Vol. 37, (1969). Reprinted by permission of Heldref Publications, 4000 Albemarle St., N.W. Washington, DC 20016.

basis of evaluation for making decisions.

The principal purpose of this research was to develop an instrument which could systematically assess the variations in performance, involving the acquired mathematical concepts and skills of kindergarten children.

Background for the Study

Neither child growth and development specialists, mathematicians, nor professional educators seem to be in accord as to what mathematical concepts a child has developed at the preschool level or what the curriculum should encompass at this age. Research has been limited in scope and the results do not lead one to make conclusive decisions. Opinions differ, some lead one to believe that the child has a very superficial concept of numerosity while others, pertaining to children of a socially biased culture, state that an extensive background of mathematical acumen has been acquired prior to that developed by the organized school program.

The studies of the developmental stages by Piaget (9) serve as a basis for much discussion and argument concerning the mathematical abilities of children, including ages 4 and beyond. Dodwell (2 and 3), Holmes (6), Inhelder (7), Elkind (4), and Wohlwill (12), have done replications of Piaget's studies and have tended to support his findings, but in so doing these researchers have had to improve upon the investigative procedures. Research by Estes (5), however, refutes many of the findings mentioned. The author suggests a careful scrutiny of the book by Wallace (10) as a source of not only the studies mentioned by many others which are relevant. Although most of these studies indicate some evidences of stages of development, no agreement appears.

Recent studies substantiate the statements that children come to kindergarten with considerable knowledge upon which the school can build an interesting, challenging, and sequential curriculum. Studies by Sister Josephina (8) and Brace and Nelson (1) involved individual evaluations of children. The first studied thirty children in one kindergarten, and the second used a sampling of 124 children drawn from a population of 3,000. Williams (11) administered a group test to 595 kindergarten entrants and reported a positive response ranging from 6.9 to 81.3 percent of the sixty-three items given.

As far as could be ascertained there are no commercial tests available to specifically measure the cognitive mathematical status of children ages 3 to 6 or to evaluate progress as they are intensively subjected to formal instructional procedures.

Purposes

The main purpose of this investigation was to develop a group pencil and paper instrument to assess the mathematical achievement of kindergarten children. Secondary concerns were: (a) assessment of the physical requirements involved in the procedures, such as turning pages, holding a pencil, and attention span, (b) assurance that the response of the individual can be accurately recorded, and (c) evidence that the response is individual rather than a "cooperative" endeavor.

Development of the Instrument

In preparation for the development of the Schwartz Early Mathematics Inventory (SEMI)[2] three primary sources were used

to develop concepts and the initial item pool. First, a literature survey was made of material regarding individual or group testing which might have implications for measuring mathematical achievement. Tests, whether general or for specific subject areas, were investigated regarding such areas as: format, manner of presentation, giving directions, and recording pupil response. Available materials and workbooks, methodology books, early childhood curricula, and general child growth and development releases were also included. A panel of educators reviewed the items.

Second, the author conducted individual assessments of 268 kindergarteners.

Third, kindergarten teachers were interviewed in respect to their number experiences with children.

Since small muscle control must be taken into consideration, it was determined to use but one vertical line, in a majority of situations, for responding to each item. Whenever feasible sets were represented by circles and squares so that required vocabulary would be reduced for those with backgrounds of cultural deprivation.

As a result, eighty-one items[4] were selected having a range from easy to difficult within specific areas. The areas ranged from simple to complex in mathematical learnings which might have probable relevance to this age group. Items were presented in numerous ways to give variety and to ascertain adaptability of the children.

Pre-inventory exercises of approximately 15 minutes duration were given to the children in order to familiarize them with the social setting, the test carrels and mechanical procedures. The children were asked to mark with pencil or crayon, whichever was most frequently used in the classroom, and were instructed to void any marks they did not want by making two horizontal marks across the vertical mark they had made. The double line was used to differentiate from X which many children were prone to use. In general, the test booklets contained one item per page—eighty-one items on 64 pages—to avoid complicating the task of responding by requiring even rudimentary reading skills.

Subjects

Complete data were obtained from 215 kindergarteners residing in northern Georgia whose age range was 5 years 0 months to 6 years 5 months. The children attended public and private schools from varied socio-economic, racial, and ethnic backgrounds as follows:

a. rural, low socio-economic children were obtained from the total kindergarten enrollment of one county in three schools, one of which was Negro. Total N = 66.

b. suburban children were obtained by the stratified sampling of the total enrollment of 5-year-olds in a county in a metropolitan area of approximately one million population, proportion 9 percent Negroes. Total N = 57.

c. urban, low economic children were obtained from the total enrollment of three schools, selected under a Title I grant as being culturally deprived, in a city of 18,000. Approximately 50 percent of this group were Negro and were enrolled in one school. Total N = 60.

d. urban, high socio-economic culturally advantaged children were obtained from the total enrollment in a private, all white kindergarten. Total N = 32.

Administration of the SEMI

The children were examined during the first 3 weeks of February in rooms and hallways with which they were familiar, and in their own classrooms if their peers were assigned to carry on activities in another place. The children were seated six at a table, separated by "carrels" of interlocking one-fourth inch plywood 1-foot high, with a minimum work space of $15'' \times 32''$. A maximum of twelve children were tested at any one period. Each group of six children were supervised by either the administrator, a graduate student or a teacher aide. The tests were administered by graduate students or the author but not by the classroom teacher, although she may have been an observer at an administration. The only assistance given during the time the inventory was being administered was to see that the child was on the correct page or to see that he understood where the response was to be placed.

During the approximately 15 minute pre-inventory exercises, the administrator or the assistant gave any aid required or requested which would help the child in understanding the activities and the task to be accomplished.

The items for the SEMI were read once to the children unless the task was somewhat involved or the statement lengthy. The tempo of administering the items was as rapid as feasible to eliminate "peeking," talking and other distracting incidents. The average of two items per minute was suggested as a guide. In order to reduce fatigue, the SEMI was administered on separate days, in three sittings besides the pre-inventory session.

Presentation of the Data

The SEMI booklets were hand scored on a right or wrong basis regardless of the number of foils for the item. No partial credit was allowed. Responses were placed on data cards and computer processed by the TSSA Program (13).

Inventory Statistics

The general test data for the SEMI is presented in Table 1 as computed from data gathered from 215 kindergarteners.

TABLE 1

Moments of the *SEMI*

Mean:	43.19	±	1.02
Standard deviation:	14.97		
Skewness:	−0.42		
Kurtosis:	−0.53*		

*Significant at .05 level

The data indicates that the population did not fall into the normal curve pattern but are leptokurtic and skewed—a rather common outcome with some kinds of empirical data. The kurtosis is significant at the .05 level. The inventory reliability equals .94 using the Kuder-Richardson Formula 20.

The mean inventory score was 43.19. The scores earned by the children ranged from a high of 70 to a low of 8. The latter child omitted fifty-four items. Fifty-two children did not omit any items. The range of administration time for the SEMI was: part I, 12–25 minutes; part II, 10–18 minutes; and part III, 12–28 minutes

Item Analysis

An analysis of the eighty-one items of the SEMI is summarized in Table 2. The difficulty level of each item is indicated in terms of the percentage of correct responses. The proportion of the children selecting a correct response for particular items ranged from .85 to .12. Seven items can be considered comparatively easy as they were answered correctly at least by 80 percent of the children. Eleven items can be considered relatively hard as they were answered correctly by less than 30 percent of the children. No items fell within the extremely easy (p > .95) and the extremely difficult (p < .05) range.

Point-biserial correlations were computed for each item and total test score. They ranged from .62 to .11. Items with point-biserial coefficients above .40 were considered to discriminate effectively. The coefficients for forty-nine items fell into this category.

Factor Analysis

Although the SEMI developed as a single-score general mathematics inventory, inter-item tetrachoric correlations were processed by factor analysis with varimax rotation. These inter-item correlations varied from .82 to random negative values as large as −.16. The number of factors to be extracted was programmed at ten. The resultant rotated factor loadings ranged from .80 to −.41 but 84 percent of the items had their highest loadings on the unrotated first factor and 52.2 percent of the common variance is accounted for by this factor, so the data did not lend themselves to interpretation by multiple discrete factors. Factor loadings of .40 or greater, on the rotated factors were given greatest emphasis in assigning the items to test parts and subparts. By combining these data with a rational analysis of the inventory, the items were categorized into fourteen comparatively recognizable and workable parts or sub-parts as given in Table 2.

General Observations

The 8½″ × 7″ format was adequate for the illustrations and materials presented. Presentation of the items in mimeographed two dimensional form did not appear to be a barrier to understanding what was expected.

The response to most items was usually immediate and the answer readily designated. Instructions were easily remembered and very little repetition was necessary. The cross-out technique for voiding responses proved invaluable and highly suitable for this age group.

Summary and Generalizations

An instrument, the Schwartz Early Mathematics Inventory (SEMI), was

Table 2

Grouping and Analysis of Items of the *SEMI*

Test Item	Description of item—reflects instructions read to children	Percent* correct	Point** Biserial Correlation
	PART 1. PROBLEM SOLVING		
A.	Number stories (If-then situations) Example: While demonstrating, "If I have two books and I take one away, then how many will I have left?"		
63.	2 − 1 = n Objects pictured. Mark the right frame	81	51
64.	5 − 2 = n Objects pictured. Mark the frame	70	49
65.	1 + 1 = n No objects. Make right number of marks	60	37
61.	2 + 1 = n Objects pictured. Mark the frame	60	41
62.	3 + 3 = n Objects pictured. Mark the frame	58	44
67.	2 − 1 = n No objects. Make right number of marks	55	35
68.	5 − 1 = n No objects. Make right number of marks	47	54
66.	2 + 2 = n No objects. Make right number of marks	47	51
B.	Reproduction		
43.	Make 2 marks	79	45
44.	Make 5 marks	68	45
57.	Make the same number of marks as circles (2)	61	51
59.	Make one less mark than circles (2)	52	21
51.	Make marks for combining a frame with a set of 1 circle with a frame with a set of 2 circles	42	45
58.	Make 2 more marks than circles (2 circles) [Identical items on different pages]	20	37
60.	Make 2 more marks than circles (2 circles) [Identical items on different pages]	20	33

Test Item	Description of item—reflects instructions read to children	Percent* correct	Point** Biserial Correlation
	PART II. VISUAL DISCRIMINATION		
A.	Matching and Analyzing Shapes		
13.	Mark two numbers or figures that are the same	82	53
14.	Mark two numbers/figures that are the same	78	62
28.	Mark something that measures table/how tall you are	66	46
27.	Mark something that measures days of month	62	42
55.	Mark the two shapes that look alike	74	54
56.	Mark two figures that look alike turned the same	39	42
B.	Recognition of sub-sets		
9.	Mark frame that has 3 squares	81	50
41.	Mark 3 of the squares in the frame	77	48
52.	Two frames, if one more than other mark it. If same number of circles in both frames mark each frame	75	48
10.	Mark frame that has 5 squares	75	47
42.	Mark 4 of the circles in the frame	73	58
34.	Mark ½ set of 4 squares (scored two ways)	51	37
C.	Analyzing patterns or classification		
16.	Frame of sticks or heavy lines, mark the stick that doesn't fit	78	39
15.	Frame of circles, mark the circle that doesn't fit	74	44
7.	Four frames, mark the two frames that have the same number (3 squares)	59	65
1.	Four frames, mark each of the two frames that look the same (four pictures of ducks)	54	60
8.	Four frames, mark the two frames that have the same number (9 circles)	53	61

Test Item	Description of item—reflects instructions read to children	Percent* correct	Point** Biserial Correlation
11.	Frame alternate circles-squares as beads, mark circle or square which will make look right	51	31
12.	Frame, square, two circles, square, etc. as beads, mark circle or square which added looks right	50	45
	PART III. COMPARISON		
A.	Semi-concrete non-equivalent sets		
5.	Mark the largest dog	85	37
6.	Mark the shortest pencil	84	40
2.	Which frame has more buttons?	82	44
35.	Draw a line from dot to dot (dots 7 inches apart)	80	44
3.	Which frame has the most pictures?	77	45
B.	Abstract non-equivalent sets		
20.	Mark frame with set greater than 3	73	38
23.	Frame has more squares than circles, mark extra squares	55	29
22.	Mark frame with set equal to 3	41	24
4.	Which frame has the least number of circles?	36	40
21.	Mark frame with set less than 3	36	39
24.	Frame has more squares than circles, mark extra squares	24	26
C.	Ordinality		
17.	Point to left. Mark the first duck.	84	45
18.	Mark the last duck.	67	58
19.	Mark the third duck.	37	42
	PART IV. GEOMETRIC IDENTIFICATION		
39.	Mark each circle in the frame	54	49

Test Item	Description of item—reflects instructions read to children	Percent* correct	Point** Biserial Correlation
36.	Set blocks or things, mark each which is all black	41	62
40.	Mark each triangle	35	36
37.	Mark each block/thing which has some black and some white	28	49
38.	Set different shapes, mark those more than two sides	14	33
	PART V. SPATIAL JUDGMENT		
53.	Pictures two pieces string, one tight, one loose. Mark the string which you think is longer.	49	20
69.	Two jars same size. Water put in other jar, how high?	46	38
70.	Two jars, one ½ dia. other, mark height water other jar.	34	11
45.	Seriation-sets of lines, make marks missing set (3)	26	35
46.	Seriation-sets of lines, make marks missing set (4)	21	30
54.	Bar graph, fill in or mark to look right	14	29
	PART VI. TIME IDENTIFICATION		
26.	Four frames clocks/watches, mark six o'clock	49	49
25.	Four frames clocks/watches, mark twelve o'clock	45	36
29.	Clock face, made two hands show 6 o'clock	35	42
	PART VII. NUMERAL-NUMBER CONCEPTS		
	The children confronted with numerals 0 through 10 for following items:		
71.	Mark the number for 3	73	47
72.	Mark number for 6	64	52

Test Item	Description of item—reflects instructions read to children	Percent* correct	Point** Biserial Correlation
74.	Mark number that shows number fingers one hand (4 or 5)	64	52
73.	Mark number that shows how many eyes you have	63	51
76.	Mark the number that comes just before 5	52	53
75.	Mark the number which shows you don't have any	47	46
77.	Mark the number that comes just after 7	45	43
78.	Mark the number that comes two numbers before 4	41	27
79.	Mark the number that comes two numbers after 3	32	22
80.	When I count 5, 4, 3, 2, mark number I should say next	29	38
81.	When I count 10, 9, 8, 7, mark number I should say next	29	37
	PART VIII. MONEY IDENTIFICATION		
48.	Mark the frame that shows a dime	71	24
49.	Mark the frame . . . which of 4 coins will buy the most (3 cents and nickel)	68	33
50.	Mark which will buy the most (2 frames)	56	14
47.	Mark the frame that shows a nickel	54	13
	PART IX. FRACTIONAL RECOGNITION		
32.	Mark the jar that is ½ full of water	41	38
30.	Mark the frame that shows ¼ or one-quarter pie	35	17
31.	Mark the frame that shows ⅓ of a pie	24	14
33.	Mark the jar that is ¼ full of water	12	01

*Percent correct is computed including errors and omits
**Point biserial correlation is correlation of item with total test score

devised to assess, by means of group administration, the mathematical achievement of children ages 3 through 5. The data presented here concern only the first stages of the process and deal only with 215 five-year-olds.

A reliability of .94 was obtained on the eighty-one items administered. The mean for items correct was 43.2. The proportion of correct responses for various items ranged from .85 to .12.

The children satisfactorily acquired the physical and emotional attributes necessary for completing the inventory, namely, holding a pencil or crayon, turning pages, recording responses in designated areas, and maintaining satisfactory attention for the 12 to 28 minutes required for administering each of the three portions of the SEMI. By using portable carrels and the usual kindergarten tables, a very high degree of individual response was maintained.

The data are encouraging in light of the purposes of the investigation. Further refining and decreasing the number of items should yield a more usable instrument. Since the youngest children taking the SEMI were able to perform the physical functions necessary, the author is encouraged to validate the instrument for three-and four-year-olds.

Footnotes

1. The research reported herein was performed as a special project as a portion of the postdoctoral education training program sponsored as part of the activities of the Research and Development Center in Educational Stimulation at the University of Georgia pursuant to a contract with the U.S. Department of Health, Education and Welfare grant No. OREG 2-6-061881-1406.
2. A complete copy of the Schwartz Early Mathematics Inventory and related materials are on file at the Research and Development Center in Educational Stimulation, University of Georgia.
3. Grateful acknowledgment is made to Dr. Warren G. Findley and staff of the Research and Development Center in Educational Stimulation, for the assistance offered in conjunction with the postdoctoral training program.
4. Numeral number connotations are used interchangeably because of usage by children, parents, and some teachers.

TABLE 3

Items Considered Comparatively Hard—
Percent of Children Answering
Correctly $\leq$ 30

Item	Percent
24. Frame has more squares than circles, mark extra squares	24
31. Mark the frame that shows ⅓ of a pie	24
33. Mark the jar that is ¼ full of water	12
37. Mark each block/thing which has some black and some white	28
38. Set of different shapes, mark those with more than two sides	14
45. Seriation—sets of lines, make marks (3) for missing set	26
46. Seriation—sets of lines, make marks (4) for missing set	21
54. Bar graph, fill in or mark to look right	14
58. Make 2 more marks than circles (2 circles)	20
80. When I count 5, 4, 3, 2, mark number I should say next	29
81. When I count 10, 9, 8, 7, mark number I should say next	29

REFERENCES

1. Brace, B. and Nelson, L. D., "The Preschool Child's Concept of Number," *The Arithmetic Teacher*, 12:126–33, February 1965.
2. Dodwell, P. C., "Children's Understanding of Number and Related Concepts," *Canadian Journal of Psychology*, 14:192–205, 1960.

3. Dodwell, P. C., "Children's Understanding of Number Concepts: Characteristics of an Individual and Group Test," *Canadian Journal of Psychology*, 15:29–36, 1961.
4. Elkind, D., "The Development of Quantitative Thinking: A Systematic Replication of Piaget's Studies," *Journal of Genetic Psychology*, 98:37–46, 1961.
5. Estes, B. W., "Some Mathematical and Logical Concepts in Children," *Journal of Genetic Psychology*, 88:219–222, 1956.
6. Holmes, E. E., "What Do Pre-First Grade Children Know About Numbers?" *Elementary School Journal*, 63:397–403, April 1963.
7. Inhelder, B. in Wallace, J. G. *Concept Growth and the Education of the Child*, King, Thorne and Stace Ltd., School Road, Hove, Sussex, British Isles, p. 82, 1965.
8. Josephina C. S. J., Sister, "Quantitative Thinking of Preschool Children," *The Arithmetic Teacher*, 12:54–55, January 1965.
9. Piaget, J., *The Child's Concept of Number*, Routledge and Kegan Paul, London, 1952.
10. Wallace, J. G., *Concept Growth and the Education of the Child*, King, Thorne and Stace Ltd., School Road, Hove, Sussex, British Isles, 1965.
11. Williams, A. H., "Mathematical Concepts, Skills and Abilities of Kindergarten Entrants," *The Arithmetic Teacher*, 12:261–268, April 1965.
12. Wohlwill, J. F., "A Study of the Development of the Number Concept by Scalogram Analysis," *Journal of Genetic Psychology*, 97:345–377, 1960.
13. Wolf, Richard and Klopfer, Leopold, "Test Scorer and Statistical Analysis 2 (with Factor Varimax Rotation)," unpublished report issued by the Computer Program Library Social Science Division, University of Chicago, p. 37.

Testing for Number Readiness: Application of the Piagetian Theory of the Child's Development of the Concept of Number

ROBERT WILLIAMS

ABSTRACT

Piaget's 3-stage theory of the child's attainment of the concept of number was applied as a number readiness criterion to ninety-six kindergarten children. Two children were found to be at the initial stage of number development, eighty-six at the intermediate stage, and eight at the stage of attainment of number concept which is inclusive of operational ability. Results were applied to mathematics curriculum goals on the kindergarten level. Curriculum goals for mathematics on this level should not include operations (addition, subtraction). Socialization to number symbols may be established as a goal at this level, but it has nothing to do with the concept of number and does not appear to enhance attainment of the concept of number.

Piaget's model of the development of the number concept identifies three stages, through which each child must progress: (1) an initial stage, (2) an intermediate stage, and (3) a stage of attainment of number concept. According to Piagetian theory (1:260–261,2,4,5), the attainment of the concept of number (Stage III) is demonstrated when a child (6½ to 7 years) is able to equalize a collection of elements (e.g., 8 disks) 1 inch apart, in a row with another collection of elements by bi-univocal correspondence between their terms. Piaget further maintains that there must be perceived equivalence of the collections after the density of the elements composing one of the collections is modified in such a way that the elements of one row no longer appear directly opposite those of the other. Before the attainment of the concept of number, the child's response takes one of two similar but incomplete forms. In the intermediate stage (Stage II), the child (5 to 6 years) makes a one-to-one correspondence of the two collections as a basis of equivalence; but after a modification of the density of the elements, the child loses equivalence of the collections. During the initial stage (Stage I), the child (4 to 5 years) responds to the elements of the model row by constructing a row equal to the length of the model but of unequal elemental distribution and composition.

Before discussing application, this model will be identified among Piaget's sequential-developmental stages. The three sequential stages toward the attainment of the concept of number seem to be within the transitional phase at the conclusion of the preconceptual phase, the whole of the intuitive thought stage, and the initial phase of the stage of concrete operations. According to Piaget, this model of the development of the number concept cannot be effectively ap-

From *The Journal of Educational Research*, Vol. 64 (May–June 1971) pp. 394–396. Reprinted by permission of Heldref Publications, 4000 Albemarle St., N.W. Washington, DC 20016.

plied before the age of 4 or the stage of intuitive thought, at which time short experiments involving the manipulation of experimental objects and meaningful conversation about the activity may be carried on (2:162, 5:129).

Procedure

An incidental sample of ninety-six children ages 5:6:26 to 7:1:0 (years:months:days) of Weller Elementary School, Centerville, Ohio, was interviewed with the intention of: (1) establishing whether Piagetian stages actually existed within the group; (2) identifying the stage of each child at the date of testing, and (3) relating the results to mathematics goals at the kindergarten level. During the interviews each child was presented with a model row composed of eight disks of the same size and color.

o o o o o o o o (Model)

The child was then asked to place down as many disks from his collection (which were the same size as those of the model but of a different color) as there were in the model. A child at the initial stage (I) might respond in the following manner:

o o o o o o o o (Model)
oooooooooooooooo (Response)

The child has constructed a row equal in length but of unequal elements and composition; yet he believes that he has established equivalence between the two collections. At the intermediate stage (II) a child responds by establishing a one-to-one correspondence of the elements of both collections.

o o o o o o o o (Model)
o o o o o o o o (Response)

The child will affirm the equivalence of the collections before a modification of the density. The test of the equivalence of this one-to-one correspondence comes when the density of the elements of one of the rows is modified:

o o o o o o o o
oooooooo

After modification of the density of the elements, a child of the intermediate

stage will affirm a lack of equivalence of the collections; however, at the stage (III) of attainment of the concept of number, the child maintains equivalence of the collections.

Every child was asked to make a manual response. The initial stage was identified from this manual response. Children making a one-to-one correspondence were interrogated after a modification of the density and a destruction of perceptual correspondence. The verbal response was the determinant in identifying the intermediate and attainment stages (2:26).

Results and Discussion

All Ss could be adequately categorized by Piaget's model of number concept development. Two children (male, 5:10:14 and female, 6:3:23) were found to be at the initial stage. Neither corresponded with the hypothesized age of the initial stage (4 to 5 years). This lack of correspondence is not a critical element. Piaget cautions against an over-literal identification of stage and age. His findings give only a rough estimate at best of the mean age at which various stages are achieved (2:20). Eighty-six of ninety-six were in the intermediate stage. Nine of the eighty-six rendered a verbal count of the number of elements composing the rows before perceptual correspondence was destroyed. As Piaget has maintained, concerning children of the intermediate stage, correspondence and the ability to count the elements of the rows were of no aid to their maintenance of equivalence after perceptual correspondence was destroyed (5:144).

Neither the initial nor intermediate stages manifest the presence of operational ability or the attainment of the concept of number. The child of the initial stage does not differentiate the disks which compose the row from the row itself and his response is regulated by what Piaget refers to as global comparison (4:86-7). The responses of children of the intermediate stage reveal that they take the immediate conditions of the model as the final and conclusive reality. The children seem to have given their attention to the end results of the transformation of the model (modification of the density of one of the collections) rather than to the transformation itself (2:157). Concerning centration on the end result of transformation Flavell states,

> *A single, isolated cognition of this sort, with little or no systematic reference to other cognitions past or potential, is the hallmark of the preoperational child (2:167).*

Eight of the children (5:11:3 to 6:8:28) were able to maintain the equivalence of the two rows after perceptual correspondence was destroyed. These children were judged to have attained the concept of number and manifested the presence of operational ability which within the Piagetian system is action or a system of bodily movements which have become internalized in the form of thought activities (1:xvi, 155–56, 167). Flavell in his explanation of Piagetian cognitive operations states,

> *A useful rule of thumb, one Piaget has used (5:32–33), is to say that all the actions implied in common mathematical symbols like +, −, ×, ÷, =, <, >, etc., belong to, but do not exhaust the domain of what he (Piaget) terms intellectual operation (2:166).*

Children of the stage of attainment do not center their attention only on the end result of transformation but also upon the transformation. The transformation that now concerns the child is merely one example of a whole system of possible transformations. Each transformation is now seen in relation to another transformation which can negate it. Here we observe a maturation of the coordination of reversible cognitive actions which distinguish the preoperational child from the child in the stage of concrete operations (2:167).

Relating the results of this study to kindergarten mathematics' goals is germane. For children identified in the first two stages we cannot have operational objectives (addition and subtraction) in mathematics. It is not realistic to have the learning of addition and subtraction as objectives. Addition and subtraction involve operations which are not congruent with the cognitive structures of the children. At this time the only realistic goal that may be considered is to give attention to the socialization of the children to the culturally accepted symbols for numbers, 1, 2, 3, 4, 5, etc. A reservation is that socialization concludes with the number 10 unless the child shows a desire to go further. It is sufficient for the purposes of socialization that children be given only the very basic numbers. What occurs in socialization has nothing to do with the concept of number. That this group of children was socialized to number symbols was verified through a study of the results of ninety-four of ninety-six of the children's Metropolitan Readiness Tests, Form A, Test 5 Numbers (MRT,FA,T5N) (3) and especially the questions from that test which seem to reveal the rote knowledge these children had of certain basic social-cultural number symbols (see Table 1).

Table 1 indicates that the children did considerably better on questions 7, 8, 9, 10, and 25 of the MRT, FA, T5N than could be expected by chance. Such responses would tend to indicate that the children in our sample had been socialized to the basic numbers, 4, 5 and 6, 5, 9, and 8 and 1 respectively. This sample of children had been socialized to number symbols for 7½ months prior to the testing. The formal instrument of this socialization was the kindergarten level workbook of the Greater Cleveland Mathematics Program, 1961. Although Table 1 would indicate that the children did possess a degree of rote knowledge of the number symbols which they were able to write and recognize in print, this knowledge was of little operational value to them: i.e., only eight of the children

Table 1

Results of Questions from the Metropolitan Readiness Tests, Form A, Test 5 Numbers Which Seem to Reveal the Rote Knowledge the Children had of Certain Social-Cultural Number Symbols[1]

		Correct N	Correct %	% of Correct Responses Expected by Chance
Q 7.	"In the next row, put a mark on the 4."	94	100	20
Q 8.	"In the box where the ducks are, put a mark on 56."	74	79	25
Q 9.	"See the box where the grapes are. Now write the number 5 in the space beside the grapes."	88	94	0
Q 10.	"Find the box where the flag is. Mark the number that comes next after 8 when you are counting."	76	81	25
Q 25.	"In the box where the book is, write eighty-one."	62	66	0

who were exposed to the structured interview were able to demonstrate that they had reached the stage of attainment of the concept of number. The only rationale which may be given in support of socialization to number symbols is that it provides children with the culturally accepted symbols with which to perform operations after the attainment of the concept of number. For children at the stage of attainment we can include addition and subtraction as goals for a mathematics curriculum.

Throughout the research, the author's concern was with the developmental status of the child and the mathematics curriculum for kindergarten (6:423–34). More precisely, the concern has been with number readiness. The recommendations are based upon the Piagetian qualitative stage-dependent theory within which the author tried to assess the child's cognitive structure at a certain time or development (6:424). The curriculum recommendations for mathematics

in the kindergarten are in accord with the cognitive status of the children as demonstrated through evaluation by means of the Piagetian model.

Footnote

1. Reproduced from Metropolitan Readiness Tests, copyright 1965 by Harcourt, Brace and World, Inc. Reproduced by special permission of the publisher.

REFERENCES

1. Beth, E. W.; Piaget, J., *Mathematical Epistemology and Psychology* (translated from French by W. Mays), D. Reidel Publishing Company, Dordrecht-Holland; Gordon and Breach Science Publishers, New York, 1966.
2. Flavell, J. H., *The Developmental Psychology of Jean Piaget*, Van Nos-

trand Company, Inc., Princeton, New
Jersey, 1963.
3. Hildreth, G. H.; Griffiths, N. L.;
McGauvran, M. E., "Metropolitan
Readiness Tests, Form A," Harcourt,
Brace and World, Inc., New York,
1965.
4. Piaget, J., *The Child's Conception of
Number,* Routledge and Kegan Paul

Ltd., London, England, 1952.
5. Piaget, J., *Psychology of Intelligence,* Littlefield, Adams and Co.,
Totowa, New Jersey, 1966.
6. Sigel, I. E.; Hooper, F. H. (eds.),
Logical Thinking in Children, Holt,
Rinehart, and Winston, Inc., New
York, 1968.

Kindergarten Mathematics—a Survey

V. RAY KURTZ

It is relatively easy to identify the mathematical concepts that first-grade and older children should master. It is much more difficult to identify with any degree of certainty the mathematical concepts that are to be mastered by kindergarten children. In the first grade, twenty to forty minutes are commonly allocated each day to mathematics, but in the kindergarten the time spent in work with numbers varies considerably. For example, two student aides who were juniors at the university insisted that the two kindergarten classes that they were observing had no mathematics period. These students were probably overlooking the casual and incidental work with numbers that the teachers were including in daily activities—calendar work and counting the children as a part of taking roll each morning—but the incidentalness of the work with numbers is further evidence of variation in the time devoted to mathematics in kindergartens. At least one major textbook company, recognizing the existing variation in the time spent on

mathematics in the kindergarten, has organized its program so as to offer alternative materials to teachers. Level A is available for teachers who want five lessons a month, Level B provides ten lessons a month, and Level C provides fifteen lessons a month. A teacher may select the three, six, or nine booklets that respectively make up the three levels, depending on the depth of mathematics desired.

How extensive is the existing variation in the standards and goals of the teachers who teach kindergarten mathematics? If standards are not set and if goals are not stated, it becomes difficult to determine what the program is and, more important, when mastery has been achieved. In the absence of grade standards, one kindergarten teacher will have one set of goals and another kindergarten teacher, a different set. The result must be first-grade children with considerable variation in their readiness for mathematics, and this situation is undesirable.

Faced with a lack of data on the scope of kindergarten mathematics and believing that teachers need more information to formulate goals at this grade, the author set out to answer two major questions:

Reprinted from *Arithmetic Teacher,* May 1978 (Vol. 25, pp. 51–53), copyright 1978 by the National Council of Teachers of Mathematics. Used by permission.

1. What competencies in mathematics are achieved by kindergarten children?

2. Are clear trends evident in the methods used by teachers of kindergarten mathematics?

Having decided that the best procedure to use in answering these questions would be to ask teachers directly about their mathematics program, the author surveyed by questionnaire one-third of the over one thousand kindergarten teachers in Kansas.

Late in the spring semester, questionnaires were sent to 340 randomly selected kindergarten teachers in Kansas. Completed forms were returned by 277 of the teachers who received the questionnaires, a return of 81 + percent. The 277 teachers taught over 11,000 children. The questionnaire, limited to forty-five questions to encourage its completion by busy teachers, was designed to determine *(a)* each teacher's assessment of those competencies in mathematics that his or her children possessed at the end of the school year and *(b)* other related information, such as teaching methods, teaching materials, frequency of mathematics lessons, and class size.

RESULTS OF THE SURVEY

Competencies

The first question, regarding the mathematical competencies of kindergarten children, could be answered by categorizing the mathematics competencies in three areas, as shown in tables 1, 2, and 3. In practically all cases, the competencies formed natural clusters. The first category (table 1) had in excess of 90 percent in the top two percentages. The third category (table 3 had less than 25 percent in the top range, with the lower range always including a greater percentage than the top range. In all cases but one, the second category (table 2) contained a total of 60 percent or more in the top two ranges.

On the basis of the evidence in this survey, the competencies in table 1 could be categorized as clearly on the kindergarten level; those in table 2, as questionable for the kindergarten level; and those in table 3, as clearly *not* of the kindergarten level.

Table 1

Clearly kindergarten competencies

| Competency | Percent of children reaching competency | | | |
	0–25	26–50	51–75	76–100
Rationally count to 20	2	3	13	82*
Recognition of numerals to 10	0	1	7	92
Identify sets of 0, 1, 2, 3, 4, and 5	0	3	8	89
Identify sets of 6, 7, 8, 9, and 10	3	4	17	76
Write numerals 0–5 in order	2	2	4	92
Write numerals 6–10 in order	1	4	9	86
Identification of circle, square, rectangle, and triangle	0	2	4	94
Identification of a circle, its inside and outside	2	5	12	81

*This is read: 82% of the teachers reported that at the end of the school year, 76–100% of the children could rationally count to 20. This percentage added to the next lower figure indicates that most all children do well on this competency.

Table 2

Questionable kindergarten competencies

Competency	Percent of children reaching competency			
	0–25	26–50	51–75	76–100
Write numerals in order to 20	13	17	37	33*
Identify sets for one more and one less	5	10	39	46
Join 2 sets to form sums to 5	7	16	30	47
Join 2 sets to form sums to 10	17	16	30	47
Separate 2 sets to form differences from 5	23	21	30	32
Add numerals to sums of five	12	23	22	32
Tell time on the hour	15	22	26	40
Locate a day of the month on the calendar	9	20	31	34
Identify penny, nickel, and dime	6	18	33	40
		18	34	42

*This is read: 33% of the teachers reported that at the end of the school year 76–100% of their children could write numerals in order to 20.

Table 3

Clearly not kindergarten competencies

Competency	Percent of children reaching competency			
	0–25	26–50	51–75	76–100
Write numerals as sets of tens and ones	66*	15	12	7
Rationally count to 100	25	22	37	16
Recognition of numerals to 50	19	31	37	13
Identify halves, fourths, and thirds	40	37	18	5
Count by twos to 20	57	24	14	5
Separate 2 sets to form differences from 10	34	24	24	18
Add numerals to sums of 10	27	22	29	22
Subtract numerals to form differences from 5	35	25	17	23
Subtract numerals to form differences from 10	48	23	21	8
Read a thermometer	49	27	20	4
Identify odd numbers to 20	64	17	14	5

*This is read: 66% of the teachers reported that at the end of the school year only 0–25% of their children could write numerals as sets of tens and ones.

Methods

There are many questions concerning the methods of teaching mathematics in the kindergarten that the literature does not seem to answer. Such information is needed if a total picture of mathematics teaching in the kindergarten classroom is to be gained. The descriptive data in ta-

ble 4 answer such questions as, What percent of kindergarten teachers have an adopted series? and, What percent of kindergarten teachers teach mathematics daily as a special subject?

A careful analysis of the data in table 4 provides some thought-provoking results. The number of kindergarten teachers who have an adopted series, 78 per-

Table 4

How kindergarten teachers answered
questions concerning classroom methods

	Percent	
	Yes	No
Adopted series	78	22
If no, do you plan to adopt	38	62
Use consumable workbooks	67	33
If no, would consumables improve program	54	46
Use manipulative materials	97	3
Mathematics taught as special subject daily	53	47
Integrate mathematics with other subjects	93	7
Mathematics program adequate	79	21

cent, is high. This also means, however, that almost one-fourth of the kindergarten teachers do not have an adopted series. Another interesting finding is that only 53 percent of the teachers in the survey teach mathematics as a special subject each day. The great variation in teaching mathematics is probably best shown by contrasting the number of teachers who use consumables (67 percent) and the number who do not (33 percent), and noting that approximately 50 percent of those who do not use consumables stated that the use of consumables would not improve their programs.

When the data revealed that 22 percent of the kindergarten teachers had no adopted series, the author was interested in knowing if further processing of the data would show that having an adopted series would contribute to a teacher feeling that the mathematics program was adequate. Table 5 shows that of the 218 teachers who reported an adequate program of mathematics, 19 percent had no adopted series. Of the 59 teachers who reported an inadequate program of mathematics, 33 percent of them had no adopted series. Thus those teachers who had an adopted series were significantly more likely to report an adequate program of mathematics than those who did not have an adopted series.

The data in tables 6 and 7 are not directly related to kindergarten content and methods, but they do provide information that helps to build a picture of kindergarten instruction. Table 6 shows, for example, that few classes of thirty or more students were reported. And table 7 reveals that in 66 percent of the reported cases, no specific method was used to assign students to the morning and afternoon sessions.

Table 6

Class size for each one-half day

Number of students per session	Percent
1–20	46
21–30	50
Over 30	4

Table 5

Comparison by percentage of teachers who feel the mathematics program is adequate to those who feel it is inadequate with having or not having an adopted series

	Have an adopted series	
	Yes	No
Program is adequate (n = 218)	81	19
Program is inadequate (n = 59)	67	33

Table 7

Assignment of students for morning or afternoon sessions

Method	Percent
No specific method	66
Age	20
Residential area	10
Ability	3
Other	1

SUMMARY

Even though this study was confined to teachers in Kansas, the writer believes that generalizations from the findings of this survey can assist kindergarten teachers across the nation in development of course objectives for mathematics. The competencies that are "clearly on the kindergarten level" could be the minimum kindergarten program. Selected competencies from those in the "questionable" and "clearly not kindergarten" categories could be integrated into the program to form average and maximum programs. Furthermore, when twenty-one out of one hundred kindergarten teachers feel that their mathematics program is inadequate, it is time to start asking some questions and looking for some answers.

Index

Two and one-half year-olds
counting ability of, 24

Underachievement, 48

Visible language concepts, 4
Vision, 45
dominance over prehension, 45
Visual discrimination, 11, 52, 53, 71,
144, 151
*Visual Pattern Recognition Test for
Prereading Skills,* 104
Visual tracking, 9, 152

*Wechsler Preschool and Primary Scale
of Intelligence,* 126
Word games, 121
Writing
child's own name, 15
letters and numerals, 15
purpose of, 15
Writing strokes. *See* Handwriting, Pre-
handwriting

Zaner-Bloser Check Lists
purpose of, 10
Zaner-Bloser Kindergarten Check Lists,
6–11
companion skills, 8–9
foundation skills, 7–8

Kindergarten Check Lists

COMPANION SKILLS

I. Task Orientation

    A. Attention span is adequate for age appropriate assigned tasks

    B. Follows directions

    C. Makes decisions

    D. Marks responses

    E. Works independently

    F. Works cooperatively

    G. Interacts appropriately with peers and adults

    H. Asks help of an adult when appropriate

II. Affect

    A. Expression

      1. Interprets feelings given pictures or facial expressions

      2. Expresses emotions appropriately

      3. Expresses self spontaneously

      4. Shares personal experiences

    B. Attitudes

      1. Respects others

      2. Has a positive attitude toward self

      3. Has a positive attitude toward school and learning

III. General Readiness

    A. Perceptual and motor skills

      1. Gross and fine motor skills are adequate for age appropriate tasks

      2. Recognizes familiar textures, tastes, smells, sounds, and sights

      3. Localizes the source of an auditory stimulus

      4. Follows moving auditory and visual stimuli

      5. Recognizes that objects and events have characteristics in more than one modality

    B. Self Awareness

      1. Identifies body parts: head, arms, hands, legs, feet, eyes, ears, nose, mouth, fingers, toes

      2. Matches body parts with their function

    C. Memory

      1. Long and short term memory are adequate for age appropriate assigned tasks

      2. Gives name and address upon request

    D. Cognition

      1. Identifies the disparity in a set in which only one element is different: B B A B

      2. Progresses from concrete to abstract

      3. Understands part to whole relationship

      4. Seeks new information

      5. Grasps fundamentals of conservation of mass and number